The Complete Book of Seafood Fishing

# The
# Complete Book
# of Seafood
# Fishing

### Rob Avery

Illustrated by Paul Dadds

**VAN NOSTRAND REINHOLD COMPANY**
NEW YORK   CINCINNATI   TORONTO   LONDON   MELBOURNE

Published in the United States in 1982
by Van Nostrand Reinhold Company
135 West 50th Street
New York, NY 10020, U.S.A.

Van Nostrand Reinhold Company Limited
1410 Birchmount Road
Scarborough, Ontario M1P 2E7, Canada

by arrangement with
Prism Press,
Dorchester, Dorset, Great Britain

16 15 14 13 12 11 10 9 8 7 6 5 4 3 2 1

Library of Congress Cataloging in Publication Data

Avery, Rob.
  The complete book of seafood fishing.

  Includes index.
  1. Fishing  2. Seafood gathering.  I. Title.
SH439.A88     639'.2     81–23165
ISBN 0–442–21073–6     AACR2

# CONTENTS

*for*

*Brooksie*

## ACKNOWLEDGEMENTS

Over the years a great many people have helped me to acquire the knowledge that has enabled me to write this book. Government fishery scientists, commercial fishermen, boat builders, marine engineers, net makers, journalists, family and friends — a whole army of people connected with the sea and sea fishing. Unfortunately they are too numerous to mention individually. Nevertheless, my sincere thanks go to each and every one of them.

It goes without saying that without the patient ministrations of my publisher you would not be reading this because I would not have written it.

# INTRODUCTION

*"The hollow oak our palace is,*
  *Our heritage the sea."*

Over the last decade, a great many people have become interested in self sufficiency. Some, because they would like a more fulfilling natural way of life. Others because they fear that the structure of society is likely to collapse, and to survive they will have to be capable of providing for themselves and their families. Yet others, particularly those with a more flexible self-employed lifestyle, have questioned the validity of going to work to earn money just in order to buy commodities that they could more satisfactorily produce for themselves.

This interest has been accompanied by a steady flow of 'how to' books. Some have touched on the possibility of obtaining food from the sea, others have ignored it. So, as comprehensively as I could, I have written this book to fill the gap that I saw on the self supporter's bookshelf.

But more than that. One of the main drawbacks of the self sufficiency dream is hard cash. Even if you are thoroughly versed in all the practical aspects, you still need capital to set you up. If you do not already own the five acres of land that it is accepted that you will need, you will have to find a substantial amount of money to acquire it. Then you will have to find yet more money to buy livestock and to equip your little farm. And yet more to see you through until you are in full production. Even then you will have to have some sort of permanent cash flow. There will always be taxes and various other payments required by the state. Should you find land that you can just rent, you will have ever increasing payments to make, and in practice this will be even more of a burden. It is very difficult, if not impossible, to be truly self-sufficient. All other things aside, the basic funding of such a project precludes the majority.

Over the years, most people interested in this way of life have come to appreciate this. But so attractive is the concept of independence, that many have reached out for it on whatever scale has been realistic for them. So has emerged an entity not totally self sufficient, but just partially along that road. Growing their own vegetables, making their own bread, brewing their own beer, keeping a few chickens. Providing many of their day to day needs on the scale of keen gardeners rather than small farmers.

Seafood fishing combines very well with such a way of life. One great advantage is that it requires no large initial capital investment. You do not have to buy your own piece of sea. In fact you cannot. So that is one major hurdle out of the way. The scale of your investment is also totally flexible. If you want you can just go fishing very occasionally, treating the whole thing as no more than a rarely indulged hobby. On the other hand, you can take it all very seriously and fit yourself out with a whole range of equipment, operating very much like a small scale professional.

Sea fishing can be the cheapest or the most expensive of all your self supporting activities. The least or the most time consuming. Unlike the actual husbandry of land or livestock, your 'crop' goes on feeding and growing without any effort on your part. When, where, and how often you gather your harvest is entirely up to you. The options are all yours. Read on and find out all about them.

Rob Avery
Dorset

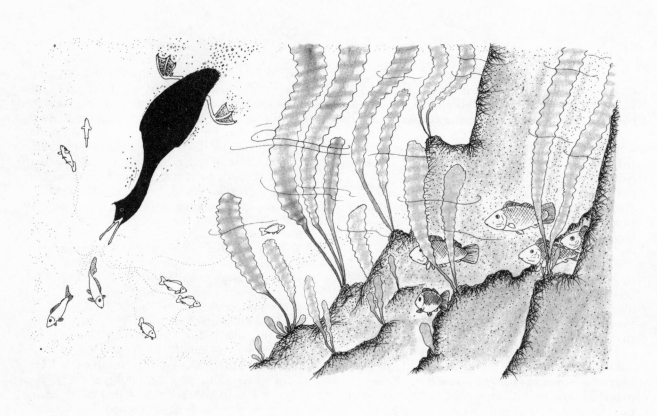

# 1. Why go Fishing?

Most people who go fishing do so either for sport, or as a way of earning their living. Food fishermen can slot in between the two, reaping the rewards that only self-reliance can bring.

Here are the main advantages:

*You save money on food. Fish and shellfish that you catch yourself are free. Luxuries like lobster and shrimp will often be on your menu.

*Fish you catch and prepare yourself tastes better. Freshness, and freedom from chemical treatments, is guaranteed.

*You will be less dependent on the dubious and often cruel activities of commercial interests.

*The level of your involvement is flexible. Small scale, big scale, wherever and whenever you want.

*If you are already trying to be a little more self-sufficient — even by just cultivating a few vegetables and keeping your own chickens; fishing will provide you with some useful biproducts. Fish meal, oil, fertilizer and sand-paper for example. (Sandpaper?)

*You will have some highly enjoyable and invigorating days away from your usual environment.

There are snags of course. These are the most important ones:

*You may not live near the sea.

*It can be cold, wet, hard work. You could get seasick or even drowned.

*Fish can be very cheap in times of glut, so why bother to go out and catch them?

*Learning about tides, charts, making and mending nets and equipment, will take up time and require too much effort.

*If you go as far as getting a boat, it will involve a large capital outlay and go on being a drain on your resources.

These then are the basic pros and cons. A look at them all in rather more detail will help us to get our perspectives right. First of all . . .

## The Cash Saving

According to the most recent official surveys, the average household spends around 5% of it's total yearly food budget on fish. But if you take into account some of the indirect expenditure on sea produce — i.e. Fish meal fed to the animals whose products and meat you consume, fish oil in margarine etc — this figure is increased by at least half as much again.

Government statistics also show that wealthy families spend more on fish than poor families. No specific breakdown of this expenditure is available, but I would have thought it likely that spur of the moment fancies for prawn cocktail and the like would be more liable to become a reality if the cost was of no great importance. If you doubt the wisdom of this, and are poor like me, attract the attention of your good lady (or gentleman) and tentatively suggest that a little Lobster Bordelaise would not come amiss for dinner tomorrow. With lobsters probably being the most expensive food that you are likely to find generally on sale, the gist of the answer is inclined to be predictable to say the least. If on the other hand you had been favoured with the good fortune to have read this book some time ago, the response might well have been — "Oh not again" or "We can't, you've eaten them all."

So what does all this mean in terms of cash saved? Well, assuming you can go fishing fairly regularly, for a start you will get an immediate 5% discount on your yearly food bill. Your fish eating habits will be taking a step up towards the money no object class, and this rise in your eating standards will mean hidden savings that will greatly increase the original basic saving. It will also mean that you will tend to eat more fish overall — simply because they will be there to be eaten; so you will save on the cost of food that you would otherwise have had to buy. This in turn will have the added bonus of making you more adventurous with your fish cookery; you will be forced on into the delightful world of the seafood gourmet. You may not have a million-aire's income, but you can certainly start to eat like one.

In basic cash terms then, we can quite safely start talking about a 15% saving for the straightfor-ward food fisherman.

Established individuals, who have already become more self reliant, and have a represen-tative range of protein hungry livestock to provide for, will be in a position to make further savings by feeding home made fish meal. Even if you were to just make enough to feed a dozen hens over the year, it could make all the difference between free eggs and simply cheap eggs.

During the year, a single breeding sow will be happy to eat as much fish as eight people normally consume annually. So imagine what the saving could be on an average holding. Clearly, you would have to make a huge amount of fish meal to be totally independent of commercial sources, but by making it throughout the year for winter use, and by feeding ordinary cooked fish in times of plenty, you will be a long way towards it.

The introduction of seaweed into your life will not only mean further savings in food costs for you and your livestock, but its almost magical influence on land and animal welfare will mean greatly improved returns on crop and stock production. As you will read later on, seaweed used as fertilizer will increase the quality and yield of many crops, and as a feed, the health and excellence of your animals and their produce. For instance, it has been shown that sheep fed on seaweed grow more wool of better quality than those not fed on it. All this is very difficult to cost in hard cash. If your potato patch can potentially produce twice as many potatoes as it did before, what do you do? Plant half as many potatoes and save on the cost of bought in seed or plant your usual quantity and sell off the surplus? These sort of answers you will have to provide for yourself, but I can think of many a worse quandary to be in.

Bi-products like oil (mainly extracted when you make your fish meal) that can be used to fuel simple lamps, and craft uses like crab claw pendants (I did quite well with those last year) and leather products, etc. will not individually save or generate much cash, but collectively they will have a noticeable contribution to make. You won't have to buy any more sandpaper either.

With all these variables it is impossible to come up with precise figures, but I think you will agree that at their worst the savings will be worthwhile, and at their best — substantial.

### Good Eating Without The Hidden Extras

Anyone who has ever been fishing and has had the good luck to tuck into the catch a few hours later, will agree that fresh fish tastes infinitely better than shop bought fish. Why should this be? Is it because the bracing sea air gives you a ravenous appetite, and anything you might happen to eat would taste delicious? — Not entirely, fish is a very delicate food, far less robust than meat; remember, it has emerged — in a sterile condition — into a hostile environ-ment that not only kills it, but actually encourages it to decay. Soon after it leaves the water, the fish is subjected to a rapid and relentless push towards ruination by self-digest-ing enzymes and bacteria, the destructive prog-ress of which is directly related to temperature. Nothing can stop this spoilage, it can only be slowed down.

So it's fairly obvious that the sooner you plug in your knife and fork or preserving activities to this spoilage cycle, the better the taste will be.

Some commercial supplies of fish may be at best 2 or 3 days old or at worst over two weeks old before either distribution as 'fresh' fish, or processing as frozen or smoked fish *even begins*. Such delays, combined with poor handling and inadequate methods of storage mean that the raw material can be stale and tasteless before it is even sent to retail outlets.

This table prepared by a government research laboratory shows what happens to white fish like cod and haddock kept in melting ice at 0°C and at 10°C.

*Age and Flavour of White Fish*

| Days in ice at 0°C | Flavour | Days at 10°C |
|---|---|---|
| 0 | fresh | 0 |
| 3 | sweet | |
| 6 | less sweet | 2 |
| 9 | no sweetness | |
| 12 | slightly stale | 4 |
| 15 | sour | |
| 18 | bitter | 6 |
| 21 | putrid | 7 |

*Torry Advisory Note No 42*

It would be wrong to say that the fish on sale in the shops is not perfectly edible, (that is to say it won't kill you) in most cases it is, but the simple fact is, that it is just not technically possible for it to be consistently as good as the fish you can catch yourself. Nor perhaps more importantly, can there be any guarantee about what 'they' have been treating it with.

## The Hidden Extras — How To Subtract The Additives
In the West, every man, woman and child eats the equivalent of well over twelve aspirin sized tablets *per day* in the form of commercially applied food additives. Which incidentally does not include your share of all the antibiotics and other veterinary medications that are passed on to you when you consume the products of agribusiness. The fishing industry makes its contribution to all this mainly in the form of Polyphosphates and various colourings and flavourings — including of course the apparently essential Monosodium Glutamate. Mankind must very nearly have Monosodium Glutamate coming out of its ears by now; it seems to be a compulsory ingredient of practically everything on the supermarket shelves. Whether it actually does you any harm or not, is anybody's guess. Controversy over its use has been well publicised during the last few years, but the arguments either for or against have never been conclusive. So I am afraid that we shall all have to wait for the results of further research before we can be totally certain of our fate.

Polyphosphates are used to inhibit drip loss in thawing fish — mainly to achieve a prettier product — and, less appealing, to mask the taste of stale fish used by manufacturing processors. Even research scientists are not quite sure how Polyphosphates actually work (and therefore what their long term effect on consumers is liable to be) but work they do, and used they

are. Inevitably it will be left to the eaters of commercially frozen fish to let us know in due course if there are any long term toxic effects or not.

This chuck it on and hope for the best philosophy is not only confined to the fishing industry. Food processors in general are all busily engaged in the same, sorry, uncertain business. But alarming as all this may be, I have cause for even greater concern. Even if you accept the assurances that individually none of these additives is doing you much harm, what about the possibility of various combinations of chemicals from a random diet producing unpredictable toxic effects? Virtually *nothing* you eat escapes the hand of the applicator. Smoked fish is dyed to make it look nice. (One of these dyes has recently been withdrawn in the U.S. as a cancer risk). Bananas are ripened in gas, traces of which you inevitably eat. Oranges are coloured to achieve standardized consumer appeal. Apples are wrapped in impregnated paper to lengthen storage life. Potatoes are sprayed to stop them sprouting. Meat is injected to give it an attractive colour. I could go on, the list is seemingly endless. Literally thousands and thousands of different chemical additives are in regular daily use. A vast hidden army of pharmaceutical concoctions, lubricating the profits of the chemifood purveyors.

We are told that government keeps the position under review, but toxicologists will publicly admit that it is impossible for them to monitor all the inter-reactive effects. By catching your own untampered with fish, you will not exactly be avoiding the situation, but at least it will be a step in the right direction, and linked with other personal food production, part of a complete solution.

## The Waste and Cruelty of Industry
It is an unfortunate fact of life, that insensitivity and inhumanity go hand in hand with the livestock enterprises of big business. Regretfully the fishermen of the world are no exception. We all know what tragedy has been wrought on the oceans' whale population, but less well known are the equally unattractive activities of the rest of the industry.

Let us take a specific example. Even as I write, a highly sophisticated fleet of Scottish seiners and trawlers is rapidly denuding the English south west coast of its mackerel stocks. Most of the boats have been displaced from their usual hunting grounds either by the new 200 mile limits or by quotas and bans necessitated by the fleet's own enormous catching ability. They have been unwelcome for numerous reasons, but what has angered the locals most of all, has been their enforced witness to the horrifying techniques employed by big business at work.

Soon after the 'invasion' began, the small local trawlers started to catch large quantities of mackerel. You can be forgiven for assuming they would have been pleased. They were not. The fish they caught were dead and decaying. Divers confirmed that in some areas the sea bed was carpeted with rotting fish. The culprits were not hard to find.

Big boats have big running costs, and need maximum catches to pay their way. Most of the interlopers were capable of pulling in 200 tons of fish for a single night's work, some as much as 400 tons. Naturally you do not catch such large quantities on spec. Refrigerated transporters and eastern bloc factory ships were waiting to carry the fish to the dining tables of the world.

Being capable of several shots during their time at sea (but with quotas restricting the amount they could land) it was discovered that skippers were slipping a particular haul if it was found to contain immature or low grade fish. Admirable you may say, they could live to grow for another day. Unfortunately not. Crushed by the net and their own numbers, most would be dead on release. The order book said prime fish of the best quality — 'So if this lot's no good, dump them and try again lads, and if the next haul's no better, sling that as well' — Cruel? Possibly. Certainly a criminal waste. They could at least have gone to the fish meal plant, but the price they would have fetched would not have been pleasing to the gentlemen in the board room. Prime fish they wanted and they were not particular how they came by it.

As well as this deliberate wastage, the fishing industry destroys large numbers of immature fish by using techniques that make such losses unavoidable. Beam trawlers are a prime example, they drag huge nets that literally plough through the sea bed. What they don't catch, they bury, leaving a barren, lifeless marine desert in their wake. Baby fish scraped up from the nursery grounds will be dead before they can be released.

The destruction is on a massive scale; the ICES Liaison Committee report for 1977 states that in 1976, Scotland and The Netherlands alone dumped 74,000 tons of immature haddock and whiting back into the North Sea. Few would survive. That is just two nations and two particular species of fish.

If profit is the name of the game, conservation becomes merely a threat to success, and under the banner of financial viability, industry becomes desensitized to what it must do in order to exist. For example, I have met no one in the fishing industry who thinks it cruel to keep lobsters in storage ponds for four months — without food, that would cause too many problems — in order that they may be more profitably marketed out of season. In fact you can even get government booklets that tell you how to do it. But then, perhaps I am too squeamish for this world.

Not being a vegetarian, I accept the fact that creatures must be killed in order that I may eat, but like any other sane person, I qualify that acceptance with the condition that the killing be done in as humane and responsible a way as possible. On these terms, how can I possibly rely on the activities of fishermen who trap crabs — break off their claws — and return the live amputees to a lingering death in the sea. Some people may find this an acceptable way of procuring their attractively packaged — easy to eat — frozen — barbecue crab claws. I do not.

## The Versatility and Enjoyment

Large scale involvement may be difficult for many of you, but that really is the big advantage of fishing. You can do as little or as much as you wish. If you happen to live very near the coast as I do, your participation can be almost on a daily basis. On the other hand just one or two fishing trips a year will at least provide a few free meals.

It can be very enjoyable as well, a few hours in that bracing sea air certainly blows the cobwebs away. Indeed for many people the mere sight and sound of the sea can be a relaxing tonic in itself. However happy your home life is, it does you good to get away once in a while; your horizons are widened and your batteries recharged.

All in all, fishing has an awful lot going for it. What more could you ask for? Fresh food — the very best — freedom from the chemifood conveyor belt and the cruelty and waste of big business. Healthy and enjoyable days out whenever the mood takes you — plus the odd cash bonus with some money-savers thrown in for good measure. I bet you can hardly wait to get started.

We ought to have a look at the snags first though.

## Location

The first problem I listed concerned your proximity to the sea. In a surprisingly large number of places this will not really be much of a problem; a few hours drive will be all that's needed to get you to the coast. In fact if you live some distance from the sea, it can be a distinct advantage in that it is just as easy to go to one particular piece of coast as it is to go to another. Your grounds can then be selected to suit the weather, your own inclinations or the type of fishing you want to do. For particularly difficult trips you could always stay with friends — or camp out perhaps. If you happen to live in Columbus, Nebraska, I admit you do have problems. I should either get the 'for sale' sign out and move a bit nearer the coast, or set up a house guest exchange system with someone more conveniently located. Failing that, read the section on netting, make a hammock, and go back to sleep.

### It's a Hard Life
Well it can be cold, and it can be wet. So wrap up in some warm waterproof clothing. (See chapter thirteen for details of how to make your own).

Hard work? Personally I enjoy it. Rather like gardening really, either you find it forced slave labour, or just an energetic episode in a fascinating part of your life.

### I Wish I'd Never Bought This Book
Seasickness can be a problem; luckily I have never been a sufferer. Determination and perseverence have been some people's salvation, but if it does cause you trouble, I am told that the various drugs that are available are very good. Have a word with your doctor about it; he will be able to make specific recommendations. It also helps if you lay off the home brew the night before. There is nothing like a rolling swell to emphasize the unpleasant after effects of any over indulgence!

The other physical dangers are obvious. People who go on or near the sea sometimes drown. If you go fishing you will inevitably be at risk. However, the likelihood of any mishaps can be reduced to an acceptable level by employing a combination of common sense, local knowledge and learnt skills. I go into all this in more detail later on, but if you use your head the chance of any accidents should be remote.

### Why Not Just Buy When Fish Is Cheap?
Why not indeed. Particular species of fish can sometimes be very cheap when catches have been heavy and the market flooded. With your soon-to-be-learnt skills of fish meal manufacture and home preserving it would be silly not to take advantage of the situation. But from a food point of view, you might find it rather boring having always to eat the same kind of fish, and you probably could have caught them yourself for nothing anyway. However, the main snag with 'glut' buying is that you are only likely to be offered the more common varieties of shoal fish. Nobody is going to give you the opportunity to purchase the more desirable types like cod or lobster or shrimp at anything less than their invariably high market value. So if you want the cream, you will have to milk the cow yourself.

### The Homework
Learning the basics of tides, charts and seamanship can be achieved simply by reading this book. On the scale we shall be operating, there is no need to have an expert's knowledge. It is only of academic interest to know how to circumnavigate the world if you are only going to be working a few hundred yards off shore all the time. So the mastery of a few elementary skills is all that you will need to start with.

### Equipment and Maintenance
Most of the gear you will be using can be constructed in a matter of hours from odds and ends that you probably have lying around, or can scrounge for next to nothing. Net making is a bit more time consuming, but once the basic principles have been grasped, it's the sort of fairly mindless task you can do listening to the radio or watching TV. A bit like knitting, but about ten times less complicated.

If you do get a boat, it may require a yearly coat of paint or varnish and probably running repairs as odd snags crop up. The engine, or whatever kind of propulsion you are going to use, will also need servicing from time to time, but I doubt whether the total time spent on these chores will amount to much more than a few days of spare time throughout the year.

### Getting Afloat
You will not necessarily have to buy a boat, but naturally if you do, it will give you considerably more scope.

New boats are prohibitively expensive, and unless some revolutionary new material becomes available they are certain to remain so. I do not even consider them as a possibility for the small scale food fisherman. So apart from borrowing one, you will either have to buy a secondhand one or make one. How much you will have to pay will depend on luck and the condition of the boat. Recently, I was offered a nice little dinghy at a price that wouldn't have bought the portable typewriter that I am slaving away to write this book on. So for a comparatively modest outlay you can be in business. A cheaper way to get on the water is to build your own little craft. The boating magazines often have articles describing how somebody or other has made a perfectly serviceable boat out of reclaimed timber or the cheapest of materials. The cost of one twelve footer that I know of, consisted in the main of the price of a few beers for the demolition gang that were pulling down an old house. They were happy to let its resourceful builder have the pick of any timber that was around. It saved them having to haul it away and burn it! So it can be done. However you go about it, bargains are around. By keeping your eyes open and letting all and sundry know what you are after you should eventually track down what you want.

(In the section on boats, I give my plan for the kind of basic boat you could build yourself.)

Again, apart from borrowing one, probably the cheapest way of all would be to share the costs of making or buying a boat with another person or a number of other people. This kind of set up does invite dispute, but it is a way in, so I discuss it in more detail elsewhere in this book.

## The Overhead

Whether you transport your boat around with you or site it permanently somewhere, you will probably have to contend with some sort of launching or mooring fees.

Later on I shall discuss this in more detail, but you will still have some annual payments to make, and in addition there will be extras like paint — engine repairs — insurance — hooks — line — fuel etc. On the bright side though, boats have shown themselves to be a good investment; representing an asset that can readily be realized if needs be. So bearing in mind the fact that you will not have to pay for fish in future and taking into account the financial and other advantages I have mentioned, you should end up well ahead on the year.

Subsequent chapters of this book contain a great deal of detailed information. How much use you make of this knowledge and how far you become involved is up to you. Self sufficiency enthusiasts can become almost entirely independent of the fishing industry, while to others fishing need be no more than a rewarding hobby. However you approach the opportunities, I hope that you do well, and more to the point, I hope this book helps you to do it.

# 2. Past, Present and Future

*The Past and Present here unite*
*Beneath Time's flowing tide,*

*Longfellow*

Now that you have read this far, the idea of catching your own seafood, has, I hope, captured your imagination. So let's begin at the beginning and use this chapter to brief you on the background you will be operating against.

Fossils from the Devonian period, some 355 million years ago, tell us that fish and shellfish have been around for a very long time. Exactly when man found out that he could eat them is not entirely clear, but our prehistoric ancestors certainly consumed large quantities of shellfish; neatly discarding the shells in the large mounds we call Kitchen Middens, which survive to this day in many parts of the world.

Gathering shellfish is undoubtedly the most logical beginning to man's harvesting of the sea. In his early nomadic wanderings he would inevitably have come to the sea shore, and it is only natural that his curiosity would have been aroused by the repetitive symmetry of the strange objects that he found lying in the sand. As soon as he found out that these stone-like 'sea nuts' were as good to eat as the ones he had found in the forest, there would be no stopping him. A new hunting ground discovered, he would begin to actively pursue the inhabitants of the shallows. It would not be long before he realised that the spear he used on his hunting trips

worked just as well in the water, and that in this simple way he could provide a large part of the food he needed for himself and his family.

Later, as man formed himself into settlements and finally nations, our now specialist fisherman found that these primitive methods could no longer meet the demands for fish from others in his society. Thus began, by necessity, a development of techniques and equipment that has continued, and will probably continue, forever.

Perhaps the first innovations would have been

in the form of traps. Based on the ones used by animal hunters, these would be adapted and developed as their effectiveness dictated. The nets used by the wild-fowlers would be pressed into service. Possibly in the first instance to block off a small creek, so that trapped fish could more easily be speared. Latterly, as the idea dawned, to enclose the fish and drag them to the shore or into a boat.

Such developments and innovations continued over the centuries. By the middle ages important fisheries for herring had been established in Europe, and as early as the 15th century, New-foundland's Grand Banks were being heavily fished for cod. The 17th century saw the beginning of the attack on the whale schools. In the Atlantic and South Pacific Oceans, ubiquitous fleets were already at work.

As with many industries, sweeping changes were to come towards the end of the 19th century. Steam had arrived and the days of the great sailing ships were numbered. At first the industry was sceptical; but when owners began to charter the new steamers to tow the trawlers on wind-less days, it was not long before the potential advantages began to be fully appreciated.

By the end of the century, many of the large fishing vessels made their way under power; with oil driven engines gradually eroding the dominance of steam.

As the century progressed, even the smallest boats had acquired mechanical propulsion; but the biggest advances were not to come until after the Second World War. Technological developments, forced through for military purposes, now became available to industry. The age of instrumentation had dawned. Echo sounders became commonplace, sonar (a kind of horizontal echo sounder) followed on in its turn, and

the new synthetic nettings began to be widely adopted.

Although power driven winches had been around since the turn of the century, and mechanized pulleys and coiling machines had gradually made their appearance, it was not until the 1950's that the power block was invented—a giraffe necked hydraulic arm, clutching the drum that could haul the nets of the purse seiners. Other developments, like trawl net drums, and stern ramps, all helped to increase the efficiency of what was by now a highly automated industry.

As refrigeration improved, the fleets could roam further afield. Giant factory trawlers prospected the oceans of the world, returning home after a year at sea with up to 7000 tons of already processed fish aboard.

Now the electronics were becoming really sophisticated. Inboard computers linked to the radar, acoustic fish finders and position indicators, could pin-point the shoals day or night, and the automatic net monitors would even tell when the catch should be hauled. Net technology kept well up with the pace, purse seine nets nearly a mile long were developed to take 600 tons in one shot. Aboard the ship, lightning fast machinery was waiting to skin, gut and fillet the catch—far more efficiently than an army of fishmongers could have done.

The industry was now no longer quaint. If the fish were there—anywhere—fleets of boats, bristling with the latest fish catching gadgetry could catch them. Coastal nations watched uneasily as their traditional stocks were looted of one species after another. Iceland was among the first to protest. Almost the whole of her economy depended on the rich supply of fish that swarmed all around her. Arrogantly the British government saw fit to reason otherwise. Cod war followed cod war, as the Royal Navy tried to re-enact the gun boat diplomacy of the days of Raj and Empire. Ignominiously defeated, their withdrawal heralded the declaration of 200 mile limits all around the world.

The effects were almost immediate. Distant water vessels left with nowhere to fish, were laid up one after the other. Most of their subsequent voyages would be in the direction of the breaker's yard.

In many respects the industry was slow to accept the realities of the situation. Hoping upon hope that in some magical way everyone would change their minds, the restrictions be forgotten and the over fishing continue. Nations haggled over reciprocal agreements so that favourite supplies could be maintained. But the possessiveness born of the newly declared limits, and the restricted quotas allowed, approached a sanity that was to be welcomed by few.

Now at this point in time, it is uncertain what direction the industry will take. In Britain, some of the big firms have switched boats to unexploited fisheries in Africa and Australia, and have met with varying amounts of success. Others have decided to throw in their lot with previously uncaught species a little nearer to home.

Relatively unknown fish like blue whiting, that live in deep water far off shore, have until now been difficult to catch. But predictably, technology has come up with the answers, and the shoals are beginning to be hammered by fleets from various countries. So that for many enterprises, it is the venue, not the tactics that have changed. The Norwegians in particular have been very quick off the mark, and their purpose built boats are already bringing in over a thousand tons a week each. With the seed corn disappearing at this kind of rate, it is certain that the blue whiting will go the way of the herring, the mackerel, the anchovy and the whale. But by then, I am sure that they will have found something else that is ripe for annihilation. The grenadier and the giant squid will be high on the list of priorities. The krill has already taken its first steps around the vicious circle of modern fishery practice –discovery – exploitation –depletion. These tiny shrimp like crustacea were once the food of the Antarctic whales, but they may now be destined to the same sad decline as their dwindling predators have been. Scientists predict 100,000,000 tons of krill per year may be safely available for processing into paste

and other products; but it is very unlikely that once the technicalities of catching and processing have been perfected, there will be much concern about stock levels. The Russians, Japanese and Chileans have been catching them for years, West German and Polish fleets have now joined them, and catch rates are proving to be enormous.

But however massive these efforts are, they still only concern a relatively small number of boats, and in general the large distant water boats are disappearing. Fish merchants must get their supplies from somewhere of course, and so the inevitable has happened, and we have seen a terrific upswing in the number of small inshore fishing boats. This has been the trend all over Britain and America, and even in my own little port the changes have been quite dramatic. Four or five years ago, you could have counted the number of full time professional boats on one hand. Now there are dozens, and more on the way by the looks of it. Whether they will make a living or not remains to be seen. Personally I doubt it. Their range is limited, and as most must make substantial monthly repayments to the finance companies, they will, as time goes on, be forced to over fish the accessible local grounds. Thus they will be cornered into trying to disprove the law of diminishing returns. I am glad that I am not one of them.

In a broader sense though, I must admit to feeling fairly optimistic about the future of world fishing. Although the World's total annual catch of over 73,000,000 tons has now risen to an all time high, the brakes of the 200 mile limits are on, and if coastal nations are unable to rationalise catches within their own waters, they have to a great

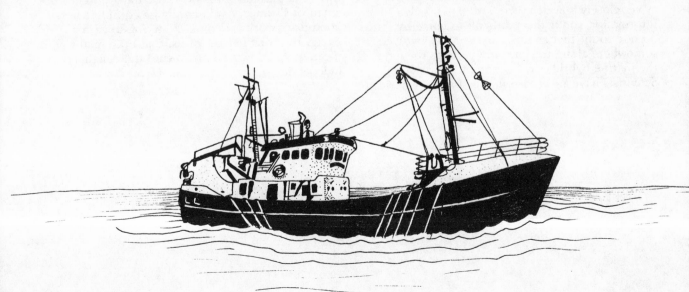

extent only themselves to blame. So hopefully catches from the most fruitful grounds will begin to be regulated, and they will not be mercilessly scavenged as they have been in the past. Fish will probably become more expensive as a result, because they will be being produced by smaller enterprises rather than mass production factories of the sea, but if we are to have any fish at all, then this must be the way of things.

Perhaps in the distant future, fishing as we know it will no longer exist, and the sea will be farmed as the land is now; but we have a long way to go before that happens, and it is no prospect for the immediate future. The main problems are economic ones. You can artificially rear most of the fish we are used to eating, but they cost substantially more than the ones that come naturally from the sea. In the main, the closest we come to true farming at the moment, is to provide sheltered accommodation for shellfish like oysters, mussels and clams, relaying them on sites that give them an enhanced chance of reaching maturity. Japan, the world leaders in fish farming, already rear many varieties of sea life, and their latest technique of releasing pound hatched chum salmon into the Pacific, to return as adults, will provide 80,000 tons of fish in the next few years. Much research is being carried out along these lines with other fish and shellfish, and no doubt, over the years the list of successfully cultivated sea life will gradually be lengthened. When you think that a hen lobster can produce up to 100,000 eggs at one time, of which only one in a thousand will survive due to predators, the possibility of being able to rear her brood for her is a very attractive one indeed.

Some areas of research, in various countries, are as yet closely guarded secrets, and naturally information about them difficult to come by; but I do not doubt that selective breeding is involved somewhere along the line, and perhaps the days of the marine hybrid may be steadily approaching. Scientists have succeeded in crossing an American lobster with a European one. The American variety of lobster has small claws and a large body—the European just the opposite. Thus the two assets have been combined.

But technology still marches on, and one German firm has developed a machine the potential of which chills my conservation instincts to the very marrow. For a few millions, they will sell you a small remote controlled submarine that automatically detects shoals of fish. Emitting soothing electronic noises, so that its presence does not frighten the fish away, it moves into the very middle of the shoal. When you and your computerized hatchet men are ready, you press a button in the mother ship and the submarine gives forth a piercing sound that acoustically stuns the fish. Senseless, the whole shoal rises to the surface, and you pump them aboard through hoses.

Where and when, you may ask, will it all end. To which I would reply—I am not exactly sure where, but I am certain very soon—if they let that little number loose.

Now you may be wondering, how on earth you can possibly fit into this highly organized and competitive scenario. It might appear that there are altogether too many at it already. But the truth of the matter is, that as with most forms of food production, we can disentangle ourselves from the commercial world, and go our own sweet way.

Professional fishermen must naturally make money at the job, and happily we will be able to stand in the wings and watch them get on with it. In all areas there are stocks of fish that do not occur in sufficient quantities to make them worth bothering with even the smallest commercial set ups. Half a dozen fish, two crabs and a pound and a half of shrimps, could hardly be considered a good day's work for someone trying to earn a living. But for the likes of us, that little haul would mean quite a few free meals, and the delights of—independence.

# 3. Before We Begin

*You see the ways the Fisherman doth take*
*To catch the fish; what Engins doth he make;*
*Behold how he ingageth all his Wits,*
*Also his Snares, Lines, Angles, Hooks and Nets.*
*Yet Fish there be, that neither Hook, nor Line,*
*Nor Snare, nor Net, nor Engine can make thine;*
*They must be grop't for, and be tickled too,*
*Or they will not be catcht, what e're you do.*

John Bunyan
*Pilgrim's Progress.* 1678.

I know how keen you will all be to get cracking
on the groping and tickling, but bear with me
for just a few pages longer, because in this
chapter I am going to give you some basic
background information that I hope will save
you time and wasted effort. Unless you are
extremely lucky, you are not really going to have
much chance of success if you just casually turn
up at the beach, with your little shrimp net in

your hand, innocently hoping for the best. So I
would like to try and give you a general insight
into the kind of way to approach any particular
method of fishing.

## Tides

The first thing we ought to know a bit about are
tides. Everyone knows that the tide comes in and
goes out again at various times of the day, and
that we get such things as high and low tides.
But what happens in detail is perhaps not so
widely understood, so for the sake of clarity, I
will explain something of the phenomenon.

Without becoming too scientific, tides are
caused by the gravitational forces of the sun and
moon. The moon's influence being strongest
because it is nearer to us, and the overall effect
greatest when the sun and moon are in direct
line on the same side of the earth. So because of
this pulling and relaxing effect as the earth

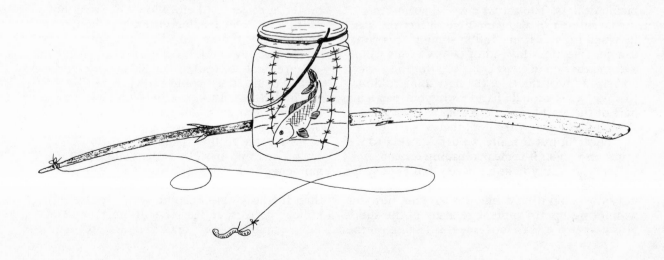

rotates, the sea flows firstly in one direction, then, after a slight halt called 'slack tide', does an about turn and flows in the opposite direction. When the tide has come in as far as it is going to, we have a state of affairs called the 'flood tide' or 'high water', and the water up until this time has been 'flowing'. When the tide turns and starts moving away again, it is said to be 'ebbing', and because of the weight of water that has built up, does so with increasing speed during the third and fourth hours, the same being true when the tide comes in. The higher the tides rise in any given spot, the faster and stronger they will be. So if you get a 24ft tide rise in your area, it will run twice as fast as your neighbours further down the coast who only gets a 12ft rise. The amount by which the tide rises and falls, and the time at which it does so, varies daily according to your location and the relative position of the sun and moon. Every full moon, greater variations occur; these are called the 'spring tides' (nothing to do with the season) and the water comes in and rises further, then recedes to a similar extreme. During the spring and autumn equinoxes in March and September, the sun and moon have their greatest effect of all, and the spring tides rise and fall to an even greater extent. Between the full and new moons, at the first and last quarter phases and about three and a half days either side of them, come the 'neap tides'. These do not rise and fall so much and consequently run less powerfully.

In most places, it takes between five and seven hours for the tide to rise from high to low, and a similar period from low to high again. Every day the high tide times are progressively later — roughly half an hour in twelve — and the exact hour and minute is given in the local press or on tide charts available from chandlers or fishing tackle dealers. The actual physical structure of the coastline can also sometimes affect the way in which the tides run, and in some places you can get four tides instead of two. Various wind and weather conditions can also alter the time and strength of the tide; the best thing to do is to study what actually happens in your particular part of the world.

Well now, I am sorry if all that was a bit complicated, but it really is worth getting to grips with, even if it means reading it over several times. If you don't have a full knowledge of what the tide is doing at any particular time, not only could it be dangerous for you, but you will not be able to appreciate many of the subtle effects that the sea's movement is having on the creatures that live in it.

Successful fishermen are not just lucky, they have reasoned out what is likely to be happening under the surface, and aligned their tactics to suit the situation. Lobsters for example, are not inclined to come out of hiding when the tide is running at its strongest, they prefer to hide up until it slackens off a bit. On the other hand, small fish fighting against the worst of the flow will make an easier prey for larger predators whom the tide is not affecting so much. Large fish will be moving inshore as the tide builds up, feeding on worms and shellfish that are emerging as the water covers them. Forced back by the falling water, the same fish will be moving offshore when the tide turns. The wise hunter will be working all this out in his mind, setting his traps with logical cunning. Experimenting, and of course making mistakes, gradually building up a picture of what happens in his own particular locality.

## Logical Observation

A good fisherman will continually ask himself questions about the reasons for his success or lack of it, looking for causes and effects — What happens when those breakers come pounding in on the beach; could they be disturbing small creatures in the sand? Does that mean big fish could be close inshore feeding on them? When the next very low tide comes, I wonder if it would be worth having a look for some clams right down by the water's edge? There aren't any higher up the beach, but you never know — The rocks on the far side of that headland are always protected from the worst of the weather; that would make a nice sheltered home for something. I think I'll try a few traps down there this evening. Why are there always seabirds sitting on those rocks just before low tide? Are they waiting for their feeding grounds to be uncovered? This is the way in which your mind must work. Nobody can tell you in precise detail what you are likely to find in any given spot, and even if they could, they would probably not be particularly keen to give the secret away to you. By using your common sense you can prospect out your own private fishing grounds and achieve some really worthwhile results.

I proved this myself a little while ago. I happened to be out for a stroll along a beach that I used to gather winkles on as a boy. Since then the beach has become very popular with holiday visitors, and as a result, no more winkles. This set me thinking. Had they disappeared from the area completely? The environment had obviously suited them, or they would not have been there in the first place. I thought about it for a while and then started to look around for the least accessible piece of shoreline close at hand. By crawling under a pier and scrambling down a sea wall, I reached an exposed patch of small rocks that was certainly very difficult to get at. It was worth it though; there by the bucket full were enough winkles to keep me going for the rest of my life I should think. Unless too many other people latch on to them, in which case I shall have to survey the area again.

## Local Knowledge

However successful you may be at this sort of prospecting though, you will not have much luck hunting for species that are simply not there. Certain kinds of fish or shellfish may just not be suited to your particular area. Others will only visit at certain times of the year. Shrimps and prawns will be offshore in the winter, only coming close to the shoreline after the winter storms are over; moving out again whenever bad weather approaches. Some fish will appear just at certain seasons when the water temperature suits their feeding or spawning habits. But whatever time of the year it is, there will be something to catch. Precisely what you can expect to find in your own particular area is something that you will have to find out for yourself. Local enquiries made to fishermen, anglers, fishing tackle dealers and anyone that has any relevant knowledge will all help to reveal what your part of the coast has on offer. In local bookshops you will find books written for anglers that deal specifically with your part of the coast. These are an invaluable source of information, since they tell you in detail what the local specialities are likely to be. Personally, I have found that one of the most accurate sources of information about what is being caught locally is the quayside fish merchant. After all he is probably buying much of what is being landed and his daily contact with the professionals makes him a natural collecting station for the most up to date fishing news. He also has no reason to want to mislead you, which cannot always be said of the full time fishermen themselves. When you have found out what kind of fish are about, you can then go on to select suitable gear to catch them.

## Types of Fish

Seafood, apart from seaweed, can be divided into two main groups. Fish that feed on or near the sea bed (demersal fish), and fish that live in the upper water near the surface (pelagic fish). Some fish will switch between the two, but it is generally true to say that in comparatively shallow water most fish will be found reasonably near the surface, actually on the sea floor, or just above it. Having established this, it becomes clear that in order to catch them, we must place our lines, traps, nets or whatever, either on or near the sea bed, or just under the surface. The crunch question of course, is exactly where and when.

## Wherefore Art They?

Now life under the sea is a vicious daily round of hunting and being hunted. Not only will the average fish be looking for smaller species to prey on, cannibal that he is, he will also have his eyes on his weaker or injured brothers and sisters as well. He in turn will be being sized up by other predators who are also feeling hungry. Many fish and shellfish therefore spend much of their time in hiding. Either to avoid being eaten, or in order to be able to spring out and surprise an unsuspecting passer by. This means that an area of good cover, say an undersea patch of rock and weeds, will contain not only resident fish and shellfish who shelter or hide there, but other predators attracted there to feed on them. This in turn will attract us, the fishermen, and traps, nets and lines worked close to such spots will produce good results, often for years, if not indefinitely.

Some fish will be in packs or shoals. Predators may be hunting as a mob, rounding up victims whom instinct has told to group themselves into the security of numbers. Other fish will be more naturally concentrated, simply because they are of the same species, and their environmental requirements will tend to be similar at any given time. These moving shoals of fish are a slightly different proposition and here again local enquiries will be your best source of information. Shoaling fish usually appear in certain areas at pretty much the same time, year after year gradually moving on as water temperature, the weather, or their supply of food dictates. Sometimes the shoals will be big and the fish in good condition, or they may be split up into smaller groups or spent after spawning. What state they will be in when they reach you will depend very much on where you are, and when you catch them. Here again only the benefit of local knowledge and experience will be able to give you all the answers.

## Practice Makes Perfect

If all this sounds a bit bewildering, don't worry too much, because once you actually become involved in fishing, you will find that it really is not as complicated and unpredictable as it may seem. In practice you will find that when the fish are around, the word soon gets about. Local gossip will tell you with remarkable speed when the first of the season's catches have been made. Eventually, after having acquired some experience, you will be able to predict what fish are liable to be around at any given time. Rather like gardeners will discuss whether the tomatoes or cucumbers will be late or early or good or bad this year, forecasting the likely pattern of events will become second nature to you. The gulls screeching and diving out in the bay will tell you that below them fish are attacking or being attacked and opportunists that they are, these birds are feeding on the floating debris of the bloody battle below. Thus you will know that fish are there and can set about catching them.

Tricks of the trade like this will become the backbone of your expertise, but don't be afraid to be unconventional. Important fisheries have been discovered by people just trying a net here or a trap there, sometimes drawing a blank and sometimes hitting the jackpot. Many people will tell you that the most productive time for fishing is two hours either side of high water, but however good a general rule this may be, don't take it as a proven fact. In winter the best catches are usually made away from the coast in deep water, because inshore, food will be in short supply. But local conditions may be such that it's not true on your particular part of the coast. 'The wind from the south, blows the bait to fishes mouth' goes the old rhyme. To which I might add 'Wind from the east, could mean you are in for a feast'. Similarly, so many fish come on to feed when it is dark or overcast, that night fishing has always been considered to be more worthwhile than day fishing. Personally, I think the place to be at night is tucked up in bed at home, but of course that does not mean that you cannot be fishing at the same time. Pots, nets and lines, left down during the hours of darkness will be working while you're snoring. The snag is that you have to make two separate trips to the place where you are fishing and by leaving the gear unattended you will risk losing it through theft or worsening weather. So unless you find that you only get worthwhile results by fishing at night, it might be just as well to confine your fishing to the daytime, or at any rate the evening, assuming that the tide is right.

## Charts

One of the most important aids that is available to fishermen are charts. These are really just maps of the sea, and can be obtained in various scales to cover any piece of coast that you care to choose. I shall be discussing charts in more detail in chapter nine, so for the time being I will mention them only briefly. Suffice to say that you will be well advised to obtain one of the largest scale you can for the area you intend to work. Among other things, it will tell you how deep the water can be in any particular place and what sort of material the sea bed consists of; be it sand, gravel, mud or whatever. This of course is a very valuable piece of information, since if you know this, you will, to a great extent, be able to deduce what kind of fish are likely to be around. On the other hand, this knowledge is liable to be of more use to you if you are using a boat. If you just intend to fish from land, you will be working only the fringes of these defined areas and the sea bed may take on a different character nearer the shore. Having said that though, the more complete the picture you have of what may be happening in the vicinity, the greater your chances of success will be.

## Where and When

In fishing from the land, there are three main types of shoreline we can work from. The man-made kind like piers and jetties, then rocks and natural outcrops and finally beaches. The nature of the first depends of course on how they were constructed in the first place. They can be solid affairs, like breakwaters and harbour walls or more open structures consisting of piles or pillars that support the platform of the pier above them. Their size and length also varies greatly, and some of them can get you quite a way out to sea into fairly deep water. But whatever you have available locally the possibilities they can offer are always worth exploring — that is if you are allowed to fish from them. In some places this may be prohibited, or there may even be a small charge. So you either pay up, get permission, or wear your running shoes. Rock fishing offers some similarly diverse opportunities. Some formations can only be fished at certain tides when they give access to deep water, at other states of the tide, flat levels of rock may be covered by water and you will not be able to work any worthwhile spots. The road to success will be through observation. Visit the area at low tide, and study how the incoming flow makes or takes away opportunities, and above all make sure that stations you intend to fish from will not be cut off as the water rises.

Beaches as such, have the most variable characteristics of all; they can be practically flat, very steep, or combinations of the two, going down to the sea bed in steps. Most will be made of either sand, shingle, pebbles or mud, with mud and sand often being present together. Rocks may or may not be around on all of them, but when they are, weed is also likely to be found, and the extra cover it gives to small creatures is inclined to make the beach more productive. At low tide study the beach thoroughly. Look out for worm casts in patches of sand or mud. When covered by the sea, fish may feed here, and a long line (see chapter four) set in the vicinity could be productive. Depressions in a similar sea bed could mean that shellfish like cockles and clams may be in residence; try a sample dig, you might be lucky. Investigate anything that could attract or give cover to small marine life. Predators will be looking for a meal when the tide comes in, and if your line is cunningly set, they could take your bait instead. Perhaps a stream enteres the sea; this could well be a hot spot when hungry fish come searching for food. Look out for craters, hollows and obstructions, anything unusual that could be of interest to passing fish; these are the places to set your traps. Combine this visual appraisal of the situation with a thorough study of your chart; even at low tide, perhaps all you can see of the beach is shingle, but does it turn into sand just beyond the water line? If the water is deep enough, a cast out line (see chapter four) could reach flat fish lying on the bottom. How strongly does the tide run here? Would it be practical to try a staked net, or might it be likely to be swept away? The more research you do, the greater will be your rewards; and I might add that with those rewards comes the very pleasant satisfaction of knowing that success has been achieved through your own observation and initiative.

## Rules and Regulations

Before we actually get down to the techniques you can use to catch fish, I ought to mention that you cannot always fish just as you please. As with most things nowadays, there are often rules and regulations that state what you may or may not do. Most of the regulations are designed to conserve fish stocks, and if you break the rules you will be deservedly fined, sometimes a substantial amount. Since the rules vary, for different pieces of coast, you will have to find out your local official's address from the telephone book, and obtain a copy of the regulations. If possible, go and have a chat with him; he will be able to dot all the 'I's' and cross all the 'T's' if you have any difficulty in understanding what you are permitted to do.

Incidentally, here again you have the chance of learning something. I was re-reading my local rules a while ago, and I noticed some comprehensive restrictions for the taking of cockles locally. Now I must admit that I had not even considered the possibility of these shellfish being around in any numbers in the area mentioned, so off I went to seek the advice of my chief advisor — a very old ex-fisherman — who told me of a particular beach where they used to be gathered in some numbers. He said that this particular spot had been very productive in the old days, but catches had gradually declined and people had stopped working the beds. I knew for certain that nobody looked for them nowadays, so off I went to investigate. After about ten minutes I was delighted to find that left alone over the years, the cockles had been able to re-establish themselves and that I was now the fortunate 'proprietor' of an extremely useful little fishery. You too will do well therefore to read your own local rules thoroughly; they might not be so restrictive as you think.

The local health department is another source of useful information. They will be able to tell you about areas of sea or shoreline that may be polluted and perhaps even indicate some 'safe' stretches of coast.

# STAGE 1

# On The Seashore

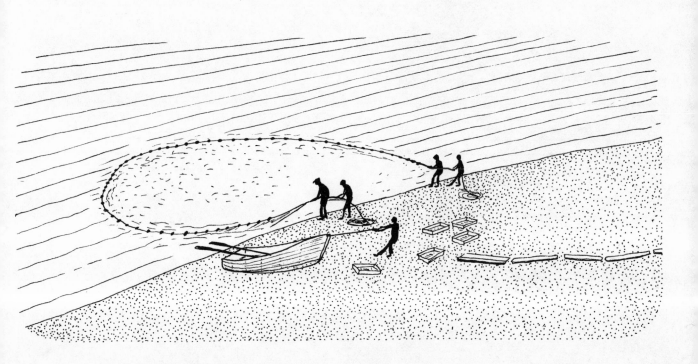

# 4. First Steps—Catching Shellfish from the Shore

In chapter two we looked at something of the history of man's harvesting of the sea, and I said that it probably began with the collecting of shellfish on the shore; so it might not be a bad idea if we start off in the same way.

## Gathering Shellfish

Not all beaches harbour shellfish, and it will be a waste of time looking for them on pebble ones. The best places will be fairly sheltered and consist of either rocky pools and gullies where there is a fair amount of weed about, or of sand, or mud, or shingle with a sprinkling of rocks.

Having located a likely spot, the first thing to do is to find out if it is polluted or not. If your hunting ground is far away from human habitation, you are unlikely to run into much trouble on this count; if the converse is true, beware. Local authorities have the disgusting habit of discharging raw sewage into the sea, and with the help of their planning department's expertise, they do their best to site such outlets as near as they possibly can to centres of human population. In many places, this will be all too obvious, in others not, so check with your local public health department. Beaches with any oil waste on them should also be avoided of course, and you will do well to steer clear of any factories that might be discharging toxic waste into the sea, even if they claim they are not.

The creatures most likely to be affected by pollution are the bivalve molluscs. These are the shellfish that have two shells hinged together, and include such animals as clams, mussels, cockles and oysters. Since they feed and breathe by filtering water through their bodies, they also extract and retain any toxic material that may be present. They can be purified by relaying them in clean sea water, but it takes two or three days for them to rid themselves of any harmful substances. So unless local circumstances make it easy for you to do this, it is probably not worth all the trouble. Crabs and lobsters (*crustacea*) are not so vulnerable to this kind of toxic attack, because, as it were, they pick up their food to eat it, but in all cases, their shells should be thoroughly scrubbed before attempting to cook them.

The next thing you have to check on are the times of the year that your local regulations allow you to gather. A number of shellfish are protected during the summer when they are spawning, so if you take them then, not only will you be breaking the law, but you will be decreasing the chances of a good supply for the future.

When you study your local regulations, you will probably find that they give precise details of the minimum size of any shellfish that may be taken from a particular fishery. There will also, almost certainly, be a clause that refers to the removal of berried (egg carrying) hen lobsters.

Such is the value of the lobster nowadays, that commercial fishermen have been known to carry a wire brush with them so that they can scrub off these eggs, allowing them to market the lobster in a state that conceals its true condition.

Apart from being a particularly callous violation of the laws of nature and human decency, these sort of activites are also against the laws of man. The penalties are, perhaps predictably, modest, usually consisting of a small fine. But I suppose that is better than nothing. Propriety does not allow me to outline my own ideas of the form that such retribution should take. Suffice to say that it would involve the vigorous and unmerciful manipulation of a large wire brush.

## Molluscs

Shellfish like the winkle and mussel are the easiest to find, because they do not bury themselves in the sand and can be found clinging to weed and rocks anywhere on the lower parts of the exposed beach. Others like clams and cockles take a bit more finding. A small depression in muddy sand is a classic indication, but the only sure way is to rake or dig. Here again there are often regulations about the type and size of tools you can use, but something like a short garden rake or hand fork is the best kind of thing. You may have to dig down as much as one and a half feet to find soft shell clams, but other fish like cockles and hard shell clams will be much nearer the surface. By the way, if you are doing any digging, remember to fill in the holes again as you go, it will help to conserve the bed and perhaps stop some unsuspecting wader from breaking his neck.

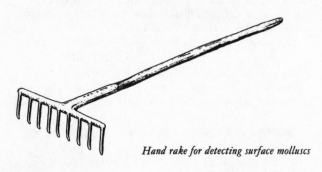

*Hand rake for detecting surface molluscs*

Other shellfish on the shore are either so rare or so unpalatable as to be hardly worth mentioning, but I suppose for the record they should at least be acknowledged. The humble limpet comes under this heading, and will be found in large numbers clinging to rocks and harbour walls that are covered at high tide. Unless you can catch them unawares, they take a fair bit of dislodging, and need to be kicked off or prised away with a knife. I tried eating them boiled once, and decided instantly that I would have to be very hungry indeed to even consider trying them again. Perhaps I didn't simmer them long enough. Some traditional recipes involve frying them. They might possibly be better minced, perhaps that would make them more chewable. Forget all about them is my advice.

On the other hand, molluscs like oysters and

pod razor shells make excellent eating, but are very difficult to find. Practically all the oysters available nowadays are cultivated ones, and you

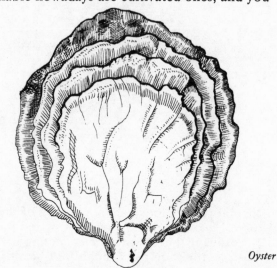

*Oyster*

will be unlikely to find any at all in the wild. The razor shell is more prolific, but all you are likely to see of him are his empty shells washed up on the tide line. Live ones will only be found in the areas of sandy beach that are exposed by the lowest of all tides, and even then you will have to dig down a couple of feet to get at them. They are very sensitive to vibration, and disappear under the sand like lightning even if you creep up on them. I have heard that if you pour salt down the hole at the top of their burrows the increased salinity annoys them, and they rise to the surface. So possibly you might give that a try if the opportunity presents itself.

When gathering shellfish, particularly the bivalves like cockles and clams, remember to treat them gently and not chuck them about. A cracked shellfish is very soon a dead one, and under no circumstances should you attempt to eat any molluscs or crustacea that are not alive immediately prior to cooking. If you do not observe this rule, you will be certain to poison yourself. You can test if a mollusc is alive by gently prising the shells apart; if it immediately snaps shut again it should be all right to eat.

## Crustacea

The other main contenders for our attention on the sea shore are lobsters, crabs and shrimps. Many books that are around at the moment claim that you will find lobsters and edible crabs in rock pools and under weed when the tide has gone out, and all you have to do is ferret around with a stick and hook them out. Perhaps I am being a little uncharitable, but I cannot help thinking that the authors of such advice have never actually tried it out for themselves. I have, and I can tell you that you will be wasting your time. But if you have all the time in the world, and feel in the mood to get your fingers trapped in a crevice by an irritated crab, (in the unlikely event that you should find a crab to irritate) good luck to you. But I can't really see the point of fooling around like this, when there are so many other far more effective and less time-consuming ways to bring them to the table. For example, a couple of traps (see also chapter eleven) strategically placed from the rocks or a pier is in my experience a far more productive proposition. All you have to do is find a suitable spot that leads to fairly deep water, bait up and lower them gently in. Having secured the end of the rope to a suitable fastening, you disappear for as long as you feel like and then return and haul them up to find out if fortune has smiled upon you. Of course I cannot guarantee that you will have caught anything. But I can assure you that your chances of success will have been much greater than they would have been scratching around rock pools and seaweed, looking for needles in haystacks.

Anyway, any lobsters and crabs discovered holed up on the shore may well be there because they are changing their shells. They do this in order to grow, and until their new shells harden up — that's why they are keeping out of the way of predators — their flesh will be watery and decidely unpleasant to eat.

### Shrimps and Prawns

There always seems to be a great deal of confusion about the difference between shrimps and prawns. In general the fish trade call small ones of both species shrimps and the bigger ones prawns. Scientifically they come in different groups, and of course these can be defined, but I think for our purposes it will be as well to go along with the old fashioned fish sellers' practice and keep it simple.

In most places, shrimps and prawns only come close inshore in the summer, temporarily moving offshore at the first sign of any bad weather that would smash them against rocks or harbour walls. Come the winter they will leave for deep water again until the following summer.

They can be caught with numerous contrivances, but perhaps the best known way is with a hand net; the kind that you may have wielded as a child. Being a bit bigger now you will be able to handle a larger one. It is likely to be of the conventional 'D' shape, with the upright of the 'D' as much as three, or even four, feet across. This part of the net is usually made of wood, while the curved part will be a metal rod. I have seen them made of bamboo, (you can permanently bend it by gentle persuasion over a flame) but I don't know if they last very long.

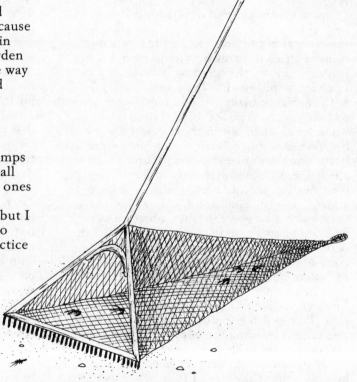

*Hand net with 'tickler' leading edge*

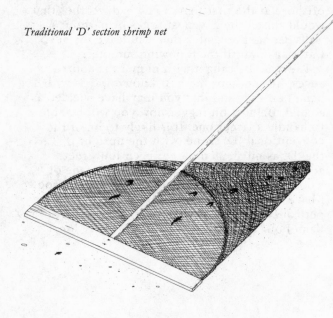

*Traditional 'D' section shrimp net*

scraping over the open patches and teasing in around the patches of weed.

In the summer, shrimps and prawns will be found in any spot that gives them a reasonable amount of shelter. I used to do very well working along the piles of an old wooden pier, scooping the net up through the weed. Alas it is there no longer, but it is the sort of hunting ground to look for. Rock pools are another possibility, but they are unlikely to be as productive as open areas of sea, and you will need a much smaller pointed net that you can work in under the rocks.

There are other, rather more complicated ways of catching shrimps and prawns that I shall be dealing with in later chapters, but I think that this one together with hoop nets and traps will be the most effective methods for the small scale fisherman without a boat.

## Hoop or Drop Nets

Like most other kinds of fishing gear, hoop nets come in various shapes and sizes, but a typical description would be a 20 inch diameter metal hoop with a 2 feet deep conical bag of netting suspended below it. Above the hoop and attached to it equidistantly, come three short retaining ropes that converge upwards to the main hauling line. The bait is often held in position by trapping it between sliding leather washers that are threaded on two pieces of twine that run parallel across the diameter of the hoop. Other methods involve tying bait to the inside of the net near the bottom, and personally I think that this way is best, because when you start to haul, much of the net will be raised above your catch before it is aware that all is not well, and escape will be far less likely. A weight set in the bottom of the net cone will help it to sit better on the sea bed if any tide is running, and will stop the net from slewing and covering up the bait. I have found that if I spread out the bait — scrap fish and the like — all around the net, I tend to get better catches; so perhaps prawn are possessive about their meals, in the way that lobsters will fight off others that try to share it.

Other variations, like purse hoops, have elaborate folding rims that close up as you start to haul, and even smarter are the French all metal folding nets. These are really terrific, but

Anyway, the one I have is of metal — except for the handle, which I pinched from an old garden rake — and the rod passes through a hole about 15 inches from the end of it. I used a piece of hardwood for the leading edge, and after binding the conical net in position I nailed on some thinner strips of hardwood to give it a bit of protection from the scraping it inevitably gets. In chapter thirteen I tell you how to make netting, but to make net of a mesh small enough to take shrimps is a real bind. I used to do it when I was a lad, but in those days I had to, because small boys' finances are inclined to have limitations. So unless you find it an attractive challenge, I would advise you to buy three or four yards of machine made stuff, and spare yourself the time and trouble. It will not cost very much, and you can often obtain it very cheaply when a manufacturer is selling off the odd lengths that he has in stock. Form a cone of netting about three feet deep, trim off the excess and then carefully tie up the seam; then in a similar way bind it to the net frame. The net needs to be pointed at the bottom, so that all your catch tumble into one spot when you raise it, making them easier to remove.

I use my net in sheltered water where the sandy bottom is strewn with weed covered boulders about the size of footballs. I usually try my luck when the water is a foot or two deep,

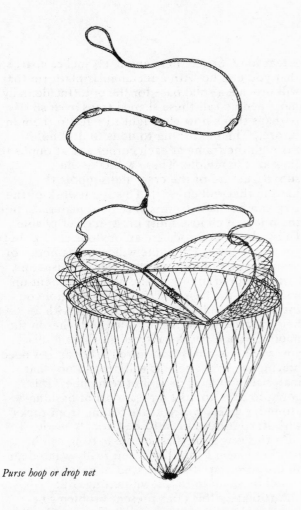

*Purse hoop or drop net*

because they take up such little space. Later on, if you do get a boat, make up half a dozen or so and attach marker floats to the ends of the hauling warps. Position them near rocks or between patches of weed, and then just cruise slowly round, pulling, clearing and resetting them.

The interesting thing about hoop nets is that you are likely to catch some really huge lobsters and crabs; the ones that are too big to get through the trap entrances, so don't be surprised if you get some jumbo results!

### Shellfish Traps
There must be at least as many different types of shellfish trap as there are pages in this book; and indeed the same could be said of the different materials they are made from. I cannot possibly discuss them all, and in fact there is no need to, because just one or two of them will suit our purposes admirably. The measurements I give for such traps are purely nominal; being those that I have found to be most suitable for my own local conditions. In your part of the world it may be common practice to use bigger or even smaller traps. A bit of local research will soon tell you what adjustments should be made to my specifications.

### Lobster and Crab Traps
Contrary to what most people think, crabs and lobsters are perfectly able to get out of most traps. Divers who have watched what happens will tell you that unless the gear is fitted with an escape inhibitor, the shellfish will come and go more or less as they please. The reason they stay in the trap is that they think they have found themselves a cosy little home, and because of the bait you have put in, that this new hideaway has a nice supply of food as well. So unless you are just going to do some 'quick' fishing, that is just leave the traps down for an hour or two, you will be liable to catch more if you make entrance to your trap easy, and departure difficult. This can be done in numerous ways: counter balanced trap doors is one popular method and pieces of wire thrust downwards across the entrance another. A funnel of netting fixed to a circular hole in the side or top of the trap is equally effective and has the merit of being easier to construct. The animal finds it fairly easy to get in, because the end fixed to the trap is held open, but if it tries to get into the tunnel from the inside the unsecured end of the netting will just flop about and escape will be difficult.

then again so are the prices, and you have to remember that you will lose a few; so unless you are rich, make up your net out of an old bicycle wheel rim and lace the bag of netting to it through the spoke holes. You can, if you want, make the net in one piece, but as I mentioned a while ago, working such small mesh netting can be very tedious, so buy sheet netting and lace it up in the same way I described for hand nets. Alternatively you could try and get hold of some of the tubular netting that the keep nets of the freshwater angler are made from — but this might prove a more expensive proposition.

These nets will not only catch shrimps and prawns of course. Lobsters, crabs and even flat fish are going to find your bait attractive as well, but if you were not interested in catching the smaller shellfish, you could use large mesh netting which would be easier to make.

Hoop net fishing is a very good method for beginners to make a start with. Worked from piers or outcrops and off rocks and gullies, they hardly ever fail to produce encouraging results, and in small boats they are particularly useful

But from our point of view, I think that the 'parlour' pot will be the most practical kind to use. In this type of trap the interior is divided into two sections. One half of the trap has two or even three entrances from the outside world, and is therefore fairly easy to get into. The other half of the pot leads off this section and has no direct exit or entry to the outside. Both parts of the trap are usually baited, and the theory is that lobsters and crabs incur no difficulty in getting into the pot initially, and having thus been almost casually tempted to their doom, move eventually into the 'parlour', from which escape is much more difficult. This ease of entry is an important point. Many traps have only one opening, and if the prey cannot quickly find it he may give up trying to get at your bait and move on in search of another more accessible meal. On the other hand if your trap has a number of entrances that are easy to get into, it is also easy to get out of, and has very little holding power at all. The parlour pot manages to combine the best of both worlds and contrives, in a rather sneaky way, firstly to lure, and then to secure.

To have a trap that keeps what it catches is not only a good thing in the obvious sense, but for the food fisherman this ability has a special significance. Should bad weather prevent you from getting to your traps, as it probably will at some time if you are working from a small boat, when you do get round to hauling them they are far more likely to contain something than is the conventional type of trap. In fact, I have a friend who makes deliberate use of the holding power that parlour pots have. He lives in a city some way from the coast and is only able to do his fishing at weekends. On Sunday afternoons he sets his pots in a secluded spot and leaves them there until the following weekend. He is very rarely disappointed with the results, although he has lost a few because of bad weather. But as he says, they cost very little to make, and the modest expenditure involved is invariably recouped during their first week's work.

## Constructing A Parlour Pot

About the simplest way to make a parlour pot is to nail some 18 inch battens of 2" x 1" timber onto two heavier pieces of timber that are about 3 feet long. Space them about 1½ inches apart so that you end up with a rectangular platform that will provide a solid base for the pot. (Incidentally, most people call these shaped traps *creels* so perhaps that's how we ought to refer to them in future.) The next thing to do is to drill holes through the frame at each corner and at opposite sides of the middle. These will take the superstructure of the creel and support the netting that will cover it. This framework of the trap can be made from a variety of materials, but the one you choose must be strong yet pliable. Fairly thin metal rods are an obvious choice, but you could use a wood like willow or bamboo, or even plastic tubing. But whatever you use, one end is secured in one of the holes then bent up and across the base and fixed into the hole on the opposite side, giving you an arch with a height of about twelve to fourteen inches in the middle. When you have fixed all three in place, you will be in a position to tell if the arches need bracing along the top. It will depend on what materials you have used, but remember, it is going to have to take a great deal of bashing around, especially if you are fishing from rocks with it; so it does need to be strongly made.

At this stage, the first of the netting can be fixed in place. I suppose if you really wanted an all purpose trap, the best kind of netting to use would be small mesh prawn netting. But unfortunately this does present problems because we have to consider the effects of the tide on the trap. The smaller the mesh, the greater the resistance to the flow will be, and even if it is heavily weighted, it is liable to take off and be lost or smashed against rocks and obstructions. So the solution will have to be a compromise based on local conditions. The best thing to do is to see what mesh size other people in your area use and do likewise.

Lace on three vertical panels of netting across the trap, secured to the curved uprights and the base. I should mention at this point, that if you want to make a deluxe version that will allow you to remove the catch more easily, you should construct one or two separate end panels that are the same shape as the cross section of the main superstructure. These will be covered in netting and hinged in some way to the end of the trap. You can do this at both ends, or just at the parlour end. If you hinge both end sections, you will of course lose one external entrance. But you could get round this by making the openings on the top of the trap.

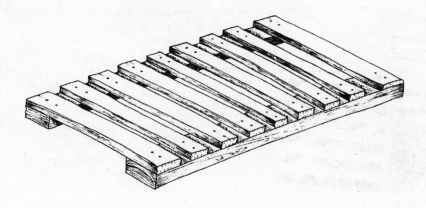

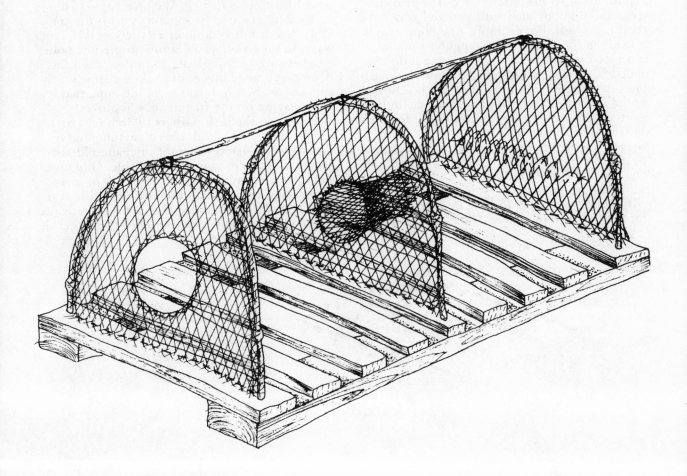

*Parlour pot construction— 1. Wooden base 2. Partially netted pot with the superstructure and bracing bar in position*

*A slatted all wooden trap—a type popular in America*

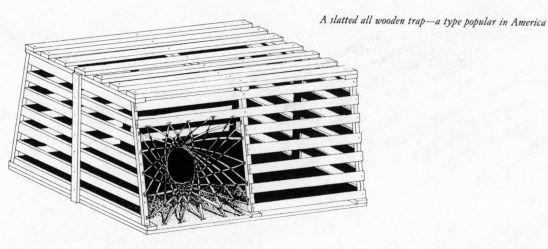

I mention all these various alternatives not, I hope, to confuse you, but to encourage you not to feel obliged to follow my particular way of making traps to the letter. Try out your own ideas and find out what suits you and your local conditions best. For example, one popular type is made in the form of a rectangular wooden crate, and instead of netting, wooden laths are nailed fairly closely together lengthwise along all the sides. But in such traps the entrance funnels would still be made of netting. Then again if you wanted to be really cunning you might feel like designing your own folding trap; perhaps on the lines of a wire framework covered in netting. That is the nice thing about fishing equipment. The possibilities for refinement and improvisation are really endless.

If you are not going to have smart hinged doors on your trap, you will now need to cut a slit across the panel that is going to be the parlour end and then attach a piece of twine to one end of the cut so that it can be laced up when the creel is fishing. We now come to a convenient stage to fit some weight to the trap. Once again, this is done in a variety of different ways, so take your pick. Some people just pour concrete all over the base, and often when this is done they imbed pieces of broken mirror on the surface just before it sets — in the hope that light playing on the fragments will prove attractive to shellfish. Others tie in bricks or lumps of concrete, and indeed anything heavy that comes to hand – lengths of chain, old sash weights, whatever is readily available. One neat and effective way is to screw on strips of metal underneath the creel on the bottom of the two long sections of the base. This not only provides the required weight, but also helps to protect the

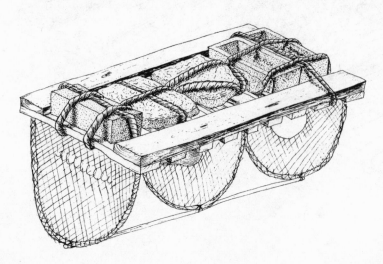

*Parlour pot with improvised weights lashed in position*

woodwork and to a certain extent balances the creel when it is being hauled. Another advantage that this particular method has is that, since the weights are attached to the lowest part of the trap, they also help it to sit the right way up on the sea floor.

Exactly how much weight you will need for your traps will depend on how hard the tide runs where you intend to set them. Anything from say 6 lbs up to about 15 lbs are accepted figures, but only experiment or local enquiry will tell you precisely the amount to use. Remember you will be the one that will have to haul them up, so the less you can get away with the better.

The next thing to do is to cut a circular hole about 6 inches in diameter in the middle panel, and on the parlour side, attach an 8 inch long tube of fine mesh netting. This will allow the prey to squeeze through into the parlour, and as I mentioned before, be an effective barrier to his escape.

The main body of the trap can now be covered in netting, which can be laced to the arches and stapled to the wooden base. Holes can now be cut on opposite sides of the entry half of the creel, and these should be about 8 inches in diameter and bound in round the edges to form a neat circular opening. These are the trap entrances through which the shellfish will initially come.

If you intend to use your trap on a fairly regular basis, it will take quite a hammering, so it will be a good idea to protect the exposed edges in the way that most commercial fishermen do. You can do this by binding the netted framework with any odd lengths of rope or with thin strips of rubber cut from old tyres. (see chapter thirteen).

## Baiting The Trap

Now you need to devise some way to secure the bait inside the trap. It needs to be placed in such a way that it is not accessible from the outside so that whatever it is that you hope to catch has to get right into the trap in order to get at it. This will stop creatures merely eating it from outside and then departing in search of another meal. Most people tie the bait to pieces of cord strung vertically or horizontally inside the trap in appropriate places, and you will probably do well to do the same. If you are using fairly firm bait, this will present few problems, but if it is in small pieces or soft like offal, you will need to contain it in some way. This can be done by putting it in a small muslin bag or by bunching it up in an old piece of nylon stocking.

While I am on the subject of bait, I might mention that it seems to be universally agreed that crabs prefer fresh bait and lobsters stale. Personally I have found that it seems to make little difference, but it might be the case in your particular area.

For commercial fishermen, obtaining large regular supplies of bait is often a continual headache; some net or line their own, while others are provided with it by the merchants who buy their catches. We will need nothing like the quantities required by the professionals, but we can obtain it in much the same way. Most merchants or mongers will give you the odd waste fish they have lying around, especially if you supply them with odd fish from time to time. On the other hand you can net or line your own for immediate use or use preserved bait that has been frozen or salted down (chapter fourteen). If you really get stumped you could

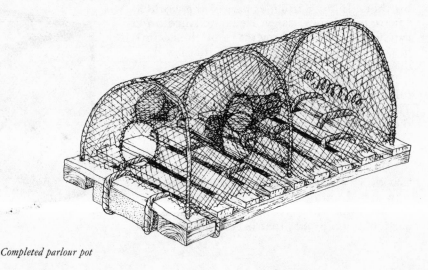

*Completed parlour pot*

always punch a few holes in a tin of cat food and use that — it works very well.

All that remains to do now, is to attach a suitable length of rope to lower and haul the trap with. Since you will almost certainly be hauling by hand (it can be done mechanically) you will need a rope that you can get a good grip on, and to this end it will need to be around 1½ inches in circumference. Sisal is about the cheapest, and its rough texture allows you to get a good grip on it; the only snag is that you will have to treat it with a copper napthalate solution (some wood preservatives are good) or it will rot. The trap will be easier to haul, not spin, and plane through the water better, if you attach the rope not directly to the creel, but to a strop fixed across the base of the end opposite the parlour section. This will also mean that when you haul the trap, gravity will tend to pull anything caught inside away from the entrances, thus making capture more certain. In a small boat it will be particularly helpful because the trap will break surface end on and be easier to bring in over the side.

When not in use, traps like these may have to be stored in the open. If this is the case and synthetic twine has been used for the netting, you may find that it will start to disintegrate. This is due to the ultra-violet element in sunlight, but deterioration can be kept to a minimum by using black netting which is the least susceptible to such ravages.

## Shrimp Pots

This kind of trap varies just as much in construction and design as the ones used for catching crabs and lobsters. But in most cases they are basically miniature versions of their big brothers. In my particular part of the world a square metal trap has evolved, and since official catching trials have shown it to be the country's most effective pot, it is the type that I will describe.

Being made entirely of metal our local pots fulfil the first basic need of any shellfish trap. They are very strong. They have to be, because they are normally set on, or very close to, rocks and other solid obstructions that would very soon smash them to pieces if they were not built for the job. Their second most valuable asset is that they catch shrimps very well indeed. Exactly why they do nobody seems to know, but my theory is that shrimps simply like metal traps — particularly old ones that have regularly been

used in the sea. In the same way that we are happier walking down a firm concrete path than we are plodding uncertainly through a snow drift, shrimps may feel more at home with the solidity of metal around them. Perhaps it is a question of association; they may know by observation or instinct that predators lurk in the soft sand of the seabed, but that attack never comes through solid objects. Anyway, whatever the reason, metal traps in general, and this type in particular, certainly have the edge on all others.

To make one of these traps you will need some right angled metal conduit of the type that bolts together to construct industrial shelving, or anything similar — parts of some old bed springs are suitable — some wire netting of the smallest gauge you can find; wire — to lace it all together with — some fairly stiff tin or zinc sheet, and a pair of pincers to cut the netting with.

The trap needs to be about 15 inches square, so first of all, lengths of the metal conduit should be cut and bolted or welded together to form the outline of a complete cube. Wire netting should now be wrapped all around the cube and wired in place leaving one side of the cube open. This uncovered part will be fitted with a door through which the trap can be baited and cleared. Circular holes 5 inches in diameter should now be nipped in four walls going around the pot leaving the base and the top opposite each other still covered in. You could have entrances

*A shrimp pot*

through the top and the bottom as well if you wanted to, but it's more work and you do not really need them. When you do this, cut the netting in such a way as to leave as many long 'threads' as possible; these will be useful when you come to wire the entrance funnels in.

Unless you have managed to find wire netting of a much smaller mesh than I have ever been able to get hold of, it will probably occur to you at this stage that the prawns and shrimps are going to be able to get through the holes. So in order to stop this we must place a further layer of netting over the first one and offset it so that it effectively halves the mesh size. Once again the entrance holes will need to be cut out in this new layer.

The entrance funnels will taper inside the trap, and should be built up of two or three layers of netting in order to achieve the required stiffness. They need to be made from panels of netting roughly 9 inches square, and are best formed by nipping out a one inch diameter hole in the centre of the sheet — then cutting across from two opposite sides almost up to the hole, and finally shaping and folding the sheet into a cone so that all loose ends of netting end up on the edge that will be fastened to the inside edge of the trap. After they have been wired in place, work can begin on the door.

If you were prepared to give them some fairly regular maintenance with penetrating oil, you could use ordinary metal hinges for your trap door. But probably the simplest solution would be to use small wire rings. In which case you would have to make sure that you got a nice tight fit or the catch would be able to escape.

To secure the door at the other end you can bend the lip of the metal back over itself to form a tube through which a wire spring bolt can be pushed. Alternatively punch rectangular holes in the closing edge of the door so that they come down over metal rings or brackets that will again allow you to bolt or tie the door securely. On the other hand you may come up with an ingenious method of your own, but whatever you do make sure that it allows the door to be really firmly secured, yet easily opened with cold wet fingers.

Some people that I know construct little wire baskets that serve as bait holders; they are about an inch deep, and a fraction smaller in dimensions than the door opening. They hang down inside the pot (and are held in position when the trap is the other way up) by means of wire hooks fitted at all four corners. I suppose that if you were regularly going to use very small pieces of bait that might otherwise wash out of the trap it would be advisable to do likewise, but as I have said before, I personally like to see the bait spread out a little more than this as I have found that it seems to improve catches.

All that remains to do now is to give the trap a good coating of tar to protect it from the ravages of salt water, and to attach the hauling line. These kinds of traps rarely need any additional weighting, but if you are going to work them where the tide runs exceptionally hard it is a simple matter to wire some suitable lumps of ballast to the inside edges. You can fit a bridle to the trap as we did with the large lobster creel, but this is not essential, and the same effect can be achieved by fixing two rings through the framework opposite the door side of the trap, and looping the hauling warp through these.

Shrimp and prawn traps are worked in more or less the same way as their bigger brothers are for lobsters and crabs; the only difference will be in the grounds they are used on. During the summer prawns will be found near rocks and weed, so likely places to set your traps will be around harbour entrances, or piers and break-waters that are fairly sheltered. The best results will be obtained during overcast weather or if the pots are set at dusk and left down overnight.

If you fish your traps on the sea bed, when working them from say a pier, you may find that all you catch are small shore crabs. Should you be troubled in this way, the solution is simple — just raise the trap a few feet and the crabs who cannot swim will not be able to crawl in.

*Suspending a prawn trap just off the seabed will help to avoid the unwelcome attention of small crabs*

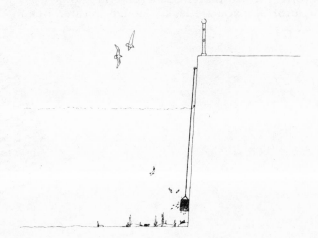

## Whelks, Crawfish and Norway Lobsters

Of the other kinds of shellfish that you are liable to come across when fishing from the shore, the whelk is one of the commonest. They are often taken as a bi-catch in hoop nets and lobster pots, and you will probably get all you need in this way; but if they are a particular favourite of yours you could make a special trap for them. The traditional kind is a heavy domed affair made of iron and rope, looking a little like an elongated miniature igloo. It consists of a solid metal base, about a foot in diameter, which has eight holes drilled equidistantly around the edge of it. Into these holes are welded 1 inch metal rods which bend upwards and inwards to a 6 inch diameter ring that forms the trap opening, about a foot above the base. Tarred rope is tied on one of the bars right at the base, then taken across to, and around the next bar, and so on, gradually spiralling upwards until the whole of the framework is filled in. A fine mesh tube of netting hangs down inside the entrance to act as an escape inhibitor and the bait is usually held on strings towards the base of the trap. These traps are extremely heavy, some 35 pounds or so, and you will need some fairly substantial rope to haul them with if you are going to do so with any comfort.

Whelks will be found in many coastal areas, but those caught offshore will be bigger and richer in flavour than the ones taken in estuaries and near the shore. If you set your traps where the sea bed consists of sand and mud you will be likely to have the greatest chance of success.

The crawfish is rather like a lobster without any large claws, and tastes very much the same. They inhabit the same sort of grounds as lobsters but are certainly not so common or widespread and do not tend to come close to the shore very often. It will therefore be something of a surprise if you are lucky enough to catch one in your creel or hoop net when fishing from the shore.

The Norway Lobster, *Nephrops Norvegious,* also known as the Dublin Bay Prawn, is probably best recognized by the name that it arrives on your plate with — Scampi. Once again, it is not very widely distributed and lives on muddy sea floors only in fairly deep water. Being much smaller than the common lobster, the traps used to catch them are similarly scaled down, generally taking the form of a miniature lobster pot. If you do have the good fortune to live in an area where you can catch them, bear in mind that although commercially only the tails are marketed as food, the claws are delicious and are well worth picking out as well.

## The Care of the Catch

At the beginning of this chapter I mentioned that it was essential to handle your catch with some care and to make sure that you kept them alive immediately prior to cooking them. This is fairly easy to do with crabs and lobsters and even with bi-valves like cockles and clams if you place them in a ventilated container with wet seaweed or sacking over them. This will keep them cool

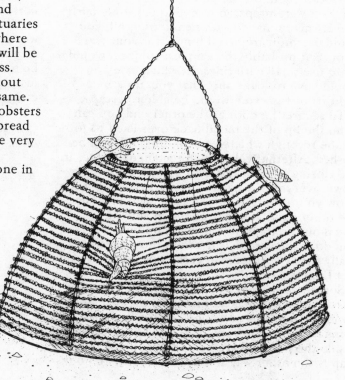

*Traditional whelk trap*

and stop them from drying out. But the sooner you can cook them the better. Shrimps and prawns are the most tricky of the lot, and need to be especially well looked after. To this end, you will be wise to construct a bag of netting that will fit inside a lidded bucket of some sort. This can be filled with sea water which can be changed at regular intervals and used to carry the catch home in. An ideal solution would be to do as many of the commercial fishermen do, and cook them as you catch them. And it may well be worth all the trouble of taking a portable stove with you if you live any distance from the coast.

Always pack lobsters and crabs tightly the right way up and remember to put an elastic band around the claws of lobsters or they will fight each other to the death.

If you should have to return any undersized lobsters or Nephrops to the water always put them gently back in tail first. This will allow them to expel any air that they have taken into their bodies and will prevent complications that could kill them.

**Tangle Bushes**
One method you might try if you can't be bothered to make a proper trap, or find yourself in a situation where you quickly need to improvise one, is the tangle bush. First of all you select a fairly dense bush of a size that will fit inside an old sack. If you feel the bush does not have enough growth to create much of a maze inside the sack, you can remedy this by winding some old rope or wool all around and in and out of it. Place some rocks or anything heavy in the sack and stuff the bush in after them. Then form an entrance by binding the mouth of the sack firmly around a piece of old pipe or a plastic container with both ends cut off it. Attach a hauling line somewhere near the entrance, drop some bait down inside and you are ready to go. The size of the entrance and indeed the sack can be varied to suit whatever you think may be around, and if you can't find a sack it will even work with just a bush, but obviously you will not have so much holding power.

*Tangle bush for catching lobsters and crabs*

## Pole Snares

These can be effective for taking shellfish like crabs where the water is clear enough to see them, and not too deep. I use one under a nearby pier, where the supporting cross members (but not the local authorities!) allow you to walk around underneath, just above the surface of the water. You need a pole that is long enough to reach the seafloor, some thin snare wire about twice the length of the pole, and a brass screw eye. Fix the eye in near the end of the pole and secure one end of the wire to its shank. Then pass the other end of the wire through the eye. To fish with it, you simply form a loop on the end, dip it down around them, pull the wire tight and then haul them in. If you find a suitable spot, and nothing seems to be around, try putting down a little ground bait for a few days. You will be surprised what this will attract.

## Your Own Fish Farm

If you can find a suitably secluded spot, you may find it worthwhile to encourage marine life to congregate there. Some old lengths of drain-pipe piled round with rocks or half buried in the sand will provide hiding holes for lobsters and crabs, and some netting strung between rocks to collect weed will give cover for shrimps and prawns. Chuck in some waste fish from time to time, and with any luck you will soon be able to start harvesting your 'crop'.

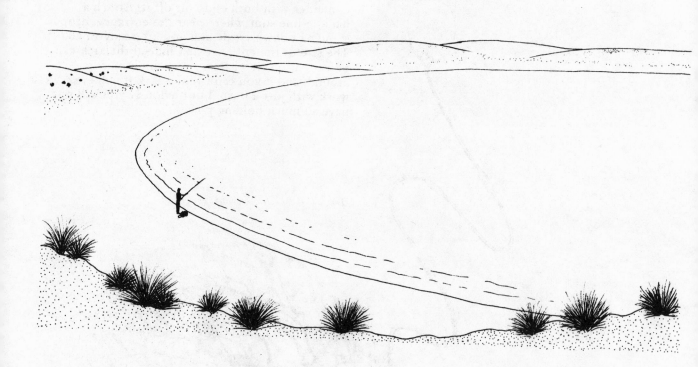

# 5. Catching Fish from the Shore

*There are as good fish in the sea as ever came out of it.*

*Scott*

As well as shellfish, many ordinary fish also come close enough to the shoreline to catch. In fact some quite large fish, bass for example, can be feeding literally just a few feet from the water's edge.

Most areas of coast will have their own particular specialities, certain varieties of fish who are more suited to the prevailing local conditions than others. So, fishing in any given area you will find in practice that your catch will be dominated by something like half a dozen types of fish. What these will be will depend on where you are and the time of year; the only certain way to find out will be through the kind of local research I mentioned in chapter three. I intend therefore not to discuss in detail each species of fish that you may possibly come across, but to concern myself principally with the variety of ways in which they may all be caught. This will give you a kind of blanket coverage, so that if fish are there, your repertoire of techniques will always be able to provide you with the means of catching them.

As with shellfish fishing, there are often rules and regulations that govern when, where and how you may fish, so check on them first.

## Rod and Line

Basically there are three different types of rod that are used for sea fishing. The surfcaster, which is 10 to 12 feet long and can get your bait out well over a 100 yards (with practice). The spinning rod, somewhat shorter in the 7 to 8 foot bracket, mainly used from rocks, beaches and piers, and the slightly smaller but much stronger boat rod. Various kinds of reels are used with each, but nowadays either multipliers or fixed spool reels dominate the scene. The multiplier is both expensive and difficult to use, and I would recommend that you go for the fixed spool kind every time. About the only type of rod that will really be of much use to us will be the surfcaster, and if you obtain one that is not too long you could also use it from a pier or jetty. Avoid at all costs the multi-purpose rods that fit together in various combinations for beach, boat or rock fishing. They are of necessity compromises, and as such are inadequate in any of their roles. But as I said, the surfcaster is the boy for us — and then only in certain circumstances. In most other situations we will have other techniques that we can use that will be more effective.

*The three main types of sea fishing rod. (From the top) boat rod, spinning rod, surfcaster beach rod*

To buy this type of rod and a suitable fixed spool reel to go with it, would at the present time set you back a substantial amount. You only have to look in a dealers' window to find that out. But as more people go fishing than participate in any other single hobby, there is a great deal of secondhand equipment floating around. You should therefore have very little trouble in equipping yourself for less than half the cost of new. Be careful though; a great deal of flashy rubbish is marketed. Look for the quality brand names — and check for damage; it may be very expensive, if not impossible, to put right.

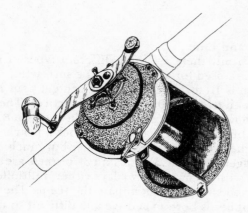

*The two most popular types of sea fishing rod. Above, the fixed spool reel and left, the multiplier*

The time to use this sort of equipment will be when fish are known to be around off a certain beach, but are either too far out to be contacted with a cast out line (the next kind of equipment that I describe) or when the weather (wind blowing inshore) makes the use of a cast out line impractical. A rod and line will also be useful to spin for fish that are more likely to take a moving bait.

As a general rule, you will need about 200 yards of 30 lb breaking strain monofilament line on your reel and a selection of weights from about 4ozs for fairly calm conditions, up to 9 ozs for rougher weather. (Making your own weights is dealt with in chapter thirteen). There are numerous ways in which to rig the business end of your line, but unless you are advised differently by local experts, it boils down to three basic possibilities. The leger for fairly placid weather, the paternoster for a rough sea, and the lure for spinning. Chapter thirteen tells

you how to make various lures and what hooks and knots to use.

As you will readily see if you visit any fishing tackle store — large numbers of commercial concerns manufacture lures, plugs and artificial baits. Most of the devices on offer are a complete waste of money; the ones that are any good can easily be made at home for next to nothing.

The best way to learn how to cast your line is to watch someone who has had a lot of practice actually doing it, and then try to do the same.

Fishing with a paternoster or leger is fairly straightforward; all you do is cast out and wait for a bite, flicking the rod tip shoreward to drive the hook home when you think something has taken the bait. Gradually reel in line if the tide is pushing your tackle back in towards you.

Spinning is really just as simple. All that you have to remember is that you are trying to make the lure or bait simulate the movement of something the fish will think is food. So you cast out your line and then wind it back in again — then cast it out again and so on. If fish are about, eventually you will catch something.

With a paternoster or leger you will need to bait the hook. You can buy artificial and frozen baits, but I must say I have never had much luck with the latter except for catching shellfish. If you possibly can, I think you will get the best results if you go out of your way to obtain fresh bait of some sort.

## Bait

Many of the shellfish that we have already learnt to catch make an excellent bait for fish of all kinds. Perhaps the most successful is the mussel, but the trouble is that it is very soft and breaks up easily, so that it has to be tied on to the hook, which is a fiddly and time consuming process. Cockles and shrimps can be deadly on occasions, and another useful standby is the limpet, which is usually available on all but the highest of tides. Small fish, or strips from large ones, will also prove effective, but the one favoured by commercial fishermen — because it stays on the hook so well — is the whelk. Certain marine worms (the lug and rag for example), are very good for a wide variety of fish. But first of all you have to locate the sand and mud patches that they live in and then spend hours digging them up. This of course is all rather a drag, and since their numbers seem to be dramatically declining — through the efforts of amateur and professional bait diggers — they are probably best left for the anglers who are willing to pay such high prices for them.

In reality you will probably end up using whatever you can readily lay your hands on, but the best advice will be to use whatever is locally successful.

## Hooks

Hook sizes are universally quoted numerically. But unfortunately the various firms that manufacture them invariably give different numbers to a particular size of hook. Luckily the variations are not all that great; but it is something to watch out for.

Hooks for freshwater fishing normally get smaller the higher the number is, but for sea fishing it works the other way round. The smallest being size 1, and the largest around the 15 or 16 mark. For general small scale food fishing the most suitable will be somewhere in the middle of the range.

## Cast Out Lines

Cast out lines are in fact launched long lines, and a very cunning and useful method of fishing they are too. Their big advantage is that they enable you to get a line out from a beach in much the same way that a beach rod can, but with all the inherent advantages of the large number of hooks that a long line can work. This means that you can be fishing right from the water's edge, up to say 80 yards offshore — a big help, since some fish can be feeding just a few feet from the water's edge, whilst they and others may be active anywhere along the extent of your line.

The line is cast by means of a 10 to 12 foot pole, and in the old days they recommended they should be of elm. Nowadays I think you would have problems tracking down a sufficiently seasoned length, so it is probably better to use a more easily obtainable bamboo one. You can sometimes acquire these from carpet sellers, but more certainly from specialized dealers in bamboo products. Female Chinese is best for the job; they use it to make the most expensive split cane fishing rods. It has small nodules and a much better action than the male bamboo. However supplies have been unreliable since the cultural revolution, so take what you can get; they are all fairly cheap. Test the pole for cracks by holding it vertically and tapping one end on a hard floor; it should 'ring' not 'clonk', and store it in a cool place or air trapped between the nodules will expand and cause serious splitting.

In days gone by they used to cut a slit in the end of the pole, and slot the line with the button on through it. But I have developed the idea slightly, and instead of the slit, I use a spike sticking out of the end of the pole, and instead of the button a ring. When casting, I find that the ring flies off the spike more smoothly than the button is released in the old method, and I tend to get more accurate results. If you decide to use my method, you will need a metal rod about as thick as a six inch nail and at least a foot long. An old stair rod is ideal. Leave about 4 inches protruding and secure the rest in the end of the pole. I used a plastic filler to bed the rod in, but a carefully shaped wooden plug would be a cheaper solution. The first casting pole I made up was of the notch kind, and after I had cut the profile of the slit across the end of the pole, it was a fairly easy job to plaster in the empty spaces with filler. It doesn't really matter which system you use; they are both very effective.

Make up the one that you think will be easiest for you; but with either method, remember to scrape off the white fibrous coating that covers the inside wall of the bamboo, otherwise the filler or glue will not be able to get a good grip.

For the line, you will need about 100 yards of spun nylon twine. Something just under pencil thickness is best (you will also be able to use it as a set long line later on); not only will it be more comfortable to haul, but its weight will prevent the wind from blowing it into an almighty birds-nest, and you will avoid many muttering hours of wasted time.

At the end of the line or about 4 feet before it (you will see why in a minute) comes the weight, which can vary from about ¾ lb up to 2 lbs, depending on how hard the sea is running and how far you want to cast. If you have a selection of various sizes at the ready, old mother trial and error will soon sort things out for you. After the weight comes either a 3 or 4 feet continuation of the main line with a ring on the end of it, or if you are using a slit pole, a similar length of thin line with a button on the end. You have to use finer line with the latter method, since the thick main line would not move freely enough in and out of the pole slot when casting. The exact length of this final part of the tackle will depend on how tall you are and the length of your caster. For a 12 feet pole like I use, the suggested measurements are about right, but then I am a very tall man; try various lengths and see what suits you best.

So now we have about 100 yards of main line, a weight attached near the end, then a further length of line with a ring or button on the end of it, plus of course one casting pole. You may have noticed that as yet we have no hooks, and if I were you, I would not even think of attaching them at this stage. I would strongly recommend that your next course of action should be to gather up the equipment so far assembled, and with your hard hat on your head, depart for the nearest deserted open space for a little casting practice.

Lay the whole of the line out in S shapes; to your right if you cast right handed, or to your left if you cast left handed. Put the ring or button on the end of the pole, and swing the weight behind you in the air. Now cast the weight overhead in the required direction. Just after the pole reaches the vertical the ring or button will detach from the pole, and the weight will hurtle upwards and away taking the line with it. Don't try to be too athletic about it all, it's

not a question of brute strength. Make the pole do all the work by flexing it against the reluctance of the weight. After about half a dozen tries you will be an old hand producing smooth effortless casts every time. It really is as easy as that.

So with yet another skill up your sleeve, nip off home and attach the hooks to the main line. In order to fish better, the hooks need to be kept away from the main line, and this is done by attaching them to short lengths of line called snoods or traces. Make up the snoods from thin nylon twine cut in 14 inch lengths. Allowing for knots this will produce 8 to 10 inch traces that should be spaced along the main line at distances that will not allow them to tangle with each other. Start off with half a dozen or so, and build up the number to fifteen or even twenty after you have gained some experience. Make the snoods shorter as they get nearer the weight; these travel fastest and furthest and have more time to twist around the main line. It also helps if you use twine that is a different colour to the main line. This makes them easier to see and position when the tackle is laid out on the beach.

Stow the line on a wooden frame that has a strip of cork on top to fix the hooks in, and use fairly firm bait, or you may lose it during casting.

The first time I ever tried this method, I unleashed the most stupendous cast, and watched proudly as the line fairly rocketed out to sea. Alas, it was all to no avail; I had forgotten to fasten the end of the line to the beach. I lost the lot, so be warned.

By substituting a heavy plastic float for the weight, and using a floating main line, you can cast a surface long line over rocks or rough sea bed, but obviously tidal conditions must be in your favour.

## Outhaul Lines

These are something of a mechanical variation on the cast out line and can be useful if used in a carefully selected spot. In principal it works like this. At low tide a heavy rock or stake with a metal ring in it is placed some distance from the shore, preferably leading down into what will be deep water. The line is taken out from the shore, looped through the ring and then taken back to the shore, and the distance is measured. A piece of timber, or indeed anything that will not pass through the ring is now tied to the line at what will be the high tide mark, followed by traces and hooks spaced at appropriate distances — the distance from the 'blocker' to the last hook being something less than the distance from the shore to the ring. When the tide has come in sufficiently to cover the line, you bait up, haul the other end of the line shoreward until the block comes fast on the ring, and hey presto — you are fishing. You can, if you feel particularly energetic, hold an end of line in each hand and with a sort of left right marching of the arms jig the line backwards and forwards, hopefully making the bait more attractive to passing fish.

I have heard of people working nets in a similar way, and although I have never tried it, I would imagine that if you found exactly the right spot it could prove to be effective.

## Set Long Lines

This method can be very productive, and involves staking out a hooked and baited line so that it is covered by the incoming tide. If you were making up a line expressly for the purpose, it would probably be best to make it up in twenty-five yard lengths for ease of handling, but it will be more economic if you enlist your cast out or outhaul lines for double duty.

You can work this type of line virtually anywhere you think there may be fish, but common sense will tell you not to try it in vicious tidal rips or where large quantities of drift weed will snag and drag the line away with the receding tide.

A line that is abandoned to the mercy of the sea in this way needs to be very securely fixed in position, and this can be done in numerous ways. The obvious choices are heavy weights or anchors, and if you located a particularly productive ground you could site your own ringed concrete blocks in permanent positions. Anchors can be made of 2 feet lengths of two inch metal tubing with 3 feet lengths of ¼ inch steel rod inserted through it. The middle rod is left protruding from one end and is bent round to form a ring to take the rope, and the ones sticking out of the other end are bent back like the ribs of an umbrella. Then you get a friendly farmer or mechanic to weld it all in position for you. If you make up a couple of these they will also be useful if later on you get a boat. Not only will you be able to anchor nets and long lines worked at sea with them, but also the boat itself, so they will be very handy things to have. Old metal buckets buried up to their handles are also very good for holding lines in place, but you have to dig the holes, and this may not always be easy on a rocky sea bed. The snag of course is that you have to lug all this equipment around with you, so if this does prove a problem, attach 6 inch squares of ½ inch wood to the line and bury these in the sand; they hold remarkably well, and need the minimum of digging in. If you use a shortish line, say 25 yards, it will only need to be anchored at both ends; but with anything longer you will find that because of the drag

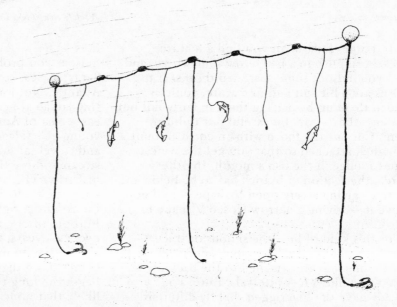

*Surface long line*

exerted by the tide the line will need to be further secured at various points along its length.

The size of hook to use will depend on what kind of fish you have deduced may be around, so you will have to find out what is generally considered most effective in your particular area. Selecting hooks is always a tricky problem, but whatever size you use, when rigging this sort of equipment, I would always advise you to go for the more expensive stainless steel variety rather than the cheaper tinned ones that rust very quickly in salt water. They are not quite as sharp as the tinned ones, but are much stronger and last almost indefinitely. So if you use them you will be spared the time consuming false economy of removing and replacing maybe a hundred hooks every season.

If you really wanted to economise and were going after flat-fish (it seems to suit only their shaped mouths) you could use a baited black-

for cast out or outhaul fishing, it will not matter all that much.

Set the line along the lie of the shore and not straight out to sea. Fished in this way they offer less resistance to the tide and are more certain to be there when you return to see what you have caught. It also often pays to cover the baited hooks with sand until the tide comes in to cover them. This will avoid the possibility of gulls or other birds pinching your bait or even getting hooked on the line, and surface weed fouling the hooks before enough water has come in for it to pass above them. Your timing must also be right, and you must be back in good time to clear the line as the tide uncovers it, or the gulls will be the only ones to benefit from your efforts.

Most people store their lines either in boxes or baskets, transfering them from one container to another during baiting, hanging the snoods and hooks out over the edge to avoid tangles.

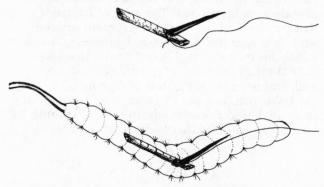

*A blackthorn gorge*

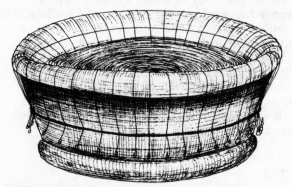

*A safely stowed long line*

thorn gorge. First of all you find a mature blackthorn bush in a hedgerow somewhere, and then you cut out some seasoned thorns. If the thorns are a bit soft and immature, you can harden them up by placing them in fairly hot but cooling ashes — but be careful not to burn them. Cut out the thorn with an equal amount of branch attached so that you get the widest span to lodge in the fish's mouth. In other words, the section of branch has to be below the thorn — giving a very open V shape — and not above it — giving a narrow closed V shape to the 'hook'.

For this kind of line, the snoods or traces — call them what you will — are normally about 15 inches long and are attached to the backline at something like 3 feet intervals. But if you already have the line rigged slightly differently

### Eels
Eels, as you probably know, originate in the Sargasso Sea, south east of Bermuda in the Atlantic. Not long after they have hatched, the tiny larvae are carried by tidal streams up the east coast of America where a proportion of the young eels (elvers) enter rivers and other outlets and travel far inland to the sheltered lakes and streams where they will feed and grow to maturity. The ones that don't make this landing continue their ride on the Gulf Stream across the Atlantic, right round to Great Britain and Europe, where, after a trip that has taken them over two years, they similarly head inland.

Some six to nine years later, the urge to spawn comes upon them and instinct tells them to begin the long trip homeward. It is now thought likely that none of the eels who manage to leave

European shores actually last the trip, and that the only ones that do return to spawn have come back from the North American coast.

During the winter, eels hibernate in the mud, emerging in the summer to feed and grow. They can be speared as they lie in the mud or caught in numerous ways when they leave it, but at this stage they are yellow and immature and not quite as desirable as the fat, mature silver eels who make for the open sea in late summer.

Some commercial interests take eels in specially constructed weirs and trawls — while smaller operators use fixed nets and traps. Such traps and staked nets will be the most practical for us, so I shall discuss them in turn.

## Fyke Nets

These are specifically designed for capturing eels, and take the form of a tunnel of netting that gradually decreases in diameter along its length. The net is held open by rings — the one at the mouth being perhaps 2 feet across, subsequent ones becoming smaller, down to say 8 inches. A typical 12 feet net would probably be rigged with six or seven such hoops and in those commercially manufactured they would invariably be made either of metal or plastic, but you could easily make them of cane.

The nets are held in place by stakes, one lashed to the entrance ring and one secured to the netting at the other end so that the net is stretched out fairly tautly. A long panel of netting — as high as the entrance ring — is also attached to the entrance stake. Weighted and floated, this is stretched out in front of the net to act as a leader, and guide the fish towards the trap. Sometimes two such leaders are attached to the entrance forming a Y shape when viewed in plan, but it is not really that much of an advantage, and if I were you I would not bother to go to all the extra trouble.

Inside the trap, attached to the second, third, fourth and fifth rings in a six ring net, are open ended cones of netting, strung in place, acting as escape inhibitors.

The mesh size of fyke nets like this is usually an inch for the leader and the main part of the net, decreasing to ¾ inch after the last couple of rings at the end where the catch will congregate. The very end of the trap is tightly laced up to form what is called a 'cod-end' and through this the catch is released into a sack or whatever you intend to carry the catch home in.

Traps like this will catch a great many eels, perhaps too many from your point of view, so unless you have reason to need them in quantity you can use the following less elaborate methods.

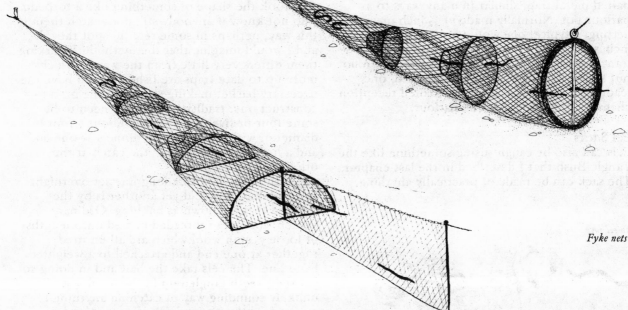

*Fyke nets*

## Mini Fyke

These have something of the form of a true fyke net, but as the name suggests are considerably smaller and naturally enough this makes them cheaper and easier to construct and work. This trap again takes a tubular form, but it need only be from 3 to 5 feet long. The rings — four of them in most cases — are all the same size, and are usually about 18 inches in diameter. The tube of netting is held open in the normal way by the rings and the whole structure braced in position by four poles attached equidistantly along the length of the trap. Both ends are fitted with entrance funnels and the two middle rings have similar arrangements that lead to the central holding chamber.

This net can be staked like a conventional fyke net if it is to be used in shallow or tidal water, but its big advantage is that it can also be used in deep water, in which case it would need to be fitted with a marker buoy or hauling warp (rope) and a little bit of weight — some old chain wrapped around a couple of the poles.

Having no leader net, it will need to be baited, and — in the case of eels — this can be anything in the meat line. But whatever you use, as in the case of lobster and crab traps, the bait is best placed fairly near the trap entrance in such a way that your prey can reach it with reasonable ease, but has to actually enter the trap to do so.

## Metal Traps

The other main way of taking eels is with a baited metal trap, similar in many ways to a parlour pot. Normally made of ½ inch mesh wire netting, a typical one would be 3 feet long, 16 inches high and 15 inches wide. Funnel entrances similar to the ones on a metal prawn pot but somewhat larger are generally used, one leading from the outside to the baited reception chamber, the other into the parlour.

## Eel Sacks

Eels can also be caught using something like the Tangle Bush that I described in the last chapter. The sack can be made of practically anything,

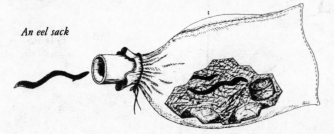

*An eel sack*

but most people construct one out of small mesh prawn netting and after baiting it, stuff it loosely with straw. The entrance pipe needs to be smaller than would be used for crabs and lobsters, and something with 3 or 4 inch diameter would be the most suitable. Once again, it will need to be baited.

## Where And When To Fish For Eels

As I mentioned at the beginning of this section, eels hibernate during the winter and are not really worth all the trouble of catching. The best time to go after them is during the early autumn when the prime silver eels are making their way to the open sea. The younger yellow eels are also active during the spring and summer and if taken then are almost as delicious. Many harbours, docks and backwaters contain eels, as do rivers and canals. But the most productive places are likely to be creeks or rivers leading to the sea, where fresh water is gradually becoming salt. As the weather becomes colder, eels move into deeper water and this will be the time to abandon the fyke net and take your chances with unstaked traps. So if you have set your gear in a likely spot, but are not catching anything, try in a different level of water. Eels do not tend to feed or move much during the day and so the best catches will be made by leaving your gear to fish all night if this is at all possible.

## Other Methods

In the old days, eels were caught in wicker traps that took the shape of something like a torpedo. I do not know if anybody still does catch them in this way, perhaps in some remote spot they do, and I would imagine that the method of working them differs very little from the way in which more up to date traps are fished. If you have the necessary basket making skills and the urge to construct one, traditionally it will need to be some four or five feet long and about a foot in diameter, with two entrance funnels at one end and a little door to remove the catch at the other.

Another way is with a long line set overnight in a suitable spot, and yet another is by the method that is known as babbing. Ordinary garden worms are threaded or tied onto lengths of loosely spun wool which are all knotted together at one end and attached to a weighted hand line. The eels take the bait and in doing so get their teeth tangled up in the wool. An unlikely sounding way of catching anything I must admit, but it works very well indeed.

# 6. More Shore Fishing

Some of the methods I am now about to describe are quite sophisticated, and will only be of practical use to those of you who live in very remote areas where you have virtually private control over a stretch of coast. Others do not have such an exclusive application. You will be able to judge for yourself which systems could be of any use to you.

## Nets

Fish are caught in nets either by enclosing them in one of a mesh size that is too small for them to pass through, or by tangling them in some way in various other kinds of nets. Set beach nets can work in both ways, but there are regulations that govern mesh sizes that can be used and the type of gear that you can work. So before you make a start you will have to check with your local authorities.

Nets that are designed to tangle fish have to be rigged in such a way that they remain baggy while they are being worked. The reason for this is fairly obvious if you think about it. If you staked the net out tightly in the same way that you might construct a fence to keep predators away from your chickens, anything coming up against it would be likely to more or less bounce off of it. On the other hand, a fish making contact with a loose swirling mass of netting stands a much greater chance of becoming caught up in it. For this reason, nets of this type are 'set in'; that is to say they are gathered in along their own length in order to achieve this baggy effect. Most kinds of nets — apart from trawls of course — are fished vertically in the water, attached to a rope with floats on at the top, and to a rope with weights on at the bottom. So if the top and bottom ropes on your net were 25 yards long, the actual length of the net might well be 50 yards long. In which case it would be set in by half. If something not quite so loosely rigged was required, the net could be 'set in' by the third and so on. In most cases though, nets are set in by the half.

## Gill Nets

If a specific type of fish is known to be in a particular area, fishermen often try to catch them with what is known as a gill net. If you take a look at most round fish, you will notice that the broadest part of their body is just behind the gill covers. It is this physical property that the gill net takes advantage of. When the fish tries to pass through the net — either because it is trying to get through the barrier it provides, or because it has not seen it — it can do so to a point past its gills, but the net then becomes stuck around his body. When he tries to reverse out of the net, his gills, being rubbed the wrong way as it were, become snagged on the mesh. Of course to do this effectively you have to know more or less how big the fish is so that you can use a net with the right mesh size. But this is not so much of a restriction as it may sound, because particular species of fish will frequent pretty much the same grounds at given times year after year, and in turn hopefully they will be very much the same size. So in using a gill net to catch them, you will merely be equipping yourself with the best specialist tool that you can possibly have for the job. On the other hand, by its very character the gill net is not particularly versatile, and because of this another type of net — the trammel — has been enjoying something of a revival over the last few years.

### Trammel Nets

A trammel net is not one net, but three — three sheets of netting hung side by side vertically in the water, attached to a single head rope and a single foot line. The middle wall of netting has a very small mesh and is very baggy; the two outer walls are made with a much larger mesh size and are not so loosely set. When a fish swims into the net, he is able to pass through the big meshes of the nets on the outside, but not through the fine mesh of the middle net. In his attempts to get free, he becomes wound up in the middle net and a bag of netting with the fish inside is pushed through one of the outer meshes. He will be very unlikely to get out.

The obvious advantage of this type of net is that it will catch more or less anything that happens along, so that for general fishing it is probably unbeatable. Faced with a shortage of specific kinds of fish, small scale commercial fishermen have, in increasing numbers, taken to using trammel nets in recent years. With diminishing catches, and in turn a more liberal market, its versatility has allowed them to catch whatever has happened to be around. For slightly different reasons, I think you too will be wise to include a trammel net among your main items of equipment. When you first start fishing, you will naturally be a little confused and uncertain. The trammel net will be your trusted fail safe companion. Later, when you have discovered what fish predominate in your particular area, you can, if you want, adopt more specialist methods of catching them, but in the beginning you will at least be able to catch something.

### Working Gill and Trammel Nets

Constructing these 'fixed' nets — as opposed to 'fixed' net traps and pushed and pulled nets that

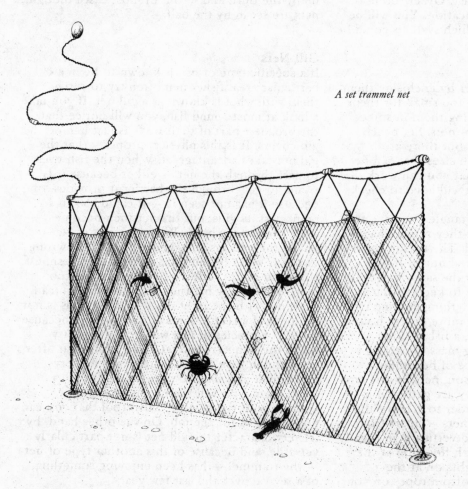

*A set trammel net*

I shall deal with later in this chapter — is dealt with in chapter thirteen. They can also be bought of course, and since we do not require such large nets as the professionals must have, this need not be particularly expensive. But however you acquire them, both types can be worked in very similar ways.

The first thing to do as far as gill nets are concerned is to establish what mesh sizes you are allowed to work with in your particular area. Then you can set about finding out what fish are around and select a suitable net to catch them. But until you know exactly what suits your purposes, it will probably be as well to find out what everybody else uses and then do the same.

Nets worked from the shore will not be as big as those that can be worked from a boat, and in some cases will only be a couple of feet deep. Regardless of size the top rope or float line is buoyed. This always used to be done with cork floats, but nowadays they have almost entirely been replaced by plastic ones. The bottom line or lead line, is — surprise, surprise — weighted with lead weights that thread on to the line. At least this has been the way in the past, but a new innovation — the lead-line — is rapidly taking over from the old system. In the new method the rope itself contains the lead, and this is achieved by manufacturing the rope so that it contains a plastic tube filled with lead particles. Apart from being a very clever idea, ropes like this also help to stop the net rolling up on itself since they spread the weighting requirement evenly along the whole of the base. With ordinary lead weights, attached at intervals along the ground-rope, the tendency for them to gyrate and foul the net above them — inducing the net to roll up like a carpet — is difficult to avoid. The obvious solution might appear to be to just put heavier weights on, but this means bigger floats would be needed, and bigger floats would need heavier weights and so on ad infinitum. An over floated net also takes some holding, so you always have to be careful to get just the right amount of buoyancy and no more. Unfortunately, lead-line is slightly more expensive than the traditional rope and weights, but after you have wasted half a day untangling a net fitted with ordinary weights you will probably agree that it is worth every penny of the additional cost.

About the simplest way of working a gill net from a beach is to anchor a weighted and floated length at right angles to the shoreline at low tide. Unless you have a terrific tidal rise where you are fishing, it need be no more than two or three feet high, and one about 20 to 30 yards long would be good for a beginner. In practice, the shallower you are able to have the net — and still make worthwhile catches — the better, because such a net will offer minimum resistance to the tide and pick up less rubbish.

Some people do away with floats and weights altogether, and stake the net in position at suitable intervals along its length. But however you rig it, you will get the best catches if it is set well in and baggy. One good tip which helps to make staked nets into more of a trap, is to tie the top of the net to the bottom every yard or so. These ties should be something less than the height of the net, say 18 inches for a 2 feet net. They can, if you wish, be alternated to different sides of the net, giving it something of the appearance of a corkscrew. This creates a net that fish can really 'get into', giving it substantially more holding power than a conventionally set gill net. I suppose it is a debatable point as to whether nets set in this way really are gill nets at all, since they begin to take on many of the functions of tangle nets (dealt with elsewhere) but in practice they become only arbitrary names, and the main thing is that they both catch fish.

These nets will not only take fish, but shellfish as well, especially if you tie some bait to it up off the ground, and if you set the last yard or so of the seaward end of the net back up the beach at an angle of 45°, it will also give you the chance of catching some quite large fish that are late going out on the tide.

## Channel Gill Nets

If you can find a suitably deep narrow channel leading out to sea, gill nets can be very productive when worked across them. If the channel is fairly dry at low tide, you may be able to wade across it to set your net; if not, you will probably need some assistance to get the gear in position. The easiest way to get the net across the channel, is to throw a light rope to someone on the other side and then use it to haul the net across. If the channel is just that bit too wide for you to throw a line, a casting pole would easily solve the problem.

Nets fished in this way need to be attended at least until the tide is approaching its height, since some manipulation may be needed to the head and foot ropes to make sure there are no tangles and that the net is fishing properly.

Fishing gill nets in this way may be all very well in theory, but in practice things may not be quite so straightforward. If the tide was likely to run strongly where you were thinking of setting the net, you might find it practical to only work it for an hour or two around slack water. Otherwise the net might not only be very difficult to hold, and fill up with weed and other rubbish, but also not fish well because it was being stretched too taut by the flow.

Another alternative would be to secure the net only at one end so that it would stream with the tide. Without a boat, it would be tricky to set it far enough away from the shore or bank, but it might be possible to get round this by throwing an anchor out on the end of a rope — and when this was fast — paying out the net from it so that it fished downstream. In this case it would be wise to have another warp attached to the business end of the anchor so that it could be dislodged when you wanted to haul the net in. It would also be wise to have a further rope at the extreme far end of the net. This would serve not only to pull the gear into position if the tide was not strong enough, but be of great assistance when the net was finally hauled.

Other channels and indeed beaches, where you get fairly high tide rises can be worked in similar ways either with surface nets or ground nets. You will need buoys and anchors, and the nets will obviously have to be weighted in different ways. A net worked on the sea bed will need enough weight to sink it and sufficient buoyancy to keep it vertical, while with surface nets, the opposite will be true.

Sometimes, for this kind of fishing, short lengths of netting are held open by upright poles attached to their ends. I do not particularly like the technique, because I think it makes the net rather too rigid, and I think you will do better to take a little trouble and adjust weights and floats to precisely the right balance instead.

Trammel nets can be worked in more or less the same ways that I have described for shore set gill nets, but the problem is that their high catching power can be their own undoing. Unless you work them in areas devoid of weed and debris, the net will very soon fill up with rubbish and it will take you the rest of your life to clear it all out. Worse still, a net in this condition offers a considerable amount of resistance to the tide and however efficient you think your anchors may be, the sea will be certain to win the whole lot from you. So unless you can avoid this sort of problem, trammel nets are best worked at sea from a boat. On the other hand, a very short length, whose loss would not bank-

rupt you, can be worked very effectively near rocks and obstructions, where they will take crabs and lobsters as well as fish.

At this point, it seems an opportune moment to mention that when you are fishing with nets, you should always make great efforts never to lose them, and even greater efforts to retrieve them if you do — whatever state they are in. Modern nets, made of synthetic fibres, do not rot in the sea like the old fashioned cotton ones, and this means that they carry on fishing for as long as they have their freedom. So a great many fish will be needlessly wasted and the lives of boat owners endangered by your rogue net fouling their propellors at a critical moment. The danger to swimmers — particularly skin divers — is likely to result in an even more certain tragedy, especially if you have been using fine monofilament netting which is very difficult to see underwater. So make it a cardinal rule never to lose or discard netting in the sea — and that goes for rope and line and any other inedible debris as well.

The best way to clear a net that has picked up a lot of debris is to allow it to dry out and then simply crush the weed and other rubbish into small fragments that will then just fall away from it.

## Baulk Nets

These nets are only of use if you have access to what is to all intents and purposes a private stretch of coast. This is because they are staked nets that remain more or less permanently in position.

Usually fixed across creeks and channels, baulk nets are hinged in such a way that they open to allow fish to go under them as the tide comes in, but close up as the tide goes out. At one or both ends of the net, pounds are constructed and fish searching for a way past the net congregate in these, where they can easily be taken in a hand net.

The siting of such mechanical nets is naturally very important, because the sea bed has to be flat enough for the net to be able to come down tight against it, or the subsequent gaps will make the whole apparatus totally ineffective. However, if you did find a spot that was acceptable in all but this respect, at low tide it might be possible to construct a wall of rocks that the net could work on.

## Stop Nets

Fished in the same kind of places as baulk nets,

these too come under the heading of mechanical nets. The net is hauled completely across the channel, and the foot rope is securely pegged or dug in to the sea bed. Stakes, with pulleys at the top, are hammered in along the line of the net, and ropes leading from the bank go through these to the headrope so that the net can be hauled up to or above the surface at high water. I suppose you could construct pounds at the ends of stop nets, but when I saw one being worked, they just waited for low tide and waded in with a hand net. They did however concentrate the fish by putting another net across the creek some way up behind the staked one, gradually bringing it down until it was right up close.

## Hose Nets

These are mainly used to catch shrimps and prawns, and are rather like small mesh fyke nets without leaders. They are not usually as long as eel nets, and normally consist only of a rectangular framework to hold the mouth open and an inner netting funnel halfway along the trap leading to the holding chamber and the staked out cod end. Hose nets are normally set in batteries and are fished on mud and sand flats that dry out at low tide. So you have to be on hand to clear them at the full ebb or the catch will be dead and useless.

## Shank Nets

Similar to the hose net, but towed along in shallow water instead of being staked to fish the ebb. They usually have a D section mouth, the upright of the latter consisting of a wedge shaped wooden bar that will skim over the sand or mud. An upright is fitted in the middle of the mouth, and a towline attached to its base, just above the bar. At the top of the upright, another line is fixed. This is called the tiltline, and allows the operator or operators to adjust the angle at which the bar skims over the ground.

If you are going to do the towing yourself, you will not want it to be too big, but quite large ones can be worked by a horse or tractor. If you don't want to get feet, hooves or wheels wet, you can work the net offset away from you by placing the towline slightly to one side or the other of the central bracing bar.

## Dangerous Fish

Before we leave the subject of shore fishing, I really ought to mention the physical dangers that may lurk for the unwary when handling the catch.

If you happen to live in a part of the world where the sea is infested with man eating sharks and suchlike, you will doubtless already be aware of the potential hazards. But apart from the fact that much smaller fish can bite or abrade you quite seriously, one important thing to be on the lookout for are poisonous fish. In my part of the world, weaver fish are the main problem. Where you will be operating things may be different. So the only advice that I can give will be to make extensive local enquiries about the possible dangers. You will be the one looking for trouble — so get yourself fully prepared for it.

And be warned — treat even the most minor scratches and bites incurred when handling fish with the greatest respect. Infection can be both swift and furious.

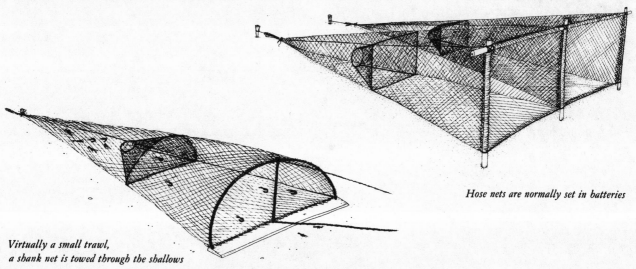

*Hose nets are normally set in batteries*

*Virtually a small trawl,
a shank net is towed through the shallows*

# STAGE 2

# Boat Fishing

# 7. Boats

*Build me straight, O worthy Master!*
*Staunch and strong, a goodly vessel,*
*That shall laugh at all disaster,*
*And with wave and whirlwind wrestle!*

*Longfellow*

Selecting a boat for any given purpose invariably turns out to be a compromise. Aircraft carriers are excellent for aeroplanes to fly on and off, but not exactly ideal craft for towing water skiers with. I cannot imagine that anyone would actually have need of a boat that could be used for doing both, but no doubt you get my meaning. A fishing boat big enough to go to sea in all weathers will be no good for exploring small creeks where the water may be no more than a few inches deep. The ideal boat for working fleets of crab traps with will not meet the design requirements for the very best stern trawler — and so on.

The largest commercial fishing boats are normally designed for a specific kind of fishing. If for some reason they wish to change to another method, they must come into port and be fitted out with new nets and machinery. Smaller boats are usually slightly more adaptable, but most will be restricted to two or three different methods of fishing; and even working within these modest confines, major compromises over deck layout and equipment will have had to have been made.

But in our case, the most important factor influencing the kind of boat we use will probably be the cost, and not the boat's specific suitability for the job. Now I could recommend some wonderful boats that would suit the small scale fisherman perfectly, and then we could go on to peruse a veritable galaxy of goodies to equip her with. She would be a darling little thing, our continuing pride and joy, fitted out with every conceivable glittering gadget that the chandler could tempt us with. We would be the envy of all who set eyes on us and we would catch lots and lots of fish and live happily ever after.

Unfortunately, in order to do that, I would have to assume that you were all very rich, because such a boat would cost a great deal of money. Obviously I cannot make that assumption, but if you are rich or have the pooled resources of any kind of syndicate at your disposal it will really only mean that you will not have to make as many compromises as the rest of us.

But however much money you have, it will be nothing short of lunatic to throw it away on a brand new boat. Present day prices of raw materials, combined with labour costs and penal taxation, have taken new boat prices through the roof, and sadly they now have no affinity with the concepts of the self supporter.

So apart from borrowing one, the only way that you are likely to be able to put to sea is either in a secondhand boat, or in one that you have made yourself.

## What Kind Of Boat

Because of local needs and conditions, numerous specialist boats have evolved for working from given areas of coast — boats whose shape allows them to be launched and recovered from steep beaches — flat bottomed boats for working the shallows — high sided boats to cope with a rolling swell — and so on.

If such a boat exists in the area you intend to work from, presumably many years of painful development have made it the best one to use, and it may be impracticable, even unsafe, to use anything else. Observation and common sense will tell you if this is so in your case. As a general rule, wherever you are, it will be the best and safest policy to be conventional and acquire a traditional local boat. Raise no eyebrows when you put to sea and you will be liable to come back into port again.

Such a boat will be the ideal, but cost or whatever may force you to make do with something short of perfection. If this is the case, only expert local knowledge — boat builders, experienced fishermen etc — will be able to tell you if the kind of boat you have in mind will be safe and suitable.

There are, however, certain kinds of boats that should be avoided at all costs — wherever you are.

## Types Of Boats To Avoid

Inflatable boats must certainly come top of this list, since they are absolutely useless for any kind of fishing. Except of course that practised by skin divers with aqualungs and wet suits, who use them to dive from in order to pinch the shellfish caught in fishermen's traps. Personally, I think their whole concept is questionable anyway. I can't really see the point of having an inflatable boat that you never deflate. Have you ever seen anyone deflating an inflatable? Of course not. They take so long to blow up, that naturally their owners can never face the prospect of ever doing so again. Once inflated, they remain ill conceived, impermanent testimonies to the success of the ad man, and the gullibility of their owners.

So unless you want to go to sea in a boat that will be extremely difficult to row, virtually impossible to work any gear from, and which will get you soaking wet while you are being blown about all over the place, avoid inflatables.

Nets and lines are tricky enough to handle on dry land, and when you are working them at sea it helps considerably if your boat is stable and not bobbing and rolling around all over the place. In order to achieve this, a boat needs plenty of beam (width) for its length. So avoid narrow boats that do not have generous proportions amidships, otherwise when you move to one side of the boat there will be a rather alarming tendency for the boat to roll over. But in a small boat, however beamy it is, the gunwales will still dip if you are working over the side, and so to avoid shipping water, you need plenty of freeboard. That is, height of boat sticking out of the water. Such a boat will also be easier and safer to work from, as you will be in it, rather than on it, and able to get some leverage with your knees against the side when hauling or setting the gear.

Undoubtedly, the best kind of boat for a beginner to start with is a flat bottom boat. This is because they are the cheapest and easiest to make, and the least expensive to buy secondhand. The problem is that they sit on top of the water rather than extend very far down into it, and although this tends to make them fairly fast under sail or power, it also means that they do not 'grip' the water very well, and you tend to get blown around a bit. On the other hand, I must mention that when I was a youngster, this was the kind of boat I did in fact use on my fishing expeditions, and I don't seem to remember it really being much of a problem. But she was a heavy, solid old lady with a removable centreboard , (I worked her under sail most of the time). So perhaps the weight and the centreboard combined put "paid" to any inclinations she might have had towards flightiness. But, as I said at the beginning of this chapter, whatever kind of boat you choose it will be bound to have some faults, and all that you can hope to do is to pick one with as few as possible. So on the whole, I think that taking into consideration the lower cost and comparative ease of construction of flat bottomed boats, they will really be as good a choice as any for the small scale fisherman. They are the type that I describe when I later talk about a boat that you can build for yourself, which shows that I am not that worried by their shortcomings.

## How Big

If you compare price lists for boats, you will notice that generally the bigger the boat is, the more expensive it becomes. Perhaps that is stating the obvious, but I mention it because it leads to another point which is not quite so apparent. If you were to express the price rise in boats on a graph, showing how the cost increased per foot of boat, you would notice a shallow climb up to about twelve feet; and after that, an almost vertical ascent. This is because that after a certain critical point, the raw materials needed to construct and strengthen the increasing bulk of the boat are rocketing with every foot, rather like a gambler doubling up on a losing run. This graph theory is admittedly more directly applicable to new boats, because they are (or should be) in perfect showroom condition; but with the sort of secondhand boat that you will be going in for, it will still be relevant, although the asking price will be rather more fluid because the condition of the boat will vary.

So from this, it becomes clear that a boat of around twelve feet is going to be the one that a small scale fisherman can reasonably be expected to afford. If you wanted a boat that you could move around on a roof rack, perhaps it would need to be a little smaller; and for more serious fishing a fifteen or even seventeen footer would be the kind of more versatile proposition to go in for. It really all depends on exactly how you intend to use the boat and what kind of bargain you can get hold of.

## Made of What?

Most small boats are nowadays made of glass reinforced plastic (GRP), with marine plywood coming a rather lagging second. You sometimes come across ones made of relatively unusual materials like ferro cement or aluminium, but these are few and far between. At the other end of the scale, you will still see many small wooden boats around, mostly of clinker construction, but

few are still being built, due to the comparative cheapness of other materials.

I should perhaps explain that a clinker built boat is one in which the planks that it is made of overlap, giving the appearance of something like assembled weatherboarding. The other main type of planked boat is made by the carvel method, in which the planks fit flush together.

Marine ply boats are mainly constructed with hulls of the hard chine type, in which the shape is not the more traditional round bilge type, but angled. This is necessitated by the difficulties involved in bending ply in more than one

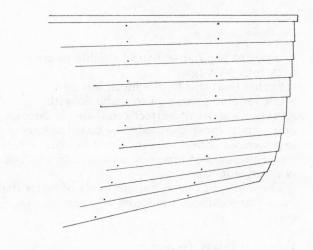

*The main methods of wooden boat construction. 1. Clinker 2. Carvel*

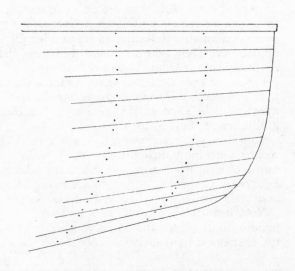

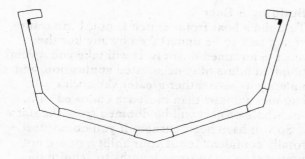

*Hard chine construction method*

direction at the same time. Another method of marine ply construction, called either hot or cold moulding — depending on whether heat is used or not — approaches this shaping problem in a rather different way. This is done by glueing fairly thin strips of plywood diagonally around a mould, gradually building up several layers of wood in a round bilge shape, so avoiding the need for any sharp angles.

You will at various times probably come across all of these various types of construction, but on the secondhand market, fibreglass, hard chine ply, and clinker boats, are the ones you are most likely to find on offer.

For the novice who wishes to build his own boat there will only be two real possibilities; it will either have to be fibreglass or wooden hard chine.

## Buying A Secondhand Boat

First, find your boat. This can be done in a variety of ways — advertisements, auction sales or the grape vine.

As far as advertising goes, it is rather a hit and miss affair to place your own adverts. I have found that the best policy is to keep a hawklike eye on your own local press. And I do mean local. It never pays to go racing off to the other side of the country in order to view what appears to be the bargain of the century. You will invariably be disappointed, and the expenses involved will be better spent if put towards something that was not quite so much of a 'bargain' nearer home.

Word of mouth is perhaps the best way of all, and it is surprising what you can turn up by simply asking around. Most people connected with boats can be extraordinarily helpful, and somehow seem to revel in the reflected glory of being the entrepreneur who 'of course' had at

their finger tips the source of a bargain for you.

Elderly fishermen are particularly worth approaching. Although they may still be working with a larger boat, they quite often have a smaller one tucked away somewhere that they acquired for some long forgotten reason, and they may be willing to sell it to you. And if they can't help, they will probably know someone who can.

Most harbours have various characters who either hang around doing odd scraping and painting jobs for people, or are paid to check on moorings and the security of unattended boats. These kind of people are also well worth contacting, because very often they are the first to hear of any boats coming up for sale. Bear in mind, also, that someone who spends a great deal of his time actually maintaining boats is often a very astute judge of their condition, and will certainly be able to offer some helpful advice.

Public sales are yet another possibility, and as well as the specialist marine auctions, it is often worth keeping an eye on the forthcoming sales of all the more general auctioneers located near the coast. They quite often sell the odd boat or two, and since these may not be typical of the kind of things that they normally have on offer, you may not encounter too much opposition and be able to come away with a bargain.

## Faults

The best way of finding out if a boat is sound or not, is to have it professionally surveyed. For a small boat this need not be very expensive, and could save you a great deal of money. However, to avoid needlessly shelling out your hard earned cash on wreck after wreck, it will be as well to be able to recognize a few of the more obvious pitfalls before you call in the surveyor.

Wooden boats seem to develop faults mostly at their ends; that is, where the planks join the stem and transom. Sometimes this will be obvious, and you will be able to clearly see where separation has occurred and perhaps been repaired (often badly). Other boats may have copper sheets (called tingles) nailed over such danger areas; of course, they may be reasonably sound underneath, but naturally you will treat such specimens with the greatest suspicion.

On a varnished wooden boat, careful inspection of every square inch will be a fairly straightforward, if tedious, operation. Nose to the hull, inside and out — prodding suspicious spots with a penknife. On a painted hull, this will be rather more difficult, and your tapping and prodding will have to be even more diligent. A freshly painted boat, recently put up for sale, may not mean that the owner just wishes her to be a credit to his painstaking care. He may be trying to land you with a cosmetized death trap, so be on your guard. React to what you see, rather than what you are told. Beware the glib remark. If the boat has a rather daunting crack in the side, let it register that it will almost certainly mean an expensive repair, and will be unlikely to 'close up when she gets in the water'.

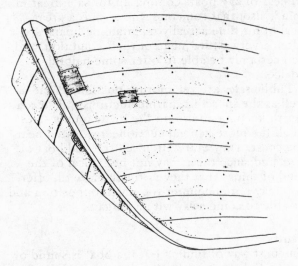

*Copper sheet patches—called tingles—are often nailed over damaged areas—so treat them with the greatest suspicion*

Checking on a fibreglass hull can be just as difficult as examining a wooden one. Look out for bubbles in the surface gel coat and cracks that have been filled in. Bear in mind that small boats sometimes get crushed against other boats or the quay, so watch out for damage around the gunwales. If any 'lifting' or separation is apparent, avoid the boat like the plague; she has probably been badly made with an incorrect resin to glass mix.

## Building A Boat

To build a boat from scratch is not, I can assure you, a task to be undertaken by any but the most determined of souls. It will take you several hundred hours of concentrated application, and unless you have rather greater skills with hammer and saw than most are endowed with, the whole project will be doomed from the start.

So you have been warned. If you do not feel totally confident about your ability, or are not prepared to go to some lengths to acquire the necessary, albeit elementary skills required, all that you will end up with will be a half-completed wreck.

## Glass Fibre

It is quite possible to build your own GRP boat at home. Various manufacturers hire out moulds, and if you can recruit a few friends to give a hand at critical stages, it will be that much easier. I do not intend to go into all the details here, simply because glass reinforced plastic technology is such a specialist subject. So if the idea appeals to you, I suggest that you obtain a publication that deals specifically with this type of construction. There are quite a few on the market.

A simpler and not necessarily much more expensive way to acquire a GRP boat would be to buy a reject moulding from one of the commercial manufacturers and then patch it up. But once again you would require specialist knowledge to be able to do this properly.

## Wooden Boats

The resin used in plastic boats is derived from oil, and is therefore expensive, and likely to become more so — and who knows, may one day be no longer available. If that happens, we will almost certainly have to get back to basics; so perhaps it will be helpful if I describe the manufacture of a simple boat made from materials that hopefully will always be available.

## Building a Flattie

The easiest and cheapest kind of boat to build is one with a flat bottom, because you eliminate as much as possible the need to cut too many angled joints. In actual fact the bottom is not entirely flat in the strict sense — it is when you lay it out — but bent from roughly the middle up toward the bow, and to a lesser extent in the direction of the stern. This gives it a bit of shape that improves its seakeeping qualities. But basically what we are building is an open box with a sharp end. The actual shape and size is not that critical and the thing to remember is that if a boat looks right, it probably will be right. The lines I give are therefore only a guide, and can be adapted, within reason, to suit your own needs and indeed the materials you can lay your hands on. I say this, because I have in mind that the wood used to build her could be secondhand, reclaimed from a demolition site or some such place, and naturally enough what is on offer may not tie in exactly with my specification.

The boat in my design is about 12 feet long with a beam of around 4 feet 9 inches and she is built mainly of pine boarding — six by one inch tongue and groove for the bottom and ordinary half inch softwood for the sides. The transom (stern board) needs to be fairly strong and should therefore be made of a hardwood like oak or mahogany. The interior woodwork could be made of softwood, but a much smarter appearance (and a stronger boat) will be obtained if the seats and other fittings are made out of hardwood that can be varnished instead of painted. Such wood is expensive to buy from merchants, but will come for next to nothing if acquired via secondhand stores and auction sales in the form of broken or unsaleable furniture. But make sure that your purchase consists of solid, not just veneered wood.

## The Workshop

Having obtained the raw materials, you now have to decide where to build the boat. You need somewhere under cover, with a level, preferably wooden floor, because you will be temporarily fixing struts of wood to the floor to hold the boat in position during construction. But it does not matter all that much; and if you build in a garage say, which will probably have a concrete floor, it just means that you will have to go to the trouble of drilling and plugging a few holes.

You will also require somewhere with a fairly low ceiling (or cross-beam), because you will need to wedge a spar between it and the bottom of the boat in order to force it into shape.

*An adaptable line plan for a basic 'flattie'*

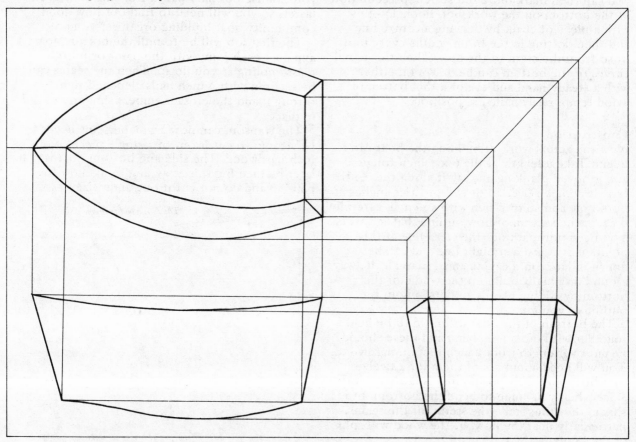

It goes without saying that you make sure that you will be able to move the boat out of the building when it is completed. It will be no economy at all if you have to call the builders in to make holes in walls for you.

## The Plan

The first thing to do is to draw a scale plan. It need not be very big, and something the size of the open pages of a tabloid newspaper will be suitable. If you use my plan as a basis, you can draw in the curves by using narrow strips of veneer held in position by pins stuck into the paper. If you use a two inch scale, you can mark off your 'ruler' accordingly, and this will be a help when you come to make up your cutting list.

Make sure that the curves on each side are identical, and that the angle of the bow (stem rake) is not exaggerated too much. The curve of the bottom should also not stray too far from the one shown in my prototype drawing, or the finished boat will not be very stable.

When the plan is drawn to your satisfaction, you can then mark out a full scale representation of the bottom on the workshop floor. Do this with a piece of chalk by drawing a centre line and then dotting in the beam widths every foot or so from the stern to the bow. Then the actual curves of the bottom can be drawn in, either with a steady hand and eye or a thin batten of wood temporarily nailed in position.

## Construction

Now the actual work of building the boat can begin. Take a length of the 6 x 1 inch tongued and grooved planking and lay it along the centre line, leaving an overlap of two or three inches at both bow and stern. Then with a pencil, carefully draw in the section of bow outline that it covers. You need not mark out the stern line at this point, as it is just a straight line and can be drawn in later on. Leaving an overlap all the way around, gradually build up the whole of the bottom by adding planks and drawing in the outline as you go.

The bottom of the boat will need to be held together with cross members, and these should be cut overlength from 2 inch section hardwood. You will need about six of them for a twelve foot boat; and their positioning is fairly critical since when you come to bend the bottom into shape, they must take the strain off the seams, particularly near the bow, or the wood will split at the joints.

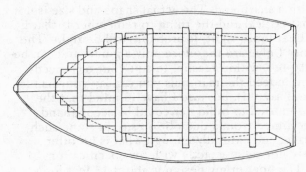

*The first stages of construction*

## Assembly

Actually fitting the parts together will need to be done as quickly as possible; because the joints have to be painted with linseed-oil-thinned putty in order to achieve a snug watertight fit. While you are working the putty will be hardening, so you will have to make haste to get all the parts in position before this happens. Assistance at this stage is very worthwhile.

If you cannot get hold of putty and linseed oil, you can use ordinary paint. But this dries even faster, so you will need to find out how good a community boat building organiser you are.

The first job will be to pull the bottom apart and coat each joint with the paint or putty — reassembling as you do so. Then the seams can be secured with 3 inch nails clenched right through, and the cross members similarly nailed in place.

The transom can now be made. This needs to be strong; so cut it out of a single piece of one inch hardwood. The side and bottom boards will later be meeting this at an angle, so allow for planing and do not cut it out undersize.

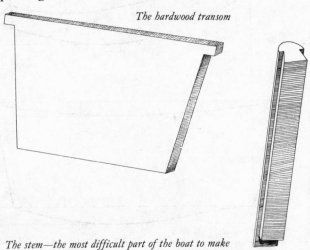

*The hardwood transom*

*The stem—the most difficult part of the boat to make*

The stem needs to be made from a length of 4 inch square hardwood, and is about the most difficult part of the boat to make. It would be quite possible to laminate one using strips of preshaped hardwood and marine glue, but it is better made in one piece; and if I were you, I would go and beg the assistance of your friendly local woodworking expert. Even if you have to pay the full going rate to have this made up for you, it will still not set you back very much.

When you have screwed the stem into position, you can bevel the bottom of the transom and similarly secure that in place at the other end of the boat. Once again the joints should be treated with the thinned putty or paint.

Now you have something that is beginning to look like a boat, but alas, we are still many cut fingers and sore thumbs away from the launching ceremony.

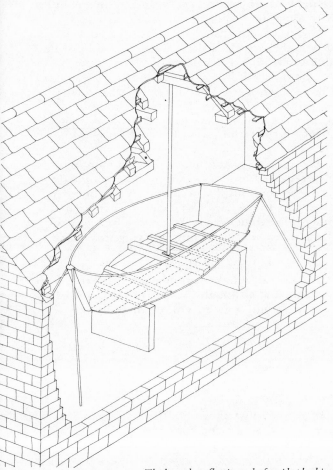

*The braced up flattie ready for side planking*

The next job is to hastily force the boat into its final shape, and this is done by raising it up on blocks near the bow and stern, and by means of a baulk of timber between it and the roof wedging the floor planking down into the curve shown on the plan.

When you are sure that everything is set up as per the plan, brace the stem and transom in position by nailing two battens to each and screwing their other ends to the floor.

You are now almost ready to start planking in the sides, but before this can be done, the final shape of the bottom of the boat must be cut out around the pencil line. This cut must be made at an angle, so that the side planks that slope upward and outward come hard up against it. In order to do this, take two lengths of thin battening and nail one end of each to the top outside edge of the transom. Then, bending the battens into the true shape of what would be the finished top edges (sheer strakes) of the boat, spring them into position at the top of the stem and nail them home. These battens must lie true, so you will have to support them in some way. Tying them to the ceiling as well as to the floor is one effective way.

The angle of the cut now becomes obvious, and by working your saw all around the boat, hard against the battens at the top and the pencil line at the bottom, all the surplus wood can be removed.

The side planks need to be about half an inch thick and as wide as possible, because each one will have to be planed to fit tightly against the one below it. So the fewer that you have, the less planing you will have to do. Cut the planks over length, and nail them on from the middle to the stern and then up towards the bow. When you reach the stem, the planks will have to be sprung tightly into place; so remember it is better to have two or three goes at cutting the plank back to the correct length than it is to risk cutting it underlength and have to start all over again. Remember the carpenter's old adage: Measure twice — and cut once.

As you build the planking up, you will need to nail 2 x 1 inch strengthening strips (inwales) over the seams inside. Clamp the wood together as you do this; and when you have finished, additional strips should be fitted inside and outside the boat on the top edge of the last planks. Then further lengths can be fixed on top of the exposed sandwich to form a neat moulding all around the sides.

At last the boat is nearing completion, and

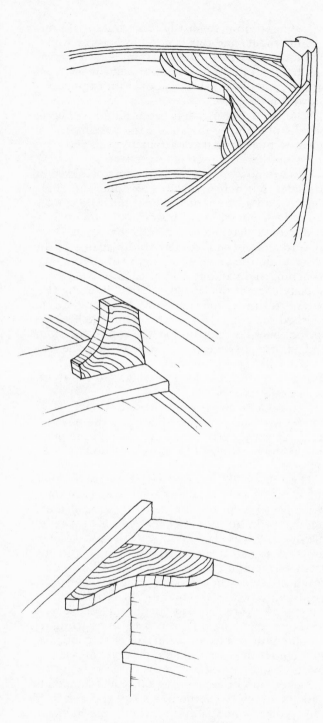

*Hardwood strengthening brackets should be fitted at the stem, transom, and seat*

after fitting a rowing seat amidships and another seat up against the transom, she should start to feel very solid and strong.

Corner brackets of hardwood should now be fitted inside the boat; at the top of the stem, on each side of the boat at the top of the transom and on top of the rowing seat against the side planking.

Underneath the boat you will need to fit a skid; and this is really just a continuation of the stem, running exactly along the centreline of the boat. It must be dead centre, or the boat will not handle very well.

When you finally get to sea, you will be bound to take in some water over the side; so unless you want to have wet feet all the time, you will need a false floor. This should consist of planks and cross bearers which should not fit very tightly inside the hull, since at times you will want to take it out for baling and cleaning.

All that remains to be done now, is to rub and plane down any rough spots, and fill in any holes with a marine stopper.

If your workmanship has been of a considerably higher standard than mine, you will just be able to give her a few coats of varnish and she will be finished. But anything more homespun will need a cover-up paint job. And for this purpose any good quality exterior household paint will be more than good enough — and cheaper than paint especially sold for painting boats.

The process of rubbing down and painting is best repeated once a year, and most people do it in the spring. But if you intend to lay the boat up during the worst of the winter weather, and can get her under cover, it is not a bad idea to spend a few winter evenings getting this chore done before then, so that you will be all set to go when the first fine weather comes.

This sort of dinghy will take an outboard of up to 5 hp., and although this is a proven type of boat, it should only be worked offshore in reasonable conditions.

## The Right Choice?

Some of you may be wondering why I have chosen to describe the construction of this particular kind of boat when you have heard so much about the ease with which plywood boats can be made. And further, why have I not fitted her out with sails?

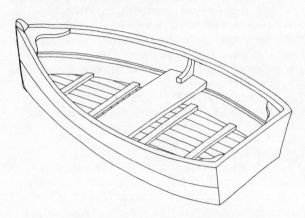

*The finished boat ready for varnishing or a cover up paint job*

on, when you feel more accomplished, go ahead and fit sails — you may have to — but not for the time being. The little boat that I have described could easily be fitted with a mast and a removable centre board (by constructing a well for it to slide down through) or with a leeboard (a sort of centreboard that hangs out over the side).

Numerous books describe the sort of rig you could use; but if you do go in for sail later on, take my advice and fit something like a standing lug — because when you are fishing, you may suddenly want to put the 'brakes' on — and with this sort of sail, if you ease off the tac line, the spar just collapses down against the mast and you are then no longer under way.

Apart from the fact that plywood may not always be available — who knows what the future holds? — I have endeavoured to describe a boat that can be built from the cheapest possible materials, secondhand ones.

Secondhand marine ply (exterior grade plywood is unpredictable for building boats with) is virtually unobtainable since people only use it to build boats with. So it does not align itself with the concept of building a boat as cheaply as possible. To build a boat in new marine ply is now a very expensive business, and I am certain that you would find it cheaper to buy an already constructed secondhand boat instead.

As far as sailing is concerned, I am of the opinion that a beginner will have quite enough on his hands during his first few seasons without even thinking of coping with sails as well. Sailing a boat is an art in itself, and is best learnt from someone with a good deal of experience. Later

*A standing lug sailing rig for a small fishing boat fitted with a leeboard*

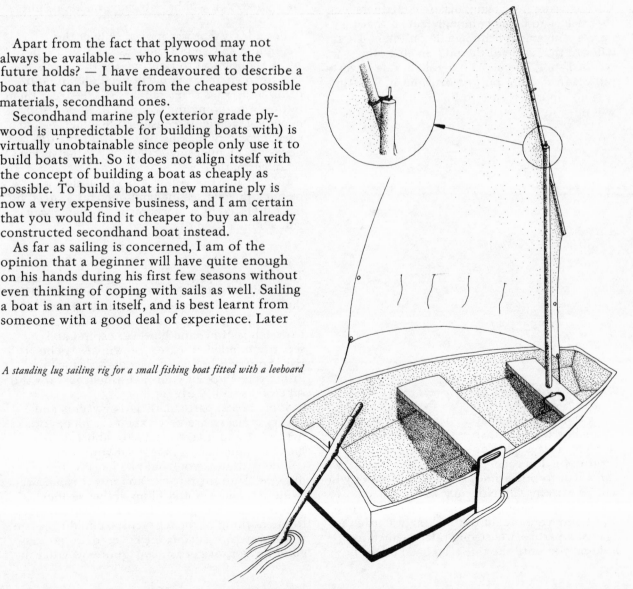

## Equipment

Unless you have been extremely lucky and acquired a secondhand boat with a comprehensive selection of equipment thrown in, you will now be faced with the prospect of obtaining one or two essential items.

Apart from safety equipment which I deal with in chapter nine, the first thing you will need will be a pair of oars. These will be used for manoeuvring in harbour and when working some sorts of gear. Hopefully they will never need to be used to get you home if your engine has broken down, but it will be reassuring to know that the marine equivalent of shanks's pony is on hand if required.

Another important item of equipment is a baler. This can be almost anything capable of shifting water, and many plastic containers lend themselves to being cunningly cut so that they have a convenient little handle on them. Tie the baler to the inside of the boat in an easily reached spot, and make it a golden rule never to put off from your mooring without it. The time it is not aboard is sure to be the one time you will need it.

*Scoop baler cut from a discarded plastic container*

I will describe in a later chapter how to make an anchor and I must stress that it is essential that you always carry one attached to a good length of nylon rope. (The warp needs to be two and a half to three times the depth of water you will be working in). Not only will you need it to hold you in position for various kinds of fishing, but if you were caught out making no headway against a particularly strong tide, an anchor holding you until the tide slackened might be the only thing to stop you disappearing over the horizon on a one way ticket to disaster.

It is not essential to have a boat hook aboard, but when you are fishing it certainly makes the job of picking up lines and marker buoys very much easier. You can buy the business end from any chandler and fix it on your own pole, but use the largest screws you can or you will lose the metal head the first time you use it.

## Trailing Boats

If your boat is not going to be permanently located, you will need to move it around either on the roof of a car or by trailer. The size of both your car and of the boat will determine if the first option is at all practical, but if it must be trailed, you will have to buy, make, or hire one.

For a boat that was moved only at the beginning and end of the season, it would be most economical to rent one for the occasion, but for regular use you will need one of your own. Numerous firms sell kits to construct them, but even by doing the work yourself you still become involved in considerable expense, and a cheaper way of making one, if you have the necessary engineering skills, is by using various scrap car parts.

But for most of you, the best solution will be to track down a secondhand one and, if need be, have it vetted by a mechanic in the same way you would a used car.

## Insurance

This really is a must, and the modest expense incurred will give you great peace of mind. The theft of small boats and particularly small outboard engines has now reached the scale of a national pastime, and however careful and security minded you are, you will always be at risk. So it will be foolish to take a chance on losing the whole of your investment just for the sake of a small yearly outlay.

Some boats, particularly glossy yachts and luxury cruisers, are very expensive pieces of hardware, and if your boat should break its mooring and damage one, or if you should collide with one, you could be faced with a massive claim for repairs. You might run down a swimmer, and if not kill him, inflict serious injuries with your propeller. Again the damages, to say nothing of the legal costs, could ruin you if you were not adequately covered. So go to a good broker, or get as many quotes as you can from specialist marine insurers, and let them be the ones to take the chances.

## Partnerships

One certain way to cut down the cost of buying and running a boat is to team up with another person, or form a syndicate with a number of people. Not only is the initial outlay shared, but also expenditure on buying or making the fishing gear. The burden of maintenance and even the boat's construction does not rest entirely on one pair of shoulders, and when actually fishing, the boat and equipment will be easier to handle if there is more than one willing pair of hands aboard.

With the financial resources of two or more people pooled, it will also mean that you will probably be able to buy a larger boat that will not be restricted to working in only the calmest of conditions. If the boat is to be trailed, the work of launching and recovery will not be so much of a struggle, and with mooring and other overhead costs shared, the actual cost of the catch to each partner will be correspondingly reduced.

From a safety point of view, it has to be said that it is in fact desirable that you work with somebody else. If you should fall overboard or become ill or injure yourself, the presence of a companion might be your only chance of survival.

The best kind of partner for someone food fishing would probably be a like-minded individual, but if you were unable to join forces with a totally kindred spirit, perhaps the best alternative would be someone who was more interested in fishing for profit. If that sounds like a contradiction of terms, consider that at least he would be keen, and not likely to want to use the boat for joyriding when the pots needed pulling and the nets a'hauling.

But partnerships can run into trouble, and because of this it is essential that the whole relationship be based on a formal contract. At first sight this might appear to be rather unnecessary and overcautious, but when you consider the difficulties that could arise, its desirability becomes obvious.

What, for example, would happen if either you or your partner wished to pull out of the arrangement? How and when would his or your financial interest be repaid? Would such payments be reckoned at cost or current value? If your partner took the boat out by himself and damaged it in some way, who would pay for the repairs? Would it be a joint responsibility? Will you or your partner be able to lend the boat to someone not in the partnership? How will the maintenance and expenses be shared? If all these potential arguing points are not defined at the outset, they will always be a threat to the partnership's success. If everything is down in black and white, arbitration is automatic and can save not only partnerships, but friendships as well. So before you begin, make a list of all the conditions you can think of, then go to a man of the law and have him draft it out properly. Then sign it and keep to it. I doubt that you will ever regret it.

# 8. Propulsion

## Outboards

For small boats, inboard engines are really non starters. Apart from being considerably more expensive than outboard engines, they take up space inside the boat, and if a major overhaul is needed, a great deal of work is involved in even getting them as far as the workshop bench.

But perhaps the biggest advantage of using an outboard engine in a small fishing boat is the safety factor. Should lines or nets become fouled around the propellor at sea, it is a fairly easy job to tilt the engine or even bring it inboard in order to sort things out. So for the type of boat that we have discussed, I would strongly recommend that your power unit be an outboard one.

## New or Secondhand

The biggest enemy of outboards is corrosion, and it is this factor, not overwork, that usually finishes them off. So a secondhand engine that has been well looked after, even if it be quite ancient, can often be a totally acceptable proposition. If on the other hand you can afford it, or are not particularly mechanically minded and able to renovate a second-hand one, it will probably be better to start off with a new one that you can gradually learn something about as you become more familiar with it. Then with your instruction manual in one hand, and your fearless spanner in the other, you can gradually learn how to do your own repairs as snags crop up.

## Choosing the Engine

Our small fishing boat will not need a very large engine, something in the 3-5hp bracket will be quite adequate and give a reasonable turn of speed. If you are tempted to think that by getting a larger engine you will drastically increase your speed, forget it, because it is a characteristic of all boats that the propeller thrust needed to gain just a small increase in speed over the boat's designed maximum is enormous. So if you put a 10hp engine on a boat that only needs a 4hp engine, you will not automatically get much of the increased speed you were hoping for. With luck, you may be able to wring an extra rather uncomfortable knot out of her, but it will cost you dearly in increased fuel consumption. All boats have a specific speed at which they perform most efficiently, and it is interesting to note that if a particular engine is matched to say a 10 feet boat, it will push it along at a maximum speed of perhaps 4 knots; but if that same engine is coupled with a 15 feet boat of a basically similar design, it could well move it at six or even seven knots.

Incidentally, if you want to calculate the top speed of any displacement vessel, multiply the square root of her length in feet at the waterline by 1.5. This will give you the answer in knots.

## What Make

Dozens of different firms manufacture outboard engines, and from a mechanical point of view I do not suppose it matters all that much whose you buy. Some have been at it longer than others, but I guess the best solution is to buy one that you can easily get serviced and obtain spares for locally. Outboard owners, like many owners of foreign cars, have found out that although initial costs of imported engines may be temptingly low, and advertising campaigns correspondingly effective, the cost, and even availability of replacement parts means that the true outlay has merely been held over for a while, and you often end up paying through the nose after all. But bear in mind that whichever engine you buy, in the final analysis it will only be as good as your care and attention allow it to be.

## Looking After Outboards

Since there are so many different kinds of outboard engines, it is impossible, when discussing them in general terms, to cover each one's particular idiosyncrasies. Therefore, the first thing to do is to study the manufacturer's instruction book, or literature, and familiarize yourself with the actual model you have acquired.

Practically all outboard engines are twostrokes, which means that they run on an oil and gas (petrol in Britain) mixture. The gas provides the power and the oil the lubrication.

The ratio of oil to gas required by different makes of engine varies considerably, and is critical; so you will have to mix the brew to the maker's specification yourself. Never use the kind of twostroke fuel that is sold for small motorbikes. The proportions will most certainly be wrong, and likely to cause you continual and possibly expensive trouble.

In order for the engine to work properly it is essential that the fuel constituents are really well shaken up together. Always do this in a clean separate container (never the fuel tank) using regular fuel. Avoid the high star grades because these contain additives which collect on the plug points and gradually stop them sparking. They can be cleaned of course (preferably sand blasted, and properly reset with a feeler gauge) but this is no solution and the problem will only arise again.

Although marine engines are designed to ward off corrosion as much as they can, they will have little chance of success without your continuing assistance. Always treat any chips or scratches to the paintwork as urgent, rubbing them down and retouching them as soon as possible. Keep an eye on likely trouble spots and wipe any salt deposits off with an oily rag. Check the fuel tank regularly for signs of rust (use a flashlight to look inside, not a naked flame) and watch out for any wear on the starting cord (always carry a spare). Don't let sand get in the engine either; it will ruin it.

## First Aid for an Overboard Outboard

Totally immersing an outboard in sea water is something to be avoided at all costs, and if you take the precaution of securing the engine with a safety lanyard it will be unlikely to happen. But if it does, and you can in fact recover it, this is what you do. Speed is essential, because sea water will start to corrode the metalwork at an alarming rate, so the first thing to do is to get the water out of it. Take it ashore and stand it upright. If your engine has a shroud, take it off and remove the sparking plugs (your engine may only have one plug, but some have two, so I shall refer to them in the plural). As you are doing this, water will drain from the underwater exhaust. With the engine on its side, try and drain out as much water as possible through the plug holes. Put her in neutral and turn the engine over a few times; this should expel most of the water from the cylinders. If everything seems in order mechanically, pour fuel into the cylinders through the sparking plug holes until they are overflowing. Turn the engine over a couple of more times and this will flush out the fuel you have just put in — hopefully leaving the cylinders clear.

Doubtless your fuel tank will be attached to the engine, so disconnect it from the carburettor in order to drain the tank so that it too can be rinsed out with fuel. Take the float chamber off the carburettor and clean this out with yet more fuel — likewide the feed pipe. Such a waste; thank heavens it's you paying for it all.

Now you can put everything back together and try the engine. If it works, rush back to the boat and run it around for half an hour. If not, water may have got into the magneto or ignition coil, and if you can remove them, an hour in a warm spot may revive them. Should the engine still fail to respond, all you can do is dry your eyes and go through the whole performance again. If you can't face that, fill up the cylinders with engine oil and pack the whole lot off to your dealer or manufacturer. In which case your only consolation will be, that when it does at last back, it will at least have had a complete overhaul.

## Laying Up

During the winter, when rough weather may prevent you fishing with your boat, the engine will need to be protected from damp and condensation. If at all possible, this is best achieved by bringing it into the house, and not leaving it in what could be a damp outbuilding or garage. But before you lodge it in a suitable temporary resting place, there are one or two routine chores that will have to be done first.

I have already mentioned how corrosive sea water is, so before the hibernation begins, any remnants of the ocean must be removed from the engine. I suppose a good way to do this would be to take a trip on an inland lake or river; but most people that I know just run the engine in a water butt for five minutes. If you can rig up a hose from a water tap so that the barrel overflows all the time, so much the better, as this will help to carry off the salt and oil debris.

With some engines it may be difficult to do this, because high propellor speeds may splash all the water out or stop the cooling system from working in such a confined space. So it will be wise to check with your dealer or manufacturer first. With some outboards, the cooling system can be flushed by applying a hose to the cylinder water outlet.

No fuel should be allowed to remain in the tank or carburettor during the lay up, since left to its own devices for any length of time two stroke fuel becomes very sticky, and will clog everything up. So these must be drained. Old engine oil must also be abandoned, and a small quantity of fresh poured in through the sparking plug holes and the carburettor intake. If you rotate the flywheel as you do this, the oil will be able to spread freely around. Don't forget the gearcase either; refill that, and similarly turn the engine over a few times.

After a few drops of lubricating oil on the throttle cable and anywhere else that you think needs it. she can be wrapped in a dust sheet and safely left (upright) until the spring.

When you feel like going fishing again, all you have to do is whip out the plugs, turn the engine over a few times to get the old oil out — give her a quick pre-season rub down — and off you go.

### Maintenance and Spares
If you acquire a secondhand outboard, or a new one for that matter, make sure that you get a manual for it, either from the person that sold it to you or the manufacturers. In this it will tell you what needs to be done to the engine when it is in regular use. This work is of vital importance, since the engine must be in tip top condition whenever you put to sea. It is difficult to attract the attention of a mechanic when you are half a mile off shore.

I have already mentioned a few of the spares that you should always carry with you, but your manual will (or should) list others. Some makers sell kits with a selection of spares that they have found to be most useful with their particular engines, and these will include such things as plugs and shear pins. Don't forget the tool kit either, and read up on the manual before the trouble occurs. Wading through the instructions as the wind freshens to force 6 will be a disastrous way of effecting any running repairs.

### Rowing
I should think that at one time or another practically all of you will have sat behind a pair of oars, and the only variable factor will be the degree of success with which you did so. But really the only way to learn how to row well is to actually get out there on the water. Before you do that though, if you can, watch one of the old timers skimming his dinghy smoothly and effortlessly across the harbour. Long even pulls, using his body weight instead of just tiring his arms out, keeping the oars driving through the water for the maximum amount of time, the return strokes just above the water. See how he anticipates the speed and momentum of the boat as he comes alongside his objective, shipping the oars with a practiced swing at precisely the right moment. He didn't learn how to do all that out of a book, nor can you; so find a nice quiet spot and just try to copy him as closely as you can. Experience will bring expertise, and before you know it, you will be the one the beginners are trying to pick up tips from.

## Oars

But the admiring novice will certainly not have the best of teachers, if you have not provided yourself with a decent pair of oars. Common sense will tell you what is about right for the boat you are using. Not too short or you will have to hold your arms out wide and dip the blades steeply down into the water; giving you little power, very tired arms, and probably lost oars. On the other hand, they don't want to go to the other extreme and be so long and unwieldy that they are difficult to row with and get back into the boat again. A nice balanced compromise is the thing to aim for.

## Copse Oars

In my part of the world, a particular kind of oar that has evolved is especially useful for fishermen. It is called the copse oar, and differs from an ordinary oar in that a slab of wood is fixed to the loom at the point where it would normally pass through the oarlocks. Instead of oarlocks, a metal peg or thole pin is inserted in the gunwale and the oar located on this by a hole drilled through the block.

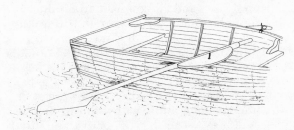

*Copse oars with their slabs in the correct rowing position*

Not only does this produce a nicely counter balanced oar that is a particular delight to row with, but it also means that if you let go of one or both oars, they will not slip unceremoniously into the water.

This is particularly useful for fishermen who may want to have both hands free for hauling lines or tying knots, because it saves them from continually having to ship their oars.

It also means that you don't have to buy any oarlocks, which like everything else are now no longer cheap, and I might add, a particular favourite of the petty thief. In this respect too the holes on the oars which take the thole pins are useful, because when leaving the boat unattended, you can ship the oars and pass a chain through the holes and around the seat and secure them with a padlock.

## Sculling

Sculling is a form of single oar rowing, and once again, a skill that can only be acquired by actually trying to do it.

The oar rests in a recess cut in the top of the boat's transom, and is made to writhe from side to side through the water by a wristy swaying action of the hand and forearm. If the boat is big enough you will get more power into it if you can stand up, but in smaller boats you will need to sit on the rowing seat or kneel facing the stern.

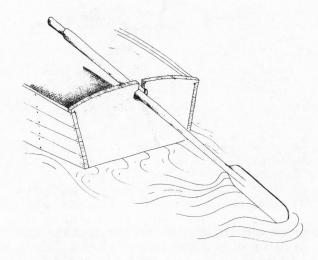

*Sculling is much easier when the recess to take the oar is the correct shape*

On most boats that I have seen, the recess cut in the transom to take the oar has been altogether the wrong shape; being just a cut out half circle. If you cut the recess into more of a complete circle, so that you must slide the oar in rather than just rest it in position, the oar will not be inclined to jump out of the slot, and you will be able to get a more consistently powerful sweep.

In order to avoid wear, leather is often nailed around the edges of the recess, or alternatively around the loom of the oar at the point of contact.

## Yuloh

This is the ancient method of single oar propulsion that is still in use in China and Japan. Since native experts can move 20-foot boats at

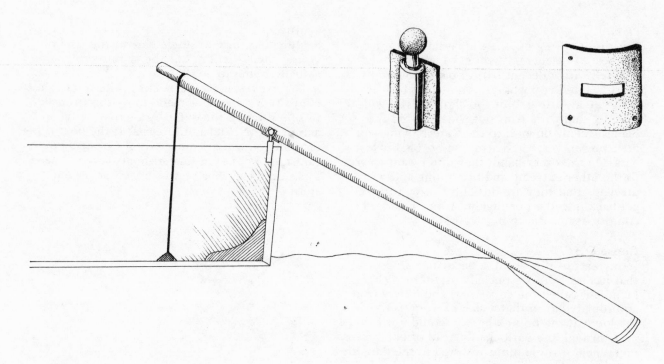

speeds that approach 4 knots, you might like to try this up-dated version. You will see from the illustration that a shanked metal ball is held in the loom of the oar by means of a slotted plate. The shank of the ball rests in a hole or bracket located on top of the transom. The inboard end of the oar is fastened to the bottom of the boat by means of a suitable rope, and by simply pushing and pulling the oar handle you are propelled through the water at an amazing speed. Far less arduous than conventional rowing or sculling, this system has the added advantage of requiring absolutely no skill at all, as the twisting action of the oar is automatic. A longish oar is best, and the fittings should preferably be made out of stainless steel. If you seek out someone with a lathe, your best winning smile will get the necessary metalwork made up for next to nothing, and all you have to do then is take a thoughtful amount of care in fitting it. Make sure the hole you drill is on a line with the edge of the oar blade, and that the ball is snugly bedded in with some plastic filler, but still has room to move. When you do this, coat the ball with soap or whatever, so that it does not stick to the filler. Take trouble with your drilling angles, and make sure that the oar can be lifted clear of the water and that you can get enough depth of blade to give you a powerful sweep.

Knots converted into Miles per Hour to the nearest decimal point

| Knots | m.p.h. |
|---|---|
| 1 | 1.15 |
| 2 | 2.3 |
| 3 | 3.5 |
| 4 | 4.6 |
| 5 | 5.8 |
| 6 | 6.9 |
| 7 | 8.1 |
| 8 | 9.2 |
| 9 | 10.4 |
| 10 | 11.15 |

# 9. Some Basic Seamanship

*"Wouldst thou," – so the helmsman answered, –*
*"Learn the secret of the sea?*
*Only those who brave its dangers*
*Comprehend its mystery!"*

*Longfellow*

Seamanship is a difficult word to define. It covers so much. Not only a knowledge of the sea and its ways, but of boats and buoys and virtually anything connected with being afloat. A true seaman not only has a comprehensive range of learnt skills at his fingertips, but the ability to continually juggle them all in his mind, computing subconsciously the correct way to put them into practice.

All this only comes with experience, and the novice will initially have to work only in the most sheltered of conditions, gradually acquiring the expertise that will allow him to go further afield. There is no short cut through this apprenticeship. The lessons must be learned, and learnt thoroughly, or you may not live to regret it.

## Swimming
If you cannot do so already, you must learn to swim before you put to sea. All public swimming pools run courses for beginners, and the fees are very modest. Even the most experienced boatmen sometimes take an involuntary dip, and if you can't swim, what could be a laughable incident, will turn into a nightmare struggle for your life. So don't take chances, and if possible, get in some practice fully clothed, because that is how you will be when you go over the side.

If you fix a rope strop inside the boat, near the middle of the transom — so that you can reach it from the water — you can use it as a step to get back into the boat, a manoeuvre which can otherwise be very difficult in heavy wet clothes.

## Life Jackets
No matter how good a swimmer you are, it is essential to wear a life jacket whenever you take to the water. Accidents can happen not only on the open sea, but in harbour as well; so make it a cardinal rule never to set foot on your boat without a life jacket on. If you knocked yourself senseless as you went over the side, only your life jacket could support you until you recovered or help was able to get to you. In a cold sea, your energy would rapidly desert you, and in a matter of minutes you would be exhausted, and totally dependent on the buoyancy of your jacket.

Now unfortunately a great many people take absolutely no notice at all of advice like this, and go merrily on their way working their poor guardian angels right into the ground. Professional fishermen are about the worst offenders, usually defending their lack of a life jacket by saying they are difficult to work in. Which is odd when you think that those same fishermen manage to do a very good job indeed when they come to manning the local rescue boat and the regulations force them to wear one. Admittedly it is difficult to change the habits of a lifetime, and they do feel a bit strange to work in if you are not used to them. But if you start off by wearing one, right from the beginning, they become an integral part of your clothing, and are no more of a hindrance than your shirt or shoes are.

## Safety Equipment
Apart from life jackets and other essential equipment like oars and anchors that have already been mentioned, a well found boat needs a number of other items aboard before she can safely put to sea.

As well as a baler, a fixed bilge pump is a good thing to have, even on the smallest of boats. Preferably sited near the helmsman, so that he can steer and pump at the same time.

If your boat hasn't got a waterproof locker, it will be advisable to fit one. Under the whole length of the rowing seat is a good place. Not only will it provide dry storage for matches, torch, blankets, and your first-aid kits, but it will also give the boat extra buoyancy should she become awash, allowing her to remain on the surface while you bail the water out.

It may seem strange to include food and water under safety equipment, but always carry plenty of both with you, even if you intend only going out for an hour or two. Something unforeseen may happen and you could get stuck somewhere. Hunger and thirst might panic you into doing something stupid, when the best course of action would have been to sit it out until the fog lifted or the tide turned.

Even if you are just working half a mile off shore, you will need distress flares, and a small boat should carry, at the very least, two red hand flares and two orange smoke signals. The flares hopefully attract attention to your predicament, and the smoke signals make it easier for your rescuers to home in on you.

Another useful item of equipment is a small hand compass. If in good weather you practice various courses with it, and learn to allow for the wind and tide, should fog or darkness catch you out, getting home will be nothing more than a routine affair.

Following on from this, you will also need a tri-coloured lantern — exhibiting white, green and red filters, to serve as emergency navigation lights, and some sort of audible fog signal — a bell, whistle, or aerosol fog horn — to warn others of your presence.

Apart from all these tangible pieces of equipment, there is one further item of 'insurance' that should not be forgotten. Always tell someone (who is going to remain on shore) when and where you are going, and the time at which you plan to return. Then if you do get into trouble, you will have the comforting knowledge that your absence has at least not gone unnoticed. And remember, always report in when you do get back from your trip — otherwise rescue services may needlessly be put into action.

## Getting Ready for Sea

On your first few trips to sea, it will be best not to try any actual fishing, and instead concentrate on familiarizing yourself with your boat and local conditions. But before you untie the mooring ropes, there are still a few things that you have to brush up on first.

## The Weather

Before I begin this section, I must mention that the wind directions I am going to refer to are relative only to the northern hemisphere. If you happen to live in the southern hemisphere, things will be different. You can clarify how this will affect you by consulting one of the specialist books on weather forecasting, or the relevant sections in any seaman's almanack.

Knowing what the weather is likely to be going to do is a vitally important part of any boating activity; and for the fisherman this is particularly relevant, because once he has set his gear, he has, to a certain extent, committed himself. True, at the first sign of bad weather he could up anchor, abandon his nets or lines, and run for the safety of home, but that would hardly be very seamanlike, and certainly very expensive. So it will be very helpful if he has as much idea as possible about what the elements are thinking of throwing at him beforehand. Then he is not likely to be caught unawares.

Unfortunately, weather forecasting is not an exact science, and the predictions broadcast by the various radio and television stations can be no more than guidelines for you to come to your own conclusions about. Obviously it will be a waste of time heading for the coast if gale warnings are being shouted all over the place; but when conditions are less clear cut you will need specific local information about the area you intend to work, and the man who can give you that is the local coastguard. After all he is on the spot, and likely to be actually looking at the sea as he talks to you on the phone. He will also have a great deal of personal experience of the area he is discussing, and the benefit of being able to collaborate with other stations up or down the coast. He is therefore, as near to the horse's mouth as you are liable to get. So if you have any doubts at all, you will do well to consult him before putting to sea.

Of course if you live near the coast, you will be able to reason out much of the likely pattern of events for yourself, and to this end an extremely useful thing to have is a good old fashioned barometer.

## Barometers

As you probably know, a barometer functions by being sensitive to changes in the atmosphere. Luckily for us — the very same changes that bring good or bad weather with them.

Variations in air temperature always precede altering weather conditions, and it is the difference in atmospheric pressure so caused that barometers measure. So if you have a mercurial barometer, it is important to place it in a particularly equable spot so that it doesn't just act as a thermometer.

A warm air flow will cause the atmosphere to lighten, and the barometer will fall. A cold air stream condenses the air producing an opposite effect.

Before strong winds, atmospheric pressure decreases quite sharply; so if the barometer suddenly falls you will know that gales are on the way. When these have blown themselves out, the hand will slowly rise again as the air condenses and the pressure builds up.

The speed with which the actual weather conditions follow the barometer's predictions can also point to their likely duration. Bad weather quickly following a fall will not usually last very long, and conversely, good weather coming soon after a rise should not be relied upon. As the old sailor's rhyme so aptly puts it

"Long foretold, long last;

Short warning — soon past."

So if the barometer has fallen appreciably and you are beginning to think that it has made a mistake, expect the worst.

## Typical Barometer Predictions

If the barometer rises, and both temperature and dampness also increase, snow, or wind and rain will usually follow — invariably from the South East, South West or South.

The worst Northern gales and shifting winds occur when the barometer rises from a very low point; and a sudden fall when the wind is from the West will often be followed by rough stormy weather coming in from the North and North West.

A rapidly rising barometer usually means that unsettled weather is on the way, while a slow steady rise accompanied by dry weather means that conditions are likely to improve and become less changeable.

The barometer will fall to its lowest with gales from the South, or South East and South West, and rise to its highest when the wind blows from opposite points in the North.

Admiral Fitzroy, the 19th Century meteorologist and inventor of the now much prized Fitzroy Barometer, had two basic rules:-

*An Admiral Fitzroy barometer from the late 19th century. Now a much prized collectors item*

*The Barometer Rises* for northerly wind (including from N.W. by the N. to E.), for dry or less wet weather, for less wind, or for more than one of these changes, except on a few occasions, when rain (or snow) comes from the N. with strong wind.

*The Barometer Falls* for south wind (including from S.E. by the S. to W.), for wet weather, for stronger wind, or for more than one of these changes, except on a few occasions, when moderate wind with rain (or snow) comes from the northward.

All of this can be confirmed by observation, and if you get into the habit of making a diary

note of what the barometer predicts each day —
against what actually happens — you will soon
see just how helpful a barometer can be.

So when official weather forecasts indicate
good weather, and your barometer has remained
nice and steady for some length of time, you
should safely be able to put to sea.

But use your common sense and keep an eye
on the horizon. In winter particularly, the
situation can rapidly alter. At the first sign of
even the slightest change, haul the gear and
make for harbour. The place to be when the
storm breaks is ashore, reminiscing about your
outstanding skill as a fisherman, not struggling
to prove it in a small boat at sea.

### Forecasting by Observing Natural Phenomena

Less scientific perhaps, but this is how fishermen
and farmers used to do it in the old days. So for
what it's worth, here are a few old fashioned
conclusions that I have collected.

If objects in the distance are clear and
apparently raised as if by reflection, rain, and
possibly wind, are on the way.

If the moon is clear, but has a halo around it,
gales and wind are imminent.

When the high ground is shrouded in mist,
expect south-west gales and rain.

When broken portions of rainbow — 'Wind
dogs' — can be seen to windward in the early
morning, it is certain a gale is on their tail.

If in the morning the wind is blowing from the
west, but backs against the sun to the east in the
evening, bad weather will follow.

Should the sun rise or set behind banks of
cloud, rough weather will soon set in.

The wind will follow the sun in settled
weather, blowing from the east in the morning,
and the west in the evening.

Ragged streaks of cloud — Mare's tails — that
hover ominously on the horizon warn of the
gales that will sweep them away.

At sunset, a pale yellow sky is a sure sign of
rain, while a bright yellow sky will be followed
by wind.

A dark blue gloomy sky is a sure sign of wind;
but a light blue sky means the weather will be
settled and fine.

In fine weather the sea birds will fly far out to
sea, but if bad weather is on the way, they will
come far inland.

If large numbers of jelly-fish come close
inshore, good weather is on the way.

When the sea is phosphorescent, the fine
weather will certainly continue.

If porpoises should move into shallow water or
make their way up river, stormy weather will
follow.

Finally, the old favourite that everyone knows

*Red sky at night, sailors' delight.*
*Red sky in morning, sailors' warning.*

I suppose it will always be a debatable point as
to whether (an unintentional pun) all these
observations should be taken very seriously; but
they have stood the test of time, and many are
now known to be based on scientific fact. We
shall need all the help that we can get.
Therefore, if the official forecast, our barometer,
and the old wives' tales all agree, why not bring
them all into the reckoning?

### Clouds

A great deal can be learned about the ensuing
weather by studying what the various ever
changing cloud formations foretell. It does
however require a fairly detailed specialist
knowledge of the subject, which in all honesty is
best acquired by studying one of the various
books on the subject. A very good one that I
have come across is — 'Instant Weather Forecasting' — by Alan Watts — published by Adlard
Coles Ltd of London. Being illustrated with
colour photographs it makes the whole thing
easier to understand, and will I think make
interesting and worthwhile reading not only for
the fisherman, but for farmers and indeed
anyone who needs to know what the weather
may be going to do.

### Charts

A large scale, up to date chart, of the area you
intend to work, is an essential part of a
fisherman's equipment. To all intents and
purposes, you will initially be a foreigner in a
foreign land, and like any other sensible tourist,
you will be wise to arm yourself with a map of
your unfamiliar surroundings. For that is all
charts are, maps of the sea, but in essence more
revealing, because they define a world that would
otherwise be unseen.

Most of the information marked on a chart is
self-explanatory. As well as the high and low
tidelines, the depth contours will be indicated in
fathoms, (sometimes feet or meters) and under-
lined figures will tell you how much water is left
above obstructions at low water.

The various marker and navigation buoys will
also be shown, and the direction and speed of

tides clearly marked. This latter piece of information will prove particularly useful to owners of small boats, since it will help them to 'work the tide'. Which simply means getting your timing right, and hitching a ride on the flow. But you must get it right. Many boating fatalities are caused by people racing along at full throttle on a fast tide, only to find out that they can make little way against it when they try to come back. For example, if the tide is running at six knots, and you join it moving at your top speed of four knots, you will very quickly be moving at ten knots, and covering a considerable distance in no time at all. On the return trip, you will only be able to make two knots against the flow, and it will take you five times as long to get back to where you started from.

Only of course you won't make it back, because you will have run out of fuel long before then, and be well on the way to becoming yet another very lifeless statistic.

As far as fishermen are concerned, probably the most useful thing about charts is the information that they give regarding the nature of both the shore and the sea bed. At a glance the practised eye is able to tell what sort of fish are liable to be around, and what sort of gear may possibly be used to catch them. If the foreshore consists of sand and mud, maybe bivalve molluscs are in residence. A rocky coast may indicate the presence of other shellfish, crabs and lobsters perhaps. Or if the bottom is of sand, it could be that flat fish will be around. Wrecks and obstructions will also be marked, and even if not in very deep water, they may be teeming with fish.

Thus your chart becomes your underwater eyes, and by observation and deduction you can select suitable grounds, and begin experimenting with various kinds of gear to find out what brings the best results.

Bear in mind though that charts gradually become out of date because of changes on the coast and seabed. For a fee, chart agents will periodically make the necessary corrections; so enquire about this when you buy your *new* one.

## Navigational Marks

Also shown on your chart will be the various lights and buoys used to indicate danger spots and guide boats safely around the coast.

The lights will be of little practical interest to the beginner, since he will not be operating at night, but it will be as well to familiarize yourself with the purpose of the ones in your area, just in case of unforeseen circumstances.

In some small harbours and rivers the navigable channels may be marked merely by branches or poles stuck into the mud; but elsewhere and at sea, proper buoys will be used.

Many different systems of buoyage are used off the coasts of various countries around the world, the shape and colour of the buoys or the way they are lit indicating how they should be navigated around. Your local harbour officials will be able to provide you with a booklet

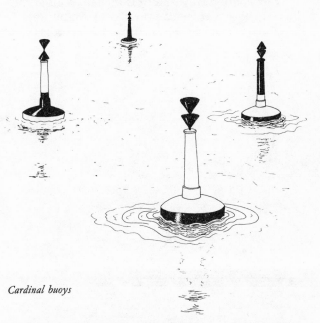

*Cardinal buoys*

(usually free) that will concern the safety of small boats, and you will find in this your own relevant system explained.

But in order to achieve some kind of international uniformity, the Cardinal system is gradually being introduced to combine with all these differing methods. Cardinal buoys are placed in any one of the four segments of a compass point based on the danger. The shape of their tops (or flashing rhythm) showing how they should be passed.

However, within reason, much of this will only be of concern to larger boats, at least as far as channel buoys are concerned, and a small boat with a shallow draft will be able to nose around all over the place. But of course the chart must be studied to see if this is wise, and weather conditions taken into account. If you do your exploring at low tide, at least you will have the comforting assurance that if you do get stuck aground, the tide will soon rise and float you off.

## Position Fixing

As well as showing the sea and seashore, your chart will also make note of any prominent landmarks that can easily be seen from offshore. This will be useful because these marks can be used to roughly fix your position, allowing you to return to gear that you have set, or particularly good fishing spots that you have discovered. Position fixing can be done quite accurately with a compass, but the bearings need to be layed off on the chart with a parallel ruler, and this is not really practical in a small boat. So the only way that we can do it is by lining up these marks against other marks or features.

Suppose you can see a church tower that is noted on the chart, and that just in front of it, or slightly to one side of it is another quite prominent object. By making a note of the relative position of these two objects, you can as it were fix one half of your position. If you then look to another part of the coast and select another mark — possibly a headland or the end of a pier — and again fix that position with another feature near it or in line with it, you have obtained a cross reference to your own position. If you and the two pairs of marks make an angle of as near 90° as you can get, so much the better, since this will help to make the whole

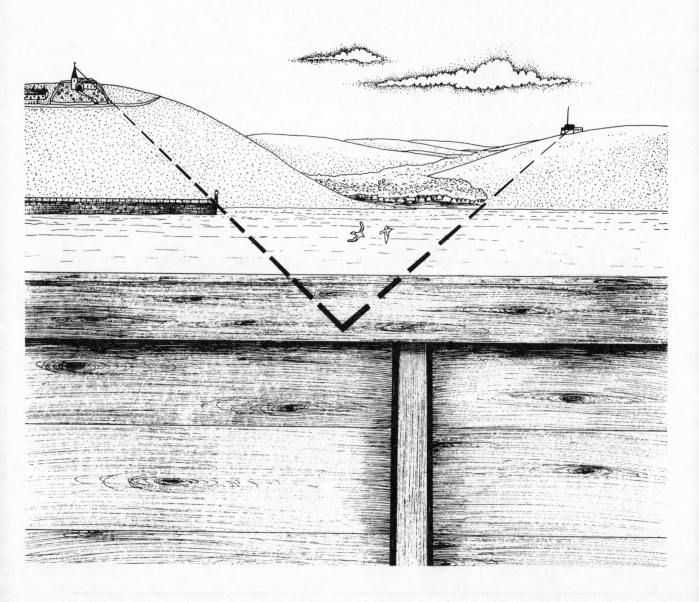

calculation more accurate.

It will be helpful if you actually make a physical note of the relative positions, because you will be sure to forget how you worked them out if you don't. Such a memo might read as follows:

"When the church tower is directly in line with the end of the pier in the foreground, one position is correct. And when the flag pole is just visible round the side of the coastguard building, the other one is correct."

## Rules of the Road
In order that boats should have some hard and fast code of practice to help them avoid bumping into one another, the 'Collision Regulations' have been formulated by a congress of representatives from all over the world.

As might be expected of any set of rules drawn up by an international committee, there could never be the slightest chance of them being anything other than lengthy and complicated. But fortunately, in as far as they affect us, they can be condensed into a few brief paragraphs.

1. The first basic principle to understand is that if two powered boats are converging towards a head on collision, both must take avoiding action by altering their courses to starboard, so that they pass each other on the port side.

This rule applies mainly to narrow channels and busy inshore waters where boats will be fairly close to each other, and not so much to the open sea. In other words, you do not have to go looking for boats to pass on the port side, scanning the horizon and making five mile detours.
2. If a boat is approaching you from the starboard side, she has right of way, and you must give way to her.
3. A vessel under sail may not be so manoeuvrable as a power drive boat, so power yields to sail.
4. You also give way to boats that are hampered in some way. Deep draft vessels may be forced to keep to specific routes in order to avoid running aground. Other fishing vessels may be trawling, or working other gear, so give way to them as well.
5. In harbours, channels and rivers, make your way on the right hand side.
6. Check on local regulations; there may be other rules besides.

But whatever you think your rights may be,

remember that you will be very small fry indeed. Do not expect large boats to do very much yielding on your account. They may not even have seen you, and if they have, bear in mind that some big vessels may need at least a mile to get out of your way in.

Assume therefore that nobody else has even heard of the collision regulations, and are in fact under the illusion that the whole purpose of their being afloat is to hit as many boats as they possibly can.

So make your manoeuvres decisive, your intentions clear, and give other craft as much room as possible.

## Moorings
If you are not going to move your boat around with you, or moor her at the quayside, you may have to lay your own moorings. Local regulations often dictate how this should be done, but one of the following two very similar methods is usually acceptable.

When left unattended, you don't want your boat to be slewing around all over the place, so she will need to be fixed in position by mooring her at both the bow and the stern.

Obviously you will need to be able to find your moorings when you return to them, so they will have to be marked with buoys — which can be made from discarded plastic containers that have been brightly painted.

The end of the mooring that is on the harbour floor can be either just a heavy weight, or two anchors set opposite each other on a bridle of chain. From this, a length of chain with a swivel in the middle leads to the surface and aboard the boat. Attached to the end of the chain is the buoy rope, and finally the buoy. When the boat is moored, she will be held by the chain; but when you cast off the moorings, all the chain will sink to the bottom leaving just the rope leading to the surface marker buoy.

## Dropping and Picking Up Moorings
This is really quite straightforward, especially if you have a nice big loop on the buoy, and all you have to watch out for is getting rope or chain around your propellor. So initially, when you cast off, it will be advisable to row clear before you start your engine, and reverse the process when you return from your trip.

When you are more experienced you will probably be able to do both manoeuvres under power, and practice will allow you to judge when to cut the engine but still have enough way to reach your objective. You will also learn how to take advantage of the fact that single screw vessels tend to slew to one side or the other unless corrected by the helm; and you will be able to power clear or onto the mooring by a quick burst of the engine turning the boat at the critical time. The reason that one prop boats do this is because the bottom half of the propeller is turning in denser water than the top half and gets more of a grip; so if the blades turn clockwise, the bow will veer to port and the stern to starboard, and vice versa.

## Mooring at the Quayside

Before you actually tie up at the quay or pier, you will have to run in alongside. A procedure that is not always easy if damage is to be avoided. As when picking up moorings, it will be best to come in against the tide (or wind if it is more powerful), then you will be able to gently ease the bow in and use the flow to swing the stern in alongside. If the tide is not strong enough to do this, you can either just haul yourself in with the boat hook, or 'kick' her in with a quick flick of the throttle and the helm hard over.

The kind of fenders you will need to protect the boat with will depend on the type of structure that you are mooring against. If it be a solid stone quay, a couple of strategically placed buffers should be adequate, but if you are alongside a more open kind of pier, or the harbour wall is faced with piles, there may be gaps that will make these inadequate, and you will need to hang a long wooden spar or plank outside them.

## Tying Up

For short term mooring, lines from the bow and stern, or even just the bow will be good enough; but if the berth dries out or you have to cope with a large rise and fall of the tide, things can be rather more difficult.

One solution is to tie up on the outside of a larger boat, then her ropes do all the work, and your boat just sedately rises and falls with her. But you can run into problems if your mother ship takes the ground at low tide, for she may roll over and crush you. So you will have to pick your harbour if this is to be a proposition.

If you do have to cope with a large tidal fluctuation, it may well be impractical to moor alongside the quay, and you will have to rig up some sort of outhaul arrangement, so that you can pull her in when you need her, and pull her off when you don't.

On the other hand, if you can moor alongside the quay, the classic way is with six ropes as shown in the drawing, but if I were you, I would forget about breast ropes, because being short they don't accommodate tidal variations as well as the long springs and the bow and stern lines, and on a small boat they will be rather unnecessary anyway.

If you have to make fast to a bollard, remember to slip your loop up under any others that are already on it — and then over the top. It will only be common courtesy, and anyway, if people have to take your rope off in order to remove theirs, they may not worry too much about putting yours back again.

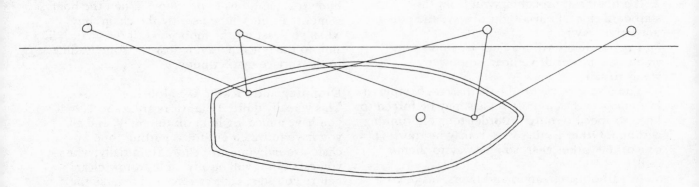

*The classic text book way of mooring alongside with six ropes. However, with a small boat the two shortest ropes can be dispensed with*

## Working from a Beach

A great deal of thought should be involved in selecting a suitable beach to work from — the most important consideration being the conditions you will be faced with at various states of the tide. It will be no good launching your boat into a decent level of water, only to return later and find that a wide expanse of mud or sand lies between you and the shore. Similarly, a steeply shelving beach may be easy enough to slither down into the sea from, but extremely difficult if not impossible, to land on. So a shoreline that allows you access at all states of the tide will be of primary importance, unless of course you know the beach's limitations, and are able to allow for them.

In general terms, if other fishermen regularly use the beach it should be suitable, but take into account their extra experience, and always have an alternative landing site worked out beforehand. It will obviously be better to have a three mile walk back from a sheltered cove down the coast, than not to be able to land at all.

For this sort of fishing, the efforts of two people are generally required, since the boat will probably have to be manhandled some distance; and if any sort of sea is running, it will make launching much easier if one of you steadies the stern from the shore, while the other clambers in and prepares to row off to deeper water and start the engine.

Even if the nature of the beach allows it, never start the engine while one of you — or anyone for that matter — is in the water near the boat. A wave could whip the boat round in an instant, and the resultant injuries from the propellor could be horrifying. So wait until you are both in the boat and well clear of the shore before you put the propellor in the water and get the power going.

Landing again is usually rather easier than launching, since you are already in the boat and able to keep her nice and straight. If you cut and tilt the engine inboard in good time, and then bring her in on the oars, it will be fairly straightforward for your companion to wait in the bow with the rope and then hop ashore when she bumps. In calm conditions you can then simply follow him; but if the sea has become at all choppy you will do well to stay where you are, steadying the boat with the oars until the wave action and your companion's heaving have taken the boat firmly onto the beach.

On a steep beach, you will need to come in fairly fast so that you have enough momentum to get a good grip before the undertow takes you back; but on a shallower gradient this will not be so much of a problem.

## Heavy Weather Beach Landings

According to a long gone relative of mine, who many years ago used to work off one of the most treacherous steep beaches in the world, it was accepted practice when they had to run in on a bad sea to row hell for leather until they struck the pebbles, and then swing the boat round hard on the helm sideways to the surf — so that the waves would hit her broadside and drive her up out of the water. Not a manoeuvre to be recommended, but for a desperate man it might prove helpful.

On a flat beach in rough weather, things would be rather different. Instead of the waves just breaking on the shoreline, as they would mainly be doing on a steep beach, the broken water would extend some way out to sea. In fact the worst of it would probably be the farthest out; so if you did have to come in on that sort of beach, at least you could be comforted by the knowledge that things would be improving the nearer you got to shore.

The big danger when you have to run before this kind of sea is the boat turning head over heels. This happens because you are travelling in the same direction as the sea, and offer very little resistance to it. So when a wave catches you up, you are lifted and carried along by it in much the same way as a surfer. But since your stern meets the wave first, the tendency is for your bow to dip as your stern climbs the wave; so unless you can keep up with the wave until it is spent, at some point your bow will dip and over you go.

There are several ways to combat this in a small boat, but about the easiest is to back into the first of the broken water and come in with your bow facing the waves. In that way you can row or power seaward into the worst of it, and in the lulls between the big waves make what progress you can towards the beach.

If you have ever been out in any sort of rough weather, or taken note of what happens from the shore, you will have observed that not all waves have the same height and power. You will get, say, three large waves, then a series of smaller ones, then some more big ones — or some other combination. It is this rhythm of the waves that makes backing in through surf possible.

If the surf was not bad enough to warrant this sort of approach, another way would be to move extra weight near the stern to stop her rolling over, and put an oar out over the stern to act as a rudder and to stop her turning broadside against the sea. Yet another way would be to tow a heavy weight or a drogue (a sea anchor made of a conical bag of canvas, exerting a considerable drag on the boat) which would not only hold the stern down, but also stop her turning broadside as well. But such methods are only for desperate emergencies, and if you use your head, you should never have need to use them.

### At Sea

Small boats and rough seas are certainly not the best of bedfellows, and the necessary skills needed to deliberately put to sea and cope with heavy weather are a study in themselves. As a beginner, the only reason you will need to know anything at all about handling your boat in such circumstances is in case the unforeseen happens, and not because you had any intentions of being afloat in any but the kindest of conditions.

If you do get caught out in bad weather, it will almost certainly be because you have made a whole series of errors of judgement. That is how things happen at sea. First of all one thing goes wrong, and because you fail to take effective action, the whole situation rapidly snowballs towards catastrophe.

For example, the engine breaks down, and instead of dropping anchor to fix it — usually it is something quite simple — you start drifting out to sea as you try to find out what the trouble is. Now would be the time to row back while you can, but still you carry on tinkering, trying to get the power back on. Out of the shelter of the headland the tide gets hold of you and the wind becomes much fresher. Now you are over two miles down the coast from your original position, and an hour has simply flown by. It is becoming increasingly obvious that the weather is on the change, with storm clouds rolling in ominously from the horizon.

At last you get the engine going again. Panic over, you head for home. But the wind is against the tide, and the waves are getting bigger by the moment. It would be best to pocket your pride and run in on the beach across the bay, but still you try to make it round the headland. But the nearer you get, the less progress you can make, and the sea is so big now that you have no choice but to keep heading into it. If you turned you would be swamped.

Luckily for you that big boat that you have just noticed bearing down on you, has indeed come to your rescue. Twenty minutes ago, the coastguard — who has seen it all before — made the radio call that saved your life.

Although it may not sound like it, avoiding that sort of situation is really quite straightforward. Because if you do your homework, and plan your trip carefully, you will be able to spot the danger signals as they occur. But you must have a plan. For without one you will have no way of knowing how successful you have been in keeping to it. If you have an established norm to work to, any deviations will immediately come to light, allowing you to at least recognize that something has gone wrong, and that corrective action needs to be taken. Initially you will have to make a positive effort to do this, but experience will make the whole process rather more automatic, and after a while most of your reasoning will be done subconsciously.

For the complete beginner it would be helpful to make an actual written note of the proposed schedule. Nothing elaborate, just a brief outline of what sort of fishing was going to be done, and how, where, and when, it was proposed to do it.

After having established that the weather conditions were settled enough to be relied upon, the first thing to do would be to work out how the tide would be running at all stages of the trip, and how it could be used to help you. It might not be possible to have the flow in your favour all the time; but if you got what assistance you could from it, and worked out where it would take you if you had no power, you would be able to cover yourself by having emergency landings already in mind.

In order to use the tide as an ally in this way, you would need to work to a predetermined time table that would tell you where you should be at any given time. But don't turn yourself into too much of a clock watcher, racing to get things done just in order to keep bang up to the minute. Make the schedule flexible and unhurried. If you give yourself plenty of time to do everything you will be able to keep a watchful eye open for any problems, and by continually appraising the situation, not blunder from one mistake to another.

### Waves

At least our unfortunate friend who had to be rescued, knew enough about the sea to keep heading into the waves. Or perhaps he didn't know, but just sensed that was the only course open to him. I have already mentioned that not all waves are of the same size and power, so if the sea is picking up at all it will be important to establish quickly just what kind of rhythm it is that you are facing.

Small boats are usually best headed into waves, be they either natural ones or those made by the wash of other boats. This is not much of a problem if the waves are coming from the direction you want to go in, since you then just keep plodding on through them. But if you find them opposed to your course, and they are too big to run before, you will have to keep turning into them, and proceed zig zag fashion, making your required course in the lulls. Similarly, if the wind and sea are abeam (from the side), it might be safest to head into the wind, and then turn back for your destination with it in your favour.

In a big rolling sea, small boats are not quite so vulnerable as one might imagine them to be, since they will rise and fall with the waves rather than plough through them as a larger boat would; and often a short choppy sea will prove much more of a problem.

Since different types of boat vary in the way that they need to be handled at sea, it is difficult to generalize; but in the case of other hard chine and round bilge hulls it is best to slow down for really big waves in order to stop digging in. On the other hand, most hard chine craft are designed to skim over the water. So in a short head sea they need to be driven in fairly fast in order to keep their bows from going down into the troughs.

In a longer sea the approach would be slightly different, and the bow would best be kept up by sliding the boat down the back of the wave at a slight angle, then squaring her up again to meet the next wave head on.

Few boats handle well when the sea is on the quarter (coming in the direction of the area just forward of the stern), but hard chine craft are particularly vulnerable in this respect, and will tend to veer round beam to the sea no matter what course you are steering. So if the sea is coming from behind you, be careful to keep it there, and not let it suddenly take you unawares on the quarter.

At sea, discretion is always the better part of valour, and only fools will take risks. Always have alternative landings worked out, and bear in mind that it may be safest to anchor up for an hour or two and wait for conditions to improve. What for the moment could be a dangerous passage, could rapidly become a safe one when the tide turns or the wind slackens.

## Fog

There are two things that you can do if you get caught in fog at sea. Either stay where you are, or try and make your way home. If you are not far off shore, the latter will usually be possible, especially if you have taken a compass bearing before it descended. But if you were in a nice sheltered spot, and had to face the prospect of some tricky navigation or risk crossing a particularly busy stretch of water, it might be best to anchor up and stay where you were until it cleared.

One problem with fog is that it plays havoc with sound waves at sea, and although it is obviously useful that lighthouses and other installations should sound warnings at such times, you should not rely totally on them to warn you of any danger. Such is the effect of fog sometimes, that although you may be very near to a signal, you will not be able to hear it, while another boat a considerable distance away, is receiving it loud and clear.

But moored or moving, you will need to warn others of your presence, and I would recommend that you acquire an aerosol fog horn from a chandler for the purpose. They are not too expensive and make more of a noise than you are likely to be able to create by blowing a whistle or bashing a bucket with a oarlock. This is important, because bigger boats with noisy diesel engines may otherwise have difficulty in hearing you.

Such signals should be made every two minutes or so; and if you read through a copy of the collision regulations and study your chart, you will be able to familiarize yourself with the warnings that other ships, buoys, and lighthouses will be making.

If you hear another boat, and are not quite sure of her course, cut the engine and listen. If she appears to be bearing down on you at some lunatic speed, I would say abandon all caution and get the hell out just as fast as you can — and watch out for her wash. On the other hand, if she is proceeding in a seamanlike and legal fashion, which will allow her to stop and reverse her engines in order to avoid a collision, you should be able to sensibly manoeuvre past each other.

About the only good thing concerned with fog at sea is that when it's around the water is usually very calm; so anchored or otherwise, at least that will be in your favour.

## Lead and Line

If you do try to make your way home, a very helpful thing to have is a lead and line. This piece of equipment consists of a lead weight and a long length of line that is marked off in fathoms to indicate the depth of the water. You simply lower the weight down to the sea bed, and read off the depth on the marks. Then by consulting your chart, you can obtain a very good idea of your position, and gradually feel your way along.

At the bottom of the weight, there is traditionally a scooped out hollow, and if you fill this with soap or tallow — 'arm it', as the term is — it will pick up samples of the sea bed. Not only helpful for this sort of blind navigation, but also when prospecting the sea bed for likely fishing grounds.

The weight only needs to be about three or four pounds, and the fathoms can be marked in any way you choose. In the old days on big boats, the weights were 20lbs or more, and the lines twenty five or even thirty fathoms long. They were usually marked as follows:

At  2 fathoms, Leather with two ends.
At  3 fathoms, Leather with three ends.
At  5 fathoms, White calico.
At  7 fathoms, Red bunting.
At 10 fathoms, Leather, with a hole through it.
At 13 fathoms, Blue serge.
At 15 fathoms, White calico.
At 17 fathoms, Red bunting.
At 20 fathoms, Strand, with two knots in it.

The idea of the marks consisting of various different materials was so that the leadsman could identify them by touch alone, and so be able to take accurate soundings in the dark, or indeed in fog.

The spaces between the marks are called deeps. Thus on the old sailing ships the sailor would shout — "By the mark five" — for 5 fathoms. And for 11 fathoms — "By the deep eleven". Although they wouldn't be marked on the line, he would also sing out the halves and quarters of fathoms as well. For 8½ fathoms — "And a half eight" — and for 12¾ fathoms — "A quarter less thirteen".

All of which instantly conjures up visions of Hollywood deeds of daring on the high seas of studio three — "Let the flogging commence, Mr Gable."

## Echoes

In fog, that normally useless phenomena, the echo, can be put to use to tell you how far you are from the shore. It will work best when you are off cliffs, but in fact most shorelines will give some sort of response.

If you sound the horn and count the seconds that pass before you hear the echo, then multiply the number by 1,130; the product, divided by two, will give you the distance in feet. This information, combined with your gleanings from the lead and line, will remove a great deal of the guesswork involved in finding your position, and combined with the compass, keep you effectively on course as you creep towards home.

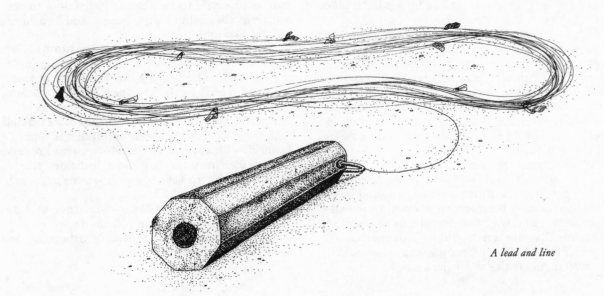

*A lead and line*

*Fisherman pattern*

In case you forget the magic numbers, tape or scratch them on the fog horn cylinder before you stow it, then the information will always be handy.

### Anchoring

At some time or another you will want to anchor your boat at sea, either to hold her in one spot while you do some fishing, or cope with some emergency, such as engine failure, or too strong a tide.

Two things are required of an anchor. First that it should hold you, and second, that it can be recovered when no longer needed. The type of anchor and the kind of seabed will dictate the degree of success of the first requirement, while tricks of the trade will take care of the second.

There are numerous types of anchors on the market, and I have already described a kind that you could make for yourself, but the four shown in the illustration are about the most popular. For a small dinghy, one of around 5 or 6 lbs would be suitable, but at this weight it will not be much good for penetrating thick weed; so if you are faced with that particular problem, you will have to seek local advice, which will probably recommend something more in the order of 25 lbs.

The rope for working the anchor with will need to be 1¼ to 1½ inch circumference hemp or nylon. Don't skimp on the length either; you should reckon on having at least two and a half to three times the depth of water you will be working in.

Whatever type of anchor you use, I always think it wise to trip it. This simply means tying the bower cable (anchor rope) to the actual business end that digs into the seabed and not to the end you would obviously tie it to. If the

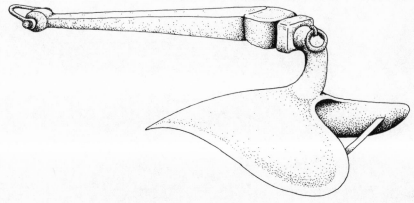

*Plough anchor*

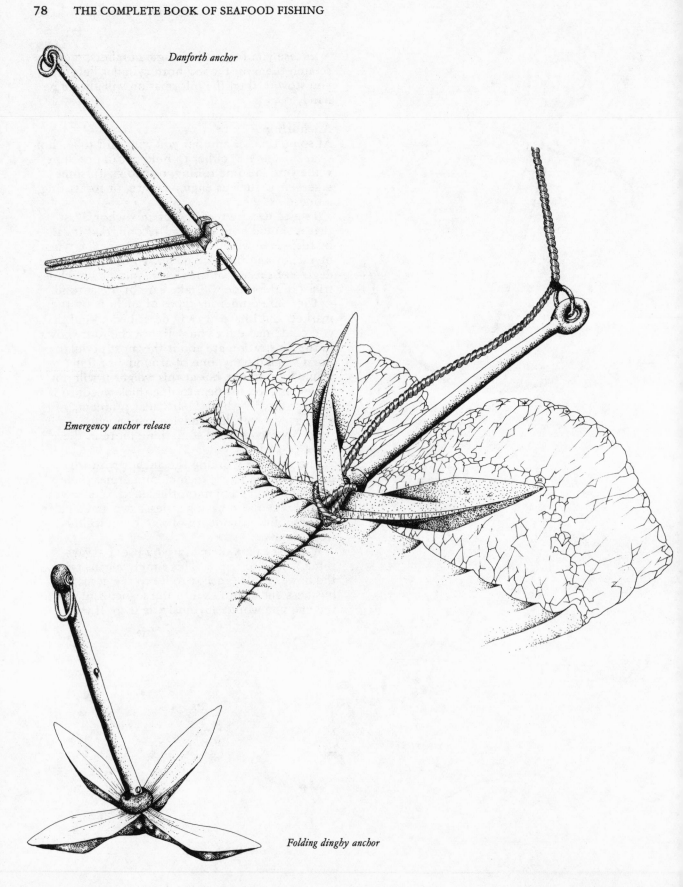

*Danforth anchor*

*Emergency anchor release*

*Folding dinghy anchor*

cable is then also secured to the shackle or ring that it would conventionally go through with a length of much lighter twine, should the apparatus get stuck on the seabed, a hefty tug will break the thin twine and the anchor can be pulled out bottom first.

Although this method of tripping will be the most suitable for small boats with small anchors, on a larger boat with a bigger anchor, it would probably be better to buoy the business end instead. Then if the anchor got stuck you could pick up the buoy and haul it clear on the line.

## A Final Word

This has been a long chapter, and if space had permitted, I would have liked it to have been at least ten times longer. But of necessity I have only scratched the surface of the kind of knowledge that all true seamen have. I can do little else in a general work of this kind; and all I can hope, is that what information I have given, will at least keep you out of trouble long enough to acquire some sort of local expertise.

But remember — however experienced you become — never take even the slightest chance with the sea. She will give to you many times, but take you only once.

# 10. Emergency Drills

If things do go wrong at sea, you will stand a much better chance of effectively doing something about it if your reactions to the situation are more or less automatic.

In an emergency, time will be of the essence, and precious, possibly critical moments will be lost if you have to think very much about what you ought to be doing.

So, I would advise you to read this chapter very carefully, and commit to memory the meaning of all the various visual and audible signals that you may receive, or have need to give. If the crunch ever comes, a life may depend on your skill — and that life may well be yours.

## Distress Signals

These can be made in a variety of ways, but the simplest officially recognized method of indicating that assistance is required, is to repeatedly raise and lower your outstretched arms, or a brightly coloured piece of material on the end of something like an oar.

The snag with that particular kind of signal is that it is really rather difficult to see from any distance, and seems somehow to communicate little of the drama that would attend a desperate situation. But it is a standard signal, and in the event of more effective methods not being available, it could prove a useful standby, so store it away in the memory bank.

A slightly better way is by the manufacture of a continuous noise with something like a whistle or fog horn. Both of which could also be used to give the audible morse signal SOS, Save Our Souls (··· ––– ···).

## Flares

Using a flare is probably the most effecive way of attracting attention in inshore waters. If someone sees a dense cloud of red smoke out at sea, even if they know nothing about signalling, they are going to know that something is wrong and hopefully do something about it.

If you need to be rescued, let off two red flares over a period of a couple of minutes, and when you see help arriving, follow this up with an orange smoke signal (red in darkness or poor conditions) so that they can home in on you.

When shore based life saving stations see such signals, they will acknowledge them by orange smoke signals in daylight, or three white star rockets at night.

## Flag Signals

Very small boats don't usually carry flags, but here is an internationally agreed flag code that is used at sea, and at least the following part of it should be understood.

We need only be concerned with five signals which are shown on the opposite page.

The signals made with them will be understood by any seamen throughout the world — whatever language they speak.

NC—I am in distress and require immediate assistance.

W—I require medical assistance.

U—You are standing into danger.

V—I require assistance, but am not in danger.

The fifth flag signal is designed to take care of the need for improvisation, and means simply — 'I need help'.

It takes the form of a square flag, or anything resembling a square flag, hoisted with a ball strung either above or below it. Like the flag, the ball doesn't have to be made of anything in

particular, and something like a sweater roughly
lashed into shape will do.

   You may also want to give some of these
signals in morse (either by light or sound), and
the following will be about the most useful:
   I require medical assistance      · – – (W)
   You are standing into danger      · · – (U)
   I require assistance,
   but am not in danger             · · · (V)
To attract attention to such signals it is
permissible to fire a white flare.

   In certain areas you will also come across red
flags flown prominently from the shore. These
mark firing ranges and suchlike, so keep clear, or
you will probably be kept clear.

*International flag signals*

*NC–'I need help'*

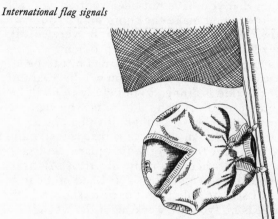

*One to improvise for an emergency, it means 'I need help'*

*'W'—'I require medical assistance'*

*'V'—'I need help, but am not in distress'*

*'U'—'You are standing into danger'*

## Signals From The Shore and Other Boats

I know I keep on saying it, but it really is essential to keep a good lookout at sea, constantly darting your eyes around like an over-enthusiastic hawk and maintaining a careful running check on everything going on around you. By doing this, not only will you avoid the possibility of being caught unawares by any of the various hazards that might come your way, but you will also be able to notice if anyone is trying to attract your attention. If this is another boat, the skipper is probably seeking your assistance or trying to warn you of some impending danger. If the latter is the case, he will be flying the appropriate code flag U or flashing its morse code equivalent (·· -), or making other appropriate audible or visual signals (of course he may not be doing any of these, but if it is painfully obvious he is in trouble or that he is trying to warn you, you will naturally do your best to get the message).

Signals of recognition or warning are also likely to be directed at you from the shore, and apart from those that tell you that you are running into danger or that your distress has been observed, you may also come across the following that will indicate safe or unsafe landing areas.

## Landing Signals

'Land Here' is indicated by an up and down movement of a white flag or flare, or by both of the signallers arms — fully extended — flapping in a similar movement.

Morse can also be used, and in the case of a safe landing, it will be the letter K (- · -).

If you notice a further flag, light, or flare, positioned below the first one, keep them in line as you come in.

For a 'Dangerous Landing', the signals will take the form of side to side movements, or the morse letter S (···).

Apart from the morse signals, these are easy to remember, if you just think of nodding and shaking your head.

After a 'Dangerous Landing' signal, an indication of the best direction to travel in will also usually be given. If the signaller has two lights or flags he will leave one in place, and move the other in the direction that you should travel in. If not, he will simply move the signal that he does have in the correct direction.

If morse is being used, the signal will be S & R for go right (··· ·-·) or S & L for left (··· ·-··).

## Man Overboard

If you work by yourself, this is something that you will have to avoid at all costs; because if you lose contact with the boat the situation could well become critical. But with your ever present life jacket on, your chances of coming out of it will be pretty good. The main thing is not to panic. If you can make it back to the boat, stay with her even if she be swamped or overturned. It may be possible to make her usable again, but if not, still remain with her. Helping hands will be far more likely to see the boat than just you yourself in the water. Especially if you have taken the precaution of coating her bottom (or the seats) with a nice bright fluorescent paint.

Should you have lost the boat, and be pretty certain that you have not been spotted, you will have to try and make the shore under your own steam; and since you should not be very far off, this will not be too much of a problem.

Having planned what has turned out to be a disastrous trip beforehand, you will be aware of what the tide is doing. So hopefully this will be of some use to you. Should the tide be viciously against you or the sea rough, it will all be a matter of luck. All I can say is that you shouldn't have been out there in the first place. So bear this in mind when you plan your trips. Always ask yourself the question — 'If I had no boat, would I still be able to get back to shore?' If the answer is no, you are working in the wrong place.

With two of you aboard (or more correctly — with two of you originally aboard), the outlook will be much more promising, especially if you have practised the routine in shallow water beforehand. The thing to remember is that the helmsman should never take his eyes off the man in the water. This is a golden rule. If you lose sight of him, it will be remarkably difficult to find him again.

The drill to pick him up is quite simple. Approach him so that the wind or tide is pushing him towards the boat. If you bear up to him in this way there will be little danger of running him down or missing him. Remember that the propeller could kill him, so cut the engine in plenty of time. Once you have made contact, work him round to the stern and pass out the loop for him to step up with, and then haul him in over the transom. Never attempt to get him in over the side, or you will both end up in the drink.

## Disabled Boats

Should the engine break down, the first thing to do is to anchor the boat. This will allow you to mainain your position and not drift into any possible danger.

The only exceptions to this would be if it was patently easy to row back to shore, or if the tide would bring you in quickly and safely.

If you can't fix the engine, and for some reason find it impossible to make a landing in some other way, for the time being you will be best off where you are. In calm conditions with plenty of other craft about, you may simply be able to hail a tow — but we will come to the pitfalls of that later. If no help is immediately at hand and conditions are such that you are in no immediate danger, it will only be necessary to signal that you require assistance and not a full scale rescue operation.

## Aground

This is always a danger for the small scale fisherman, because by the very nature of his work — setting traps and lines near rocks — he courts disaster. Usually, the best direction off is the way that you came aground, but before you try and get clear, always check that you have not been holed first; the obstruction may be the only thing that's stopping you from sinking. If there is damage, nail or wedge a patch on as quickly as possible, then start probing over the side with the oar to establish exactly how much of the boat is fast. In most cases you will simply be able to push her off with the oar, perhaps assisting the shove with a gentle rocking of the boat. But if that doesn't work, and moving all the weight to the stern doesn't work, you will have to resort to more drastic measures.

One trick, if the tide's right, is to float the anchor off over the stern on anything that will carry its weight. Then when it's well clear, give a sharp tug on the rope, and let it sink to the sea bed. With luck, you will then be able to pull yourself clear. Alternatively, you may achieve the same effect by just throwing the anchor; in practice the further you can get the anchor away, the more likely you will be to get a good enough grip to take the strain.

If none of this works, about the only solution left, apart from being towed off, is to get out and push. In some situations this would be more feasible than in others; but if you did attempt it common sense would tell you to keep yourself in contact with the boat by means of a line.

## Helicopters

If you were in dire disress at sea, one remedy sent (at considerable public cost) might be a helicopter. Should you still be in the boat, stow all loose gear, because the downward thrust of air from the rotors is liable to send things crashing dangerously around. Steer into the wind, and never under any circumstances attach the wire sent down to the boat. If you do, the winchman will probably let the whole lot go.

If your boat has a mast and any rigging, they may ask you to jump clear of the boat. But in any case, do just as the crew tell you; they know what they're doing, even if you've just proved that you don't.

## Tows

Before you accept a tow, there are one or two points to consider. Firstly, is the boat offering assistance too big for you? If she can't make way at the sort of slow speed you normally travel at, you will be in grave danger of foundering.

The second consideration is a legal one. The crew towing you may be able to claim salvage on your boat. Not, I admit, very likely in the case of a comparatively inexpensive little dinghy, but should you have acquired anything less modest, it will be a point to bear in mind.

If there should be a mercenary squint in the eye of the person (I will not debase the word skipper by using it to describe this sort of money grabbing vulture) offering the tow, the best solution will be to agree on a cash figure there and then. But should this prove impossible, remember there are certain subtle points that in law are seen to reflect the degree of your distress, and in turn the amount of salvage that can be claimed. It will be important therefore to:

1. Remain on the boat.
2. Allow no one from the towing vessel to take charge of your boat.
3. Use your own towing line.

If you bear these technicalities in mind, at least it will keep their miserable pickings down to a minimum.

## First Aid

The first aid kit, that you have already been advised to have aboard, will be all very well for dealing with everyday minor cuts and grazes; but if a more serious accident occurs, you will only be able to cope if you have had some sort of formal training.

Various organizations run first aid courses, and enquiries through your local police, hospital or doctor will readily put you in touch with a suitable source of instruction.

At sea, probably the most important relevant skill needed will concern the revival of the apparently drowned, and this, only a qualified instructor can teach you.

In many books and publications various writers (some of whom should know better) casually 'run through' the various procedures for giving artificial respiration and dealing with hypothermia. But this is dangerous, because if you have not been properly trained, you can in fact do more harm than good.

So give up a few hours of your spare time and go on an official course. It will cost you practically nothing, but the saving could be immeasurable.

# 11. Basic Boat Fishing

*The lightest wind was in its nest,*
*The tempest in its home.*
*The whisp'ring waves were half asleep,*
*The clouds were gone to play,*
*And on the bosom of the deep*
*The smile of heaven lay;*

*Shelley*

After four hefty chapters of preparation, plus a few trial runs, you should now be pretty well ready for your first fishing trip at sea.

Initially, it will be best to keep it all very simple. So begin by using only the more basic items of equipment—hand lines, drop nets and traps. Then later on, when you have become a little more experienced, you can gradually move on to the slightly trickier techniques of netting and multi-hook lining.

## Hand Lines

Nowadays, fishermen who handline commercially—and for the moment I am talking about fishing from stationary or slowly drifting boats—normally use special heavy duty reels or gurdies to work their lines. These can be either hand or power driven, and vary from fairly basic winding devices, right up to sophisticated machines that automatically pay out line to a pre-determined depth, and then again automatically haul in when a fish (or a number of fish) have taken the bait.

Apart from being very expensive, most such equipment will be rather unnecessary for the small scale fisherman. But if you intended to do a great deal of this sort of fishing—especially in deep water, where a substantial amount of hauling is involved—it would obviously make things easier if you had some sort of mechanical help.

If you could get hold of one, I suppose you could use one of the large-game fishing reels that anglers take shark and tuna with, but this might prove difficult; so probably the best way would be to make one yourself.

I think that a good general purpose type would be one of open construction, rather like a small version of the contraptions that people wind their garden hoses up on. Not only would this be most likely to be the easiest kind to build, but it would also drain well, and this could be helpful in lengthening the life of some sorts of natural fibre line.

You could easily make one by taking foot long strips of inch square timber (you would need four) and cross jointing them at 90° in pairs—giving you two wooden crosses. Then, by fixing a spindle in the middle and four circular rods to keep the two sections apart, you would have a perfectly serviceable gurdy. But you would need a winding handle of course, and something to support it while you worked it.

You would also need to build in some sort of brake system so that the line would not unwind if you took your hands off the reel. This can be done quite simply by fitting the spindle with a large, easily adjustable locking nut on the end opposite the winding handle. If you didn't incorporate such a device into the mechanism, when you came to haul the last bit of line in hand over hand, fish would have to have been left floundering on the surface while you gathered up enough line to boat them. Left to their own devices in this way they would be sure to unhook themselves, because there would be no tension on the line. And I can assure you that there is nothing more irritating than watching the catch (invariably the best of the day) swimming clear at this last critical moment.

As you will see from the drawing, you will also need a roller guide of some sort to take the line over the side. But the exact design and set up will depend very much on the type and size of boat that you have acquired. For a small boat that you could not stand up in, the reel support would be best clamped directly to the gunwale.

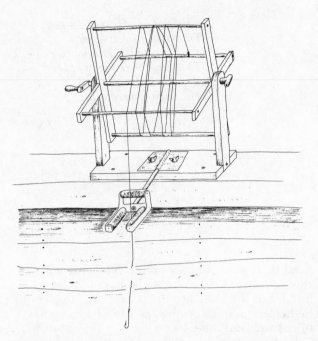

*Easily made gurdy for line fishing*

On a bigger boat, it would be a better idea to fix it on a little davit a foot or two above the gunwales. This would give you more line out of the water to play with, and be helpful when you came to swinging the catch inboard. Someone that I know, who uses this sort of reel regularly, experimented (temporarily securing the reel with woodworking clamps) until he discovered the most convenient part of the boat to work it from. Then he permanently sited it by constructing a little platform on the gunwale and bolting the reel to it. When not in use he ties a plastic sack over it to protect it from the weather.

From a cost point of view, you could argue that using a reel or gurdy would save you money, because you would be able to fish with a thinner, and therefore cheaper line—the sort that would be uncomfortable to haul by hand. But against this, you will find that you will also keep costs down if you buy long lengths of line in bulk. The more you buy, the cheaper it becomes per foot or metre. So if you can standardize as much as possible, and acquire line that can be used for a whole range of fishing methods, the savings will probably be more effective. So I would say, for handlining, use a spun nylon line about a quarter of an inch in circumference; then you will also be able to use it for longlining and as a cast out line as well. True, you would not be able to get so much of this size line onto a reel, but unless

you were working in a terrific depth of water, I doubt that this would present much of a problem for most of you.

However, the use of reels and gurdies will probably be rather unnecessary for most food fishermen, and the quarter-inch line that I have just recommended will be as good as any for hand over hand hauling.

This sort of fishing is done either from an anchored, or a slowly drifting boat. And the depth at which the bait or lure is worked will depend very much on what you think may be around. If you have not got any confident ideas on the subject, it will all be a matter of trial and error. And until you can pin-point the level at which fish are on the feed, you will have to fish at different depths before you hit on the most rewarding one.

### Rigging Hand Lines

Most fishermen have their own pet way of rigging hand lines, and after you have been fishing a while, I don't doubt that your own particular preferences will gradually be formed. Personally, I always like a hand line to have two main features: first to be inconspicuous, and second to be adaptable. The former I achieve (I hope) by making the last few fathoms of the line out of monofilament nylon. This is difficult for fish to see underwater, and must give me at least some sort of advantage over more conspicuous methods of presenting a baited hook. As to being adaptable, I always rig hand lines with loops at their extremities; then if needs be, weights and hooks can be changed in a matter of seconds.

The illustration shows how I would rig a beginner's basic hand line. To form a boom in the

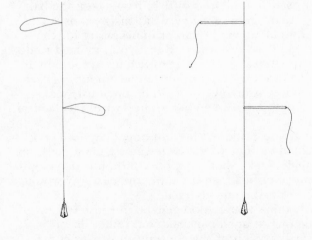

tackle—that will fish the hook inconspicuously away from the main line—I just loop out a length of some two feet of nylon, and knot it round on itself. I usually thread lengths of rubber or plastic tubing over these arms to stiffen them. Some people just knot it in various places to achieve a similar effect; but avoid this if you can. You have to remember that every knot you tie in any length of line weakens it. So try to keep their numbers down to a minimum.

To attach the leader—the final piece of line with the hook on—I tie a double overhead loop knot in the end of it (see chapter 13). Thread this through the end of the 'boom', thread the hook through the loop of the knot that I have just tied, and pull it tight. All this procedure is probably enough to make many a hardened old salt faint clean away, and I admit there are more traditional ways of doing it. But that is the way I do it; it is simple and it works. of course, if you enjoy tying knots (and undoing them... if you can), by all means go ahead with your 'four turn half blood knots' and your 'double larks head returns', and God bless you and your nimble fingers. But being basically idle (and probably of unsound mind) I will continue to take the easy way out.

I attach weights in much the same way. But since they come at the end of the line, I just tie the line back on itself—forming a loop that needs to be no bigger than will pass over the largest weight I am likely to want to use.

Doing all this allows me to make any changes in absolutely no time at all. So if my weight is not holding the line against the tide, I can just haul in and rapidly substitute one that will. Similarly, if I find that what I am catching really needs smaller or larger hooks, the necessary alterations can be very quickly effected.

I usually work with two leaders. So if the weight is touching the bottom, one hook fishes more or less on the seabed, and the other about a fathom above it. This gives some scope to my coverage, and I have found it to be the best general arrangement.

Obviously this is a very elementary set up, and you will find that for fish with particularly strong jaws and sharp teeth you will need wire leaders that they can't bite through. But the loop system would still hold good, although the whole of the leader and the hook section would have to be removed for any alterations, because the hook would be wired on.

You can also of course rig more leaders and more hooks on your line. But in the beginning it will pay you not to be too ambitious. To be able to deal with three or four fish (or more) all hooked at the same time, on the same line, needs a bit of practice. And without experience, you will be liable to spend more time untangling your line than actually fishing with it.

## Weights

It will also help you to avoid the above sort of problem if the weight that you rig your line with is rather on the heavy side. I would suggest a minimum of two or three pounds. Such a weight will keep the line vertical in the water, and enable you to deal with one fish at a time and not allow them all to swim around on the surface at once.

One problem that you may come up against, working over certain kinds of seabed, is that you continually lose half your line because the weight has snagged on the bottom. There is really very little that you can do about this, except to philosophically make provision to abandon the weight and lose as little of the rest of the line as possible. This is done simply by attaching the weight with a length of nylon of a lesser breaking strain than that of the main line. So when your weight gets caught and you heave hard on the line, it will part just above the weight, and you will be able to save most of the tackle.

In the final chapter of this section on boat fishing, I describe how you can make your own lead weights; and if you can get hold of enough scrap lead, this is all well and good. But if you can't, perhaps a cheaper solution is to use lengths of old chain. These can still be attached by the loop system, and if you require more or less weight, you simply loop or unloop the required number of links. You could attach the various lengths of chain all on the same loop. However should you become snagged, if each section is fixed to the end of the last, when you make your line breaking heave you should not lose every single piece of chain.

Suitably sized rocks can also be used—secured perhaps in a bag of netting. But their comparatively low density (weight to volume ratio) compared to lead and chain, make them a rather cumbersome alternative for anything but emergency use.

## Swivels

If you want to, you can rig swivels into the tackle. The theory is that they stop the line tangling up through the movement of the tide or the activities of particularly vigorous fish. Most anglers include them all over the place — above the boom, below the boom, above the weight, at the end of the leader, at the beginning of the leader. Swivels are probably indispensable, because they will, to some extent, take the strain off low breaking strength line. But our heavy duty equipment is designed purely for the acquisition of food, and the weight and strength of our line will mean that swivels will be rather a waste of time. Swivels may be of some use when we come to trailing lines behind a moving boat, because possibly they could help to make the bait or lure move in a more enticing way through the water. They may also be useful when rigged into set long lines. But these are different sorts of fishing, and I will deal with the various pros and cons at the appropriate times.

Incidentally, as far as I remember, I have forgotten to mention that you will need something to store your hand line on, that is if you are not using a reel. When I was about half as tall as I am now, we used great slabs of cork that had been washed up on the beach. But at that time we were not using the modern synthetic lines, and had to be careful to see that the line dried out properly or it would have rotted. Anyway, nowadays a rough wooden frame, of whatever common sense tells you is a suitable size, will do.

## Baits and Lures

I always look upon demersal fish as being the scroungers of the ocean, nosing around on the bottom looking for worms, unwary shellfish and the day to day debris of the struggle for survival under the sea. In fishing from the shore we dealt with the sort of baits to use; and in general terms, I suppose that it merely boils down to equipping your hook with the sort of tasty morsel that such browsing fish might find attractive. Once away from the seafloor, we tend to be dealing with a different kind of animal altogether. Now we are up amongst the speed merchants, the fast moving shoals and the predators who must run down their quarry and feed quickly while they can.

Now the object of the whole exercise is to convince these various kinds of fish that our baited hooks represent natural food of some sort. Such food will be mobile or immobile. In other words it would be either travelling through the water (or along the seabed), or it would be more or less stationary on the bottom.

So you will have to simulate this situation— either with genuine or imitation bait of some sort.

As I say, we have already dealt with the various natural baits that you can use (worms, small crabs, strips of fish etc.); and in a moment I will give you some information on the better known artificial ones. But, as always, you will get the best indications of what to try from your own local research.

Now remember, at this point we are talking about fishing from a stationary or barely moving boat, and we are using a fairly heavily weighted line. You can drift out a lightly—or almost unweighted line—well away from you. But I will deal with that later. For the moment, I am talking about fishing straight down over the side. So in this particular method, the movement of our bait and line will obviously be restricted to the vertical plane. Up or down.

This gives us two choices. We can just drop our bait onto the seabed and leave it there, hoping that a passing quarry will imagine it to be a piece of edible debris that has gravitated there. Or we can jig our line up and down—at varying depths—to simulate some sort of food that happens to be on the move.

## Artificial Lures

In my part of the world we use feathered lures a great deal. They are easy enough to make— consisting of a brightly dyed feather (one about twice as long as the hook) which is bound onto the shank of the hook. But they are also very cheap to buy. In fact so cheap, I doubt that a food fisherman would be able to acquire the raw materials to make such a rig for much less than the cost of the finished commercial product. So I think for a beginner it will be just as well to buy such rigs, if only just to see how the experts make them up.

As with most lures fished from a stationary boat, they are worked through the water by jerking them up and down. Passing fish are attracted by these sudden movements; and instead of being able to ponderously inspect what you have on offer, they have to grab quickly at it for fear of losing what to them is apparently a fast disappearing meal.

These feathered lures come in the general group of what I would call 'illusion lures'. They don't represent any specific sort of natural food, but just appear to fish to be something good to eat. There are a vast number of different kinds of them and every locality has it's own particular

*A feathered hook—a simple and very effective mackerel lure*

favourites. I have shown a selection of them, but again, local research will tell you what the local specialities are.

Remember though, even a lure that gives quite spectacular results for a time may suddenly cease to be effective for no apparent reason. Maybe the fish get wise to them after a while. I don't know. So unless you are constantly dealing with Kamikaze fish like mackerel, you will have to experiment and vary what you have on offer if you want to keep catching fish.

The other main type of lure is what I will refer to as a 'replica lure'. These are man made imitations of a fish's natural food, and include rubber, plastic and metal representations. Again, I have shown a selection of them and in Chapter 13 I will give you a few ideas on how you can make your own.

### Float Out Lines

The other main way of working hand lines from a stationary boat is by what I will call the float out line. These can be particularly useful when you think that it might be productive to fish near rocks or obstructions, but it would be dangerous to do so.

Now an angler would do all this by using a spinning rod (a medium sized rod in between the short boat rod and the long surfcaster). He would either cast his bait or lure to the required spot and gradually 'work' it back towards him; or he would use a lightly weighted line—perhaps with a float on—that would drift towards the required spot; or he would use an intrinsically buoyant line (weighted or not weighted—depending on what depth he thought the fish were feeding at).

The only method that will be of much practical use to us will be the latter. Your local equipment supplier will be able to tell you what the best buy is as far as the line is concerned, and experience will help you decide how much weight you will need to take the business end of the line down to a level which is likely to be productive.

The procedure is really self explanatory, and the only problem you are likely to come across is positioning yourself so that you can anchor safely away from the obstruction, yet still have the tide taking your line in the required direction.

### Grounds

Where exactly do you do all this. Again my answer must be rather vague—wherever the fish are and who really knows that? Commercial fishermen certainly don't and there wouldn't be any fish left in the sea if they did. Even expert anglers and charter fishing skippers don't or they would never come home empty handed. But we are out to catch fish; so somehow we will have to find out, or at least discover which spots will give us the best chance of success.

If you had nothing better to do, I suppose the most logical way of finding out what a given piece of coast had on offer would be to try fishing every square inch of it. But that would hardly be practical, because to achieve a truly accurate assessment you would have to fish every given spot at all states of the tide all the year round — which would mean that just to cover an area half the size of a football pitch would take you the rest of your life. So that's out. What we must do initially is to pick out some of the more likely marks and try those out for starters. With any luck, this will at least allow us to catch something. There will be plenty of time later on for unconventional experiment in spots where nobody else ever thinks of fishing.

The most obvious way of doing this is to watch or ask where more experienced fishermen try their luck, and then do the same. But if this is impossible, you will have to employ the sort of logical reasoning that I discussed in Chapter 3.

In a small boat, your range will be limited, so that will at least define the maximum boundaries of the area you will be able to work in. A study of your chart will reveal if there are any obvious marks such as wrecks close inshore, and it will also disclose the existence of any rock formations that will harbour or attract fish. Many of these will be very close inshore, nothing more than undersea continuations of the coastline itself. Others may be offshore eruptions of rock on an otherwise flat seabed. They may be marked on the chart, but the chances are that they won't be. Fish will be attracted to these sort of places like moths to a flame, so if you want to catch them you will have to be able to pinpoint such likely spots. And without a chart recording echo sounder, about the only piece of equipment that can help you do that is a rough ground locator.

### Rough Ground Locator
Although an RGL sounds like it might be the latest piece of sophisticated electronic marine equipment; it is in fact just a length of metal tubing on the end of a rope. You simply tow it along the seabed behind your boat, and with your hand on the warp you will be able to feel what sort of ground you are travelling over. If you have reason to believe that the seabed you will be testing is fairly clear of weed, the metal tube can be quite long—say four feet or so; otherwise use a slightly shorter length—two and a half to three feet long. This will not be inclined to tangle up so much. Keep plenty of spare warp inboard, and buoy the end as well. You may suddenly become fast and have to pay out line or even temporarily abandon the whole shooting-match.

### Working Handlines From a Stationary Boat
So there you are, sitting in your boat with your hand line rigged and baited, anchored or drifting around a spot that you think or have been told is a good place to try your luck. What happens next? Well, if you are going to fish on the bottom, it will just be a matter of paying out the line until you feel the weight touch ground. Then all you have to do is hold the line in position and wait for the tell-tale nibbles or heavy mouthed grabs that will mean that fish are on the feed. Some fish will hook themselves, taking the bait greedily and quickly. Others will be more tentative and will tease and try it before attempting to swallow it. These are the tricky

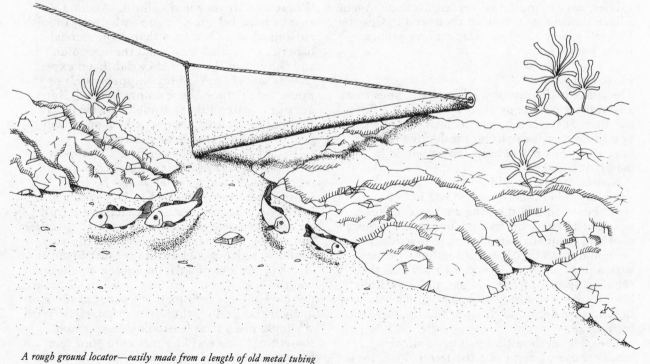

*A rough ground locator—easily made from a length of old metal tubing*

ones, and you will have to wait for the moment that you think they have taken the bait into their mouths, and then drive the hook home by quickly jerking the line upwards.

If you are working gear up off the seabed, you will be after shoal fish of some kind and will be baited with a lure or a natural bait that you want such fish to think is food on the move. So you will have to work the line up and down in a slow, rhythmic natural way to simulate this. Fishing in this way, you probably won't need to strike the hooks home — partly because the movement of your line will be doing that anyway, and partly because such fish will normally hook themselves in their eagerness for a meal.

But hooking fish is just the beginning of the battle; you are not home and dry until they are safely in the fish box aboard the boat.

Some fish will be capable of taking your line inbetween rocks or wedging themselves on the bottom in some other way. So it will be important to get them up clear of cover as soon as they are hooked, particularly with demersal fish. Pelagic fish won't prove a problem in this way; but they may make runs or passes, and you will have to stay with them keeping tension on the line and avoiding tangles with your anchor warp or propeller. Maintaining tension on the line is an important point. If you don't, the fish will more than likely be able to eject the hook from its mouth. So keep the line nice and tight until the catch has been netted, gaffed or boated.

## Squid and Cuttlefish

Of course there are always exceptions to these sort of blanket rules, the two obvious ones being cuttlefish and squid. Both of these make excellent eating, so are well worth catching. If you live in an area that they inhabit, you may, while fishing in the summer, feel a strange sucklike pull on the line. If you do, haul the line in very gently, smoothly and steadily—or you will lose him. As soon as you get him near to the surface whip him into a hand net, or once clear of the water he will let go of the line and be gone. Once boated, put such fish in a box or sack separate from the rest of the catch, or they will cover everything with the ink that they usually dispel on capture.

Should you be lucky enough to be able to catch these sort of fish in any quantity, you will be best off abandoning your ordinary hooks, and going in for a proper squid jig. These have much more holding power than an ordinary hook, and you will not need to net the fish in order to

bring them inboard. Squid jigs are available commercially, but they are easy enough to make up from a barrel weight, some brass wire and a couple of triple hooks.

## Unhooking

Small fish can often be just shaked or flicked off the line into the fish box or well. Others will need to be unhitched by hand. And if they have swallowed the hook deep down their throats, you will need to disgorge it by wriggling a spiked piece of wood down after it. Larger unidentified fish are best left on the hook with the leader cut off the main line, that is until you are sure that they are dead or you have killed them by cutting through the spinal column at the back of the neck.

## Trolling—Whiffing—Railing

All three are names for the same thing: towing a baited or lured hook behind a moving boat in the hope of catching pelagic fish.

The procedure is quite simple, and if it is an accepted method of fishing in your particular area you will probably find it very productive. You don't need to travel very fast, and a nice steady plod is the thing to aim for. Many pelagic fish can appear almost anywhere; so as soon as you are clear of the harbour or beach it will be just as well to start streaming your line behind the boat. Once you have made contact you can cut the power and just drift with the shoal,

*A multi hooked spoon*

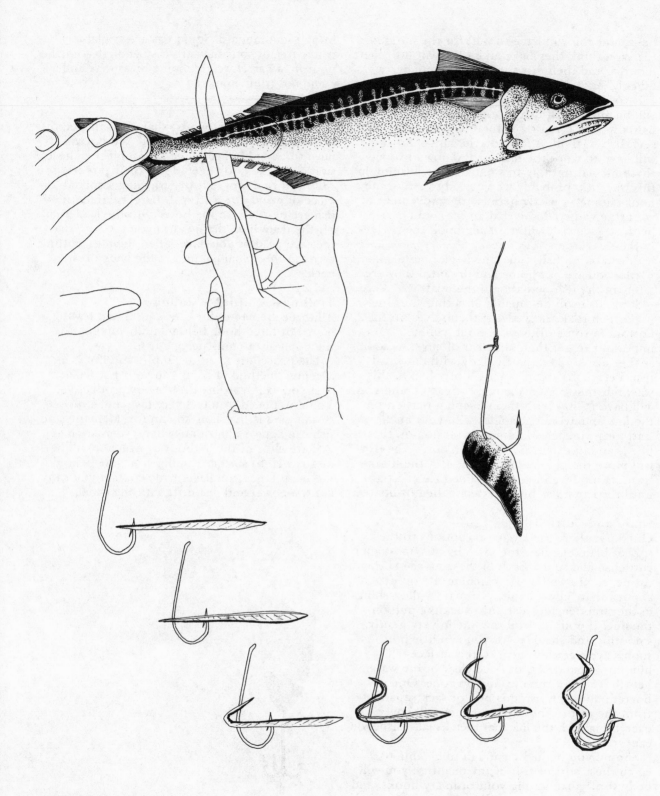

*Cutting and hooking lasks*

working your line as you would from a stationary boat. You will need about 40 fathoms of line, and it can be rigged in exactly the same way as it would be for upper water fishing, with something like a 2lb weight on the end and a hook or a number of hooks rigged about a fathom above it. What you put on the hooks will depend mainly on local practice. I use feathered lures or shiney strips of fish skin (Lasks) skimmed off near the tails of fish that I have caught or acquired for bait. But if you want to, you can experiment with a whole host of other devices. Silver paper wound round the hook. Pieces of plastic tubing hooked through the shank. Commercially made spinners and lures or homemade ones. Anything that you have reason to believe

may be successful can be pressed into service.

If you want to, you can rig spinners into the line. Some people swear by them and would never dream of setting up their gear without including them. Personally I consider them to be just an added expense and yet one more thing to go wrong. But you will have to make up your own mind about that.

Pelagic fish may be feeding right on the surface, a fathom or two or more below it; so in order to locate them, it will be helpful to stream two lines behind the boat and weight one more heavily than the other. This will allow you to sweep through a much deeper area of sea, and give you a better chance of making contact with the shoal.

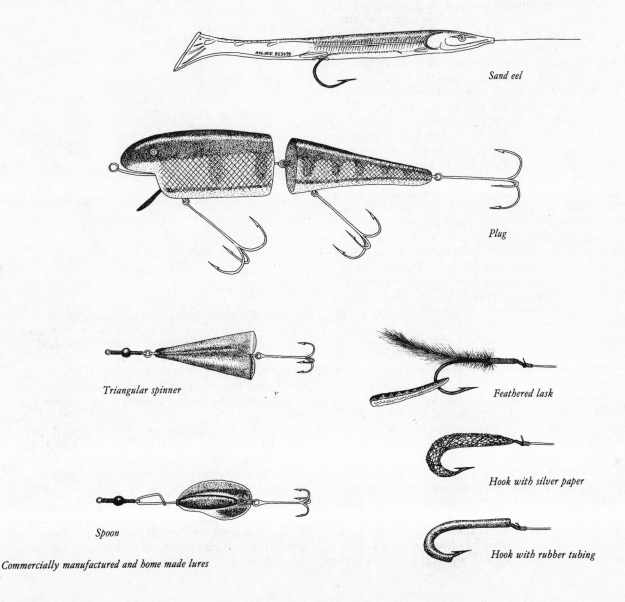

*Sand eel*

*Plug*

*Triangular spinner*

*Feathered lask*

*Hook with silver paper*

*Spoon*

*Hook with rubber tubing*

*Commercially manufactured and home made lures*

## Paravanes

For this sort of fishing you can also use paravanes, but they need to be rigged on a much lighter sort of line or they will not flight very well. You can buy very nice looking aerodynamic jobs from chandlers and tackle dealers, but if the price tag puts you off (as it most certainly will) you can very easily make one at home in half an hour. All you need are some offcuts of three-ply and a small quantity of lead. The ply should be cut into the rough boat shape of the one in the drawing. It needs to be about three inches wide and roughly seven inches overall from nose to tail. Then it requires a nose cone of lead, the weight of which you can vary, depending on how far below the surface you want it to work. Drill holes big enough for the line to go through, on either side of the centre line right up near the nose, and another one at the tail end right on the centre line.

If you want the paravane to stream to starboard behind the boat, attach the main line through the hole left of centre near the nose. If to port, then through the right hand hole. The leader—which should consist of about a fathom of line—is attached to the other end of the paravane through the centre line hole. Just push the lines through the holes and knot them off.

There are three main advantages with using paravanes. In a small boat they will allow you to work two or even three lines well clear of one another — one to port, one to starboard and possibly one in the middle. In an outboard powered boat they will also help to keep lines clear of the engine and its prop. But probably their most helpful aspect is that once a fish is hooked on the leader, the balance of the paravane is upset and it will surface, letting you know instantly that you are in business—something which it is not always easy to discover with trailed lines, because the drag from your movement makes it difficult to feel if a fish has been hooked.

When experience tells you that you have enough line out overboard, mark the line by tying a whip of coloured cotton around it at the appropriate spot.

## The Care of the Catch

Fish are best gutted as soon after catching as possible unless you have some form of processing in mind that precludes the need for this. Make your cuts smooth and clean, and rinse out the belly cavity thoroughly leaving no trace of blood or slime which will step up bacterial action

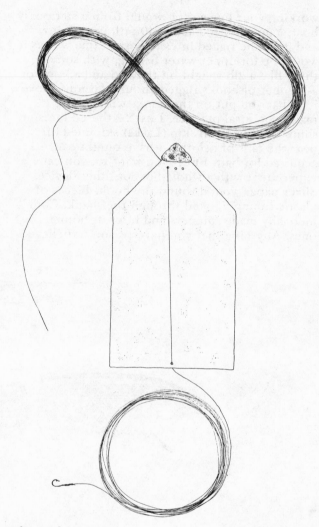

*A home made paravane*

and hasten their decay. On no account throw the fish around or allow them to become bruised in any way. Store them under cover in crushed ice or at least in an ice cold container. This is a critical stage in the fish's journey to the dining table, and the more meticulous the care you take at this stage the better and safer the eating will be.

Store such species as sole and coalfish separately because they will discolour other fish. And keep skate or dogfish on their own as well, or they will taint the rest of the catch with ammonia.

## Hoop or Drop Nets

We have already discussed the construction, use and baiting of hoop nets in an earlier chapter on shore fishing; and their use at sea will be very much the same. You may possibly need longer warps if you are going to work them in any depth of water; and you will have to have floats to mark them if you intend to leave them while you set other nets. But those will be the only major differences.

It will be best to work with about half a dozen or so. These will take up very little space inside the boat, and give you enough irons in the fire to allow you a reasonable chance of success. Six is about the right number from a time point of view as well. They need to be left down for about twenty minutes or so, and with this number, by the time you have finished setting the last one it will be time to go back and haul and reset the first one and so on.

### Where To Set Hoop Nets

This will depend very much on what you are going after. If you want shrimps and prawns, these will probably be close inshore around piers and jetties and sheltered rock formations. Although you will be able to reach many of these sort of spots from the shore, there will be other likely places that will be out of reach, and with your boat you will now be able to fish them.

Your chart and rough ground locator will help you pin-point rock patches that will be likely hiding places for crabs and lobsters, and if the water is clear enough, you may actually be able to pick out such hot spots visually. Now too will be the time to press your 'armed' lead line into service, searching for muddy or sandy ground that may be the home of flat fish.

### Shellfish Traps

In the chapters on shore fishing we dealt with the construction and use of a selection of the vast number of specialist traps that can be used for catching shellfish. Now that we can use them at sea, our chances of success will be greatly increased, because we will be able to get into deeper water much farther afield.

### Lobster and Crab Traps

In a small boat you won't be able to carry a large number of these sort of traps at one time. Unless of course you go in for fiddlesome collapsable ones or the kind that have detachable bases that will allow you to stack them. But that need not prove too much of a problem, because you will be able to carry half a dozen or so in the smallest boats; and unless you have other angles in mind, that will be more than enough for the average

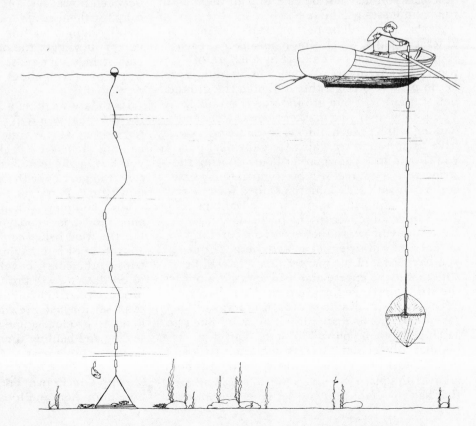

*Lobster traps*

food fisherman. If you want to work more traps than that it will just mean that you will have to make a series of trips until you have the required number out on the grounds. However if you do that, bear in mind that if bad weather suddenly descends you may not be able to haul them all in time and losses will be inevitable.

At sea, traps will be best worked in strings, or at least in pairs, which simply means that each trap is connected to the next by a length of rope. The advantages of doing this are numerous. Set in pairs or strings, they will hold the ground better if any sort of a ground tide is running. You'll only need one marker float as well, and hauling will be much quicker, because you won't have to go round searching for individual pots. If you should lose your marker float, locating the string with a grapnel will be comparatively easy compared with searching the seabed for one trap at a time. You will also find it an advantage to give saturation cover to one particular area before moving on to the next. To a certain extent you will save fuel as well, because once you have located the marker float you will be able to cut the engine and haul yourself along the string until the final trap has been cleared.

The main disadvantage of setting traps in strings like this is that you will be more likely to catch crabs than you will lobsters. This is because lobsters tend to stay near their rocky homes most of the time, while crabs range about all over the place. So if you put to sea in an area that has any crabs in it and set your fleet of traps almost anywhere, you will stand a very good chance of catching them. Lobster traps on the other hand must be set much more precisely close by the rocky formations that the creatures inhabit. But lobsters are very few and far between nowadays, and to set your traps specifically for them could mean that you will get awfully hungry waiting for one to fall victim to you. You will get the odd one or two in your crab strings anyway; so in the beginning don't worry too much about going after them in particular.

If you are working a long string of traps, space them so that you don't have more than two off the sea bed at the same time when you are hauling them. And at all costs make sure that you keep your feet clear of the warps as you send the gear over the side, or you may unwittingly join your traps on the bottom.

Most commercial fishermen set their lobster and crab traps one day and haul them the next. For the food fisherman this presents the disadvantage of him having to make two separate trips to the coast, but if it is easy enough for you to do this you will probably find it the most productive arrangement. On the other hand traps set for just a few hours will be more than likely to produce some sort of catch. So fit in the setting and hauling times with whatever suits your timetable best.

## Shrimp and Prawn Traps
Like hoop nets and lobster and crab traps, we

have already dealt with the construction and basic use of this sort of shellfish catching equipment. So there is little point in covering that ground again here. Their use in a boat will be little different than when working them from the shore, since shrimps and prawns will be found mostly close to rocks and around harbour walls and jetties. But a boat will certainly make their catching that much easier. Not only will it act as a transport vehicle and spare you the labour of lugging dozens of traps around, but it will allow you to place them in all those super attractive spots that always seem infuriatingly to be just out of reach from the shore.

Like crab traps they will be best set in strings of half a dozen or so, but they can be attached to the backline at much closer intervals—say six feet apart.

The best catches will be made in dark or overcast conditions when shrimps and prawns start to feed more actively, the general practice being to set the traps at dusk and haul them in the early morning.

This sort of fishing is certainly a fair weather occupation, because when winter weather starts to close in they will move off shore to spend the cold months in their muddy burrows. I'm not recommending that you try it, but I do know of one man who even manages to catch them when they've gone to ground in this way. In a mild winter with long periods of settled weather and no ground swell, he sets heavily baited prawn traps on the muddy grounds he has discovered well off shore. After a few days these have settled down into the seabed; and this is when he hauls them, which as you can imagine is not easy now that they are filled with wet sand and mud. Once aboard, he gently hoses the traps clean, and there, low and behold, are the prawns — fat, juicy and in the finest of condition.

In some areas, shrimps and prawns are taken commercially by trawlers in open water, and if you live near such grounds you could try your hand at it with one of the small trawls or dredges that I describe in the next chapter. But it would be unwise to set traps in this sort of area, because at some time or other the trawlers would be certain to win them from you; and because trawlermen, in general, jealously guard their freedom of activity, they would be highly un-likely to let you have them back. In fact what they would most certainly do is dump them or destroy them in the hopes of warning you off. And unless you're into quayside brawling you would be well advised to take the hint.

## The Care of the Catch

Shrimps and prawns will not live very long out of water; and since they must be alive immediately prior to cooking, you will either have to cook them on a small stove aboard the boat or keep them in a seawater container until you can get them ashore.

Other shellfish, like lobsters and crabs, are easier to handle, and will live for some time out of the water. But they must be treated sensibly. Keep them out of the sun, and pack them the right way up under layers of damp sacking. Crabs are not so aggressive as lobsters, who will fight anyone and anything, so put heavy elastic bands over their pincers. Sections cut from discarded cycle innertubes are good for the job if they haven't perished too much.

There are so many cartoon jokes about people getting nipped by shellfish that its easy to be misled into thinking that they can't do you much harm. Nothing could be farther from the truth; a big lobster or crab can smash your fingers with ease. So treat them with respect. If you do get caught, crush the body under your foot.

You will often see commercial fishermen handling crabs and lobsters by their claws, and I suppose if they have been out of the water for some time and have become a bit dozy it may be reasonably safe to do so. But when taken straight from the traps, crabs should be grasped by the body between the back legs and lobsters held firmly across the shoulders.

## A Sea Storage Box

If you regularly catch these sort of shellfish in any quantity, it might be an advantage to build yourself a sea storage box of some sort. Then hauls can be held over for a few days until you are ready to eat, process or sell them.

The actual design can vary according to the materials that you have available, but it is best made from wood which will absorb water and allow the box to be submerged below the surface. You will need plenty of holes in the sides to allow a free flow of water; and it wants to be constructed so that the movement of the creatures inside it is kept to a minimum. If you are not going to be handling all that many shellfish you can do this by making the box fairly shallow; but if it is going to need to hold any quantity you will be best off fitting drop in partitions of some sort.

Anchor it in a sheltered but unpolluted spot — if possible where someone can keep a fairly

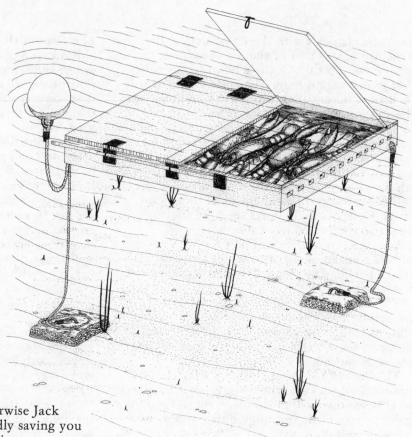

*Submerged storage box for crabs and lobsters*

permanent eye on it for you. Otherwise Jack Snatch will once again be very kindly saving you the trouble of having to lick your lips.

### Other Fish and Shellfish
In the following chapter I will describe yet more ways of taking specific kinds of fish and shellfish at sea using a boat. But of the ones that we have already discussed, many will be taken as bicatches when working other sorts of gear. If you don't get all that you want in this way, you will have to set the sort of specialist equipment that has been described in earlier chapters. So if you are particularly out of your head for whelks say, you will do best to set proper whelk pots for them, rather than rely on the numbers that your crab traps will undoubtedly provide for you.

With the 'extra arm' of a boat you will be able to work most shore gear more efficiently as well. Even if a net or trap has been set with meticulous care at low tide, it can often require attention when the sea has come in and covered it. A boat will allow you to do this, extending your range and simplifying many of the problems that will be certain to crop up.

# 12. Advanced Boat Fishing

When you have had a bit of experience with your boat at sea, you can think about some of the more complex fishing methods that I am going to describe in this chapter. Some may appeal and be practical for you, others not. But that, I think, is the beauty of sea fishing. With so many different kinds of fish, and an infinite variety of equipment to catch them with, at least you can never get bored with it.

But first a word of caution. In this chapter I will be dealing with gear that is paid out from the boat. Sometimes this can be heavily weighted, and when once in motion it is very easily capable of taking you with it. So beware, ten times beware. Keep clear of the gear. Engrave that on your mind.

## Longlining
We have already dealt with the basic construction of longlines in the chapters on shore fishing. Those very same lines can be worked from a boat. But you will need longer anchor warps, and marker floats as well. The lines themselves can be lengthier as well, or you can just join up any smaller ones that you already have. The biggest commercial longliners work with thousands of hooks on lines a mile or more long. But you will do well to limit yourself to fifty hooks on about 100 yards of line.

## Gear
The main difficulty involved with working longlines at sea is setting them — that is, actually getting them over the side into the water without the line getting snarled up. It has long been the dream of the inshore fisherman that one day someone would come up with a small mechanical device that would dispense the line into the sea, baiting up the hooks automatically as it did so. Over the years, many people have tried to invent one, but none of the patent contraptions that I have seen have been much good. Although I gather that large scale commercial equipment is now being marketed, but that is only for the bigger boats.

About the best innovation to appear so far has been the longline clip. This is a wire spring affair that can be quickly attached or detached from the main line. One way of working these is to bait up the leaders separately and have them hung out over the transom, with the hooks practically in the water. Or you get someone to hand them to you—which is easier. Then you send the anchor over the side and get it firmly positioned. As you pull away, the line is dragged out of its coiling basket, and you clip the leaders on as it goes. They also make it quicker to haul the line. You don't have to unhook each fish as it comes aboard. You just unfasten the clips and leave them until later.

But the traditional way of laying longlines is to flick the line out from the coiling basket with a stick. Deftly sending each hook clear of the boat. It needs practice of course, but in the long run it is probably the best and cheapest way of doing it. Keep clear of those flying hooks though.

Apart from the line itself, you will need an anchor on each end of the line and marker buoys leading to the surface from them. If you attach these to the business end of the anchors, then you will automatically trip them when you haul on the marker buoy warps.

Most people rig swivels on sea set longlines, and possibly it is a good idea because you may have to leave them down longer than you anticipated, in which case they may help to keep fish hooked. They are certainly not essential though.

## Grounds

The big advantage of longlines is that they can be set over the sort of rough ground that trawlers avoid, so you will be unlikely to have them carried off. These sort of patches will also be likely hidey holes for fish. So you win both ways. You will of course risk snagging them, but in practice this is not much of a problem because you can nearly always recover the main line, losing at the worst a few leaders. And what does that matter.

With the help of your chart and rough ground locator you should easily be able to find a suitable spot. But alas, as always in a small boat, you will be restricted to those areas that you can, in fact, safely get to. So set them sensibly anywhere within this range. As I keep on saying, the most unlikely spots that nobody ever dreams of trying can often be most rewarding.

## Working the Gear

Baiting multi-hooked lines has traditionally been the work of fishermen's wives, who would prepare one setting while their menfolk were at sea finding bait and working with other gear. But with relatively few hooks on our gear this will not be such a formidable problem. But I guess it will help if you get some sort of help; it is quite a fiddley job.

Coil the line down in the basket or tub as you bait up, arranging the snoods or leaders so that they are hanging out over the edge. But before you start, leave about six feet of line lying out over the basket. When you have finished, wind

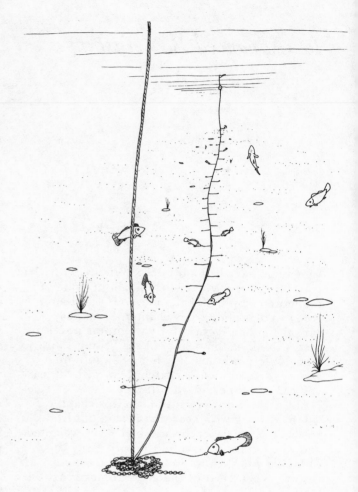

*Long line set on offshore grounds*

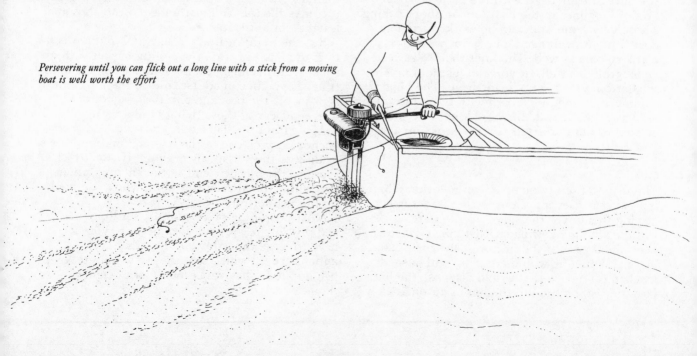

*Persevering until you can flick out a long line with a stick from a moving boat is well worth the effort*

this spare bit of line around the basket to stop the hooks swinging about and getting tangled.

When you are on the grounds and in position, unbind the basket, and attach the loose ends to the anchor. That is the one that will go in last. Now face into the tide and get the first anchor and marker float over the side. As soon as you are sure it is holding, attach the actual long line to this anchor warp. Now the line can be laid. If you don't go too fast initially, you will be surprised how easy it is to flick each leader clear over the transom. Concentrate on getting a steady rhythm. When all the hooks are out, the second anchor can go over the side on its buoy line. And that will be that.

Longlines are usually left down overnight, but whenever it is that you come to haul them, the procedure is very straightforward. Pick up the first buoy against the tide, and then haul the anchor in the boat. Now you can shut off the engine. Keep hauling until the actual longline arrives, then detach the anchor tackle and secure the hook line inside the boat.

Now you can haul at your leisure. Unhooking fish as you go, or cutting snoods and fish from the line in difficult cases. Work systematically, neatly coiling the line back in its basket, again with the hooks hanging over the side—all ready for rebaiting—and the initial six foot length arranged as before.

Most longlines are worked on the seabed, but you can also rig them to fish at any depth you want. The procedure for laying and hauling them is very much the same.

## Transom Trays

These have been around for a very long time, but they appear to have been reinvented over the last few years, and many of the small boats in my part of the world now have them fitted.

They are small platforms that are sited just above the stern, extending out away from the boat for a few feet. Most of these around our way have a railed gallery going all around the outside edges as they are used principally as additional 'deck' space to store fish baskets on. But if you were going to use them to set nets from, you would want them to be open ended. If I were fitting one I would make the gallery complete, but wholly detachable. Then I would have the best of all worlds.

They are particularly useful to set nets from, because they help to keep them clear of the propeller. Their other great asset of course is that they give you increased windage aft. Acting like a mizzen sail to keep your head into the wind when working gear.

## Gill and Drift Nets

Gill nets, you will remember, are those that catch fish by allowing them to get only their 'head and shoulders' through the mesh of the net, so that they are snagged by their gill covers. Such nets are anchored in position. A drift net is of exactly the same form as a gill net; in fact it can be the very same net. The only difference is that it is not anchored and is allowed to drift with the tide. You can hang on to the end of them as they drift, of course, but they are not

*A transom tray is a great help in paying out nets clear of a moving propeller. They also provide useful storage space and help to keep your head into the wind when setting gear*

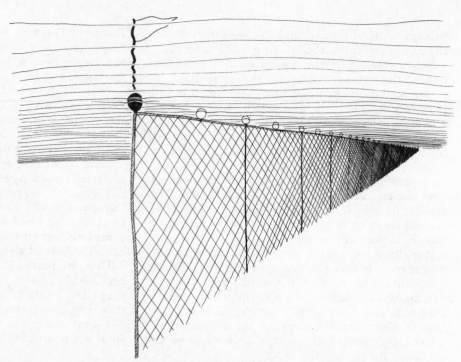

*A set gill net*

attached to the sea bed in the normal way.

As with all nets that are required to fish vertically in the water, nylon is the best material to make them from because it sinks. It therefore requires the minimum of floating and weighting to take up a more or less perfect upright position. On the other hand, if you are going to use cotton netting it will need to be cutched or barked (see chapter 13) not only to preserve it but also to stiffen it so that the net can gill more effectively.

Commercially, these sort of nets are often worked in fleets, a series of nets all being attached to each other. But I think that for the food fisherman a single net set in by half to 50 yards some 8–12 feet deep will be more than adequate. The mesh size will depend on local regulations and the size of fish you may be after.

Gill nets—drifting or otherwise—are rigged quite straightforwardly. The floatline is threaded directly through the top meshes of the net, and the lead line through those at the bottom. Marker buoys are attached in the usual way, and if they are to be moored, anchors with plenty of warp are attached to the lead line.

Gill nets are used to catch pelagic fish mainly, and these will be near the surface. But you can fish them a fathom or two down, if you want to, by increasing the weight on the lead line to take the float line below the surface. In which case you will obviously need longer marker buoy lines or you will have no idea where the net is.

## Working Gill Nets

Gill nets can be shot from a transom tray, but if you are going to send them on their way over the side of the boat, which is the usual practice, it will help them to run out better if you spring a length of split plastic tubing over the gunwales to smooth the way. Alternatively, a sheet of plastic draped over the side will serve the same purpose.

If you are going to moor your net, it is generally best anchored at right angles to the shore. But if it is to drift, it should be shot downwind as the tide ebbs, and hauled on the next flood. You, if you want, can drift with it, your hand on the headline, waiting for the tell-tale movements that will tell you that the shoal has hit the net.

Gill nets can also be worked in the manner of a seine net to catch shoal fish. They are firstly shot, and then towed round in a circle to enclose the fish.

## Trammel Netting

I have already explained the basic idea and working of trammel nets in an earlier chapter; so all that remains for me to do now is to give you one or two additional hints on working them from a boat.

If they are to be fished close inshore, across the mouths of rivers or in generally shallow water, the nets can be rigged in very much the same way as I have described. In deeper water you will just need longer anchor warps so that net and anchor can be worked more or less separately.

Trammels are best left down over night where the tide will run at no more than two knots. To set them at slack tide and haul them at slack tide is the best general arrangement.

Some people insist that trammels should be set at right angles to the shore, others that they should always stream with the tide. Personally I have found that it makes little difference. If there are fish to be caught, the trammel will find them out. Set over a clean sandy bottom they will produce flat fish. Near rough rocky ground, practically anything. Such is their catching power that I would advise a trammel should be at the top of your net shopping list.

### Beach Seines and Drag Nets
These are enclosing nets that are worked manually (with or without the assistance of a boat) to capture shoal fish of various sizes close to the shore line.

### Drag Nets
These can be described as long narrow strips of netting that are pulled through the shallows by two men to catch fish like sand eels and shrimps.

A typical one would be a foot or two high and no more than about thirty yards long. It would be fitted with a float and foot line as conditions dictated.

If they are to be operated by just one man, they are often staked at one end and worked round in a sweep.

### Beach Seines
These are the big brothers of drag nets, and can be well over 100 yards long, and as much as 60 feet deep in the middle. Like drag nets they are weighted and floated, but the main difference is that they become deeper the nearer you get to the middle. Shaped in this way they can enclose more completely shoals of fish that come close to a steeply shelving beach. Many bulge in the middle of the deepest part to form more of a trap.

Although net manufacturers make standard beach seines for general use, they are, in my opinion, best tailored individually to suit the particular characteristics of a specific beach. The ones that are worked near where I live are all made by the fishermen themselves to a pattern that is handed down from generation to generation. One interesting feature is their lack of a

*Boulders, similar in size to those of the local seabed, will help prevent a beach seine net fouling if they are suspended from the groundrope*

weighted groundline as such. Instead large stones hang on the footline. The ground that the nets are worked over consists of sizeable pebbles, and the large hanging rocks can compete with these on fairly equal terms, allowing the net to travel as easily as possible over them. An ordinary leaded ground line would get caught up in no time at all.

The wings of the net taper rather like those of an otter trawl. When they have diminished to about a foot, they stop altogether and ordinary warps take over from the foot and head ropes. These save on netting to a certain extent, and in practice are as effective as a slim piece of netting would be in herding the shoal towards the main part of the net. Having two ropes is fairly essential, because you may need to adjust the position of the float and foot lines separately when the net is actually fishing.

### Working Beach Seines
The procedure is quite straightforward. One set of warps is retained on land, and the net is taken out from the beach by boat to encircle the shoal. Then the other set of hauling warps are landed some way up the beach, and the net can be hauled.

Some fish will be inclined to try and jump the net as it is enclosed around them, and to stop them fishermen will sometimes sprinkle sawdust around the inside edge of the net. This clouds the water near the float line and keeps the fish away from it.

The position of the float and head lines is not all that important with some fish. Mackerel, for example, will only move horizontally along the net looking for a way out. They will not be inclined to search for their freedom by trying to get over the headline or under the foot rope. This means that in such cases the head rope can be fished underwater and the foot rope can be well off the bottom until the final stages of hauling.

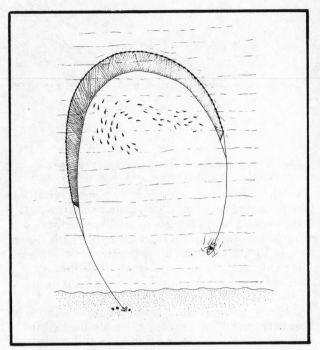

*Working a small beach seine single handed. One end is anchored on the beach. The other end is then played out in a full circle.*

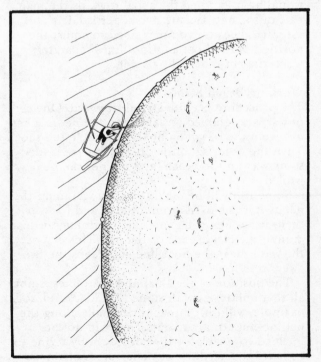

*Sawdust scattered inside the perimeter of a beach seine clouds the water and stops some fish from jumping the net*

*Mackerel will not usually attempt escape over or under a beach seine, they will invariably seek an exit in a horizontal plane along the net*

## Trawling

With a small boat and comparatively little engine power you can only play at trawling. A trawl with a mouth less than six feet wide will be of little use for anything but the most specialist forms of fishing; and to tow even a diminutive one like this you will need an engine of at least 6 H.P. So for a fisherman equipped with the sort of boat and engine that we have discussed, this form of fishing will not be a realistic proposition.

However, I think it will be helpful if I describe the basic techniques of trawling; you may possibly have use of a larger boat, and it will certainly do no harm to have a working knowledge of the subject.

Most trawls can be described as conical bags of netting that are towed either along the seabed (bottom or ground demersal trawls) or off it (mid-water pelagic trawls). Mid-water trawls are the most difficult to handle. They can in general terms only be worked by large boats—or pairs of large boats—using really sophisticated equipment. Their use is certainly not within the scope of the small scale fisherman. Bottom trawls are a slightly more realistic proposition, and I will deal with two types, the otter trawl and the beam trawl.

## Otter Trawls

If you are going to tow a conical bag of netting along the seabed in the hope of catching fish, it is a fairly obvious requirement that the cone remain open mouthed so that fish can be caught in it. So to achieve this, the bottom leading edge of the net is weighted and the top half is floated. But how do you tow it? If you attach warps to the net mouth and pull, it will just close up. You will be left dragging a useless straggle of netting that will be unlikely to catch anything.

The otter trawl overcomes this problem by having built into it slim wings of netting that extend forward of the mouth of the trawl on each side. At the ends of these wings are what amount to water kites. These are the otter boards or trawl doors. They are set in such a way that when the net is towed (by warps attached to each board), they stream out on either side of the net, extending the wings, and keeping the net wide open. As you can imagine, these open arms of the net also serve to herd fish inwards to the main part of the trap.

## Beam Trawls

The beam trawl is still the same basic conical bag of netting. But the problem of keeping the net

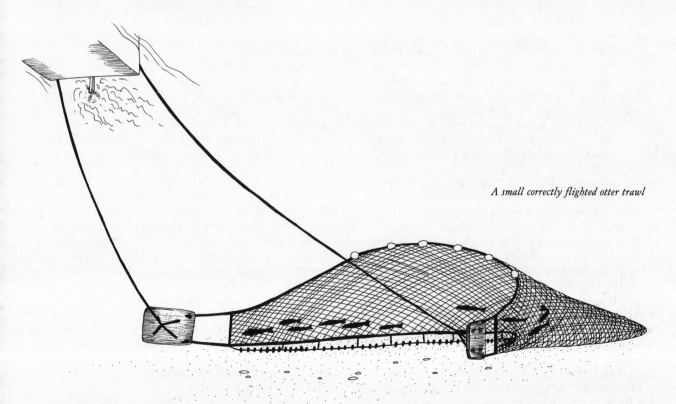

*A small correctly flighted otter trawl*

mouth open is solved in this case by attaching a pole or beam across the mouth.

Beam trawls have acquired a bad name with conservationists, but it is the way in which they are constructed that dictates the damage that they can inflict. Those that could be fished by a small boat will do little harm to the seabed and the creatures living buried in it. This is because the actual beam travels up away from the bottom on skids. The kind that are often towed by large commercial boats are the ones that do the damage. With these the beam is not raised on shoes and literally ploughs the seabed, scooping all creatures, large and small, into it's greedy mouth.

One of the main problems in using a beam trawl on a small boat is the sheer physical difficulty of manipulating the beam and all it's attached trappings in and out of the water, to say nothing of the problem of stowage. But this can be overcome to a certain extent by hinging the beam in the middle and bolting on a lock plate to hold it open when in use.

An otter trawl is much easier for one man to work, because it can be handled in three more or less separate parts. The beam trawl is just one single dead weight.

## General Features of Trawls

Apart from the method of extending the net, otter and beam trawls are basically very similar. Both have weighted ground ropes forward of a foot rope, and both have floated head ropes.

The ground rope drags back in a semicircle, with the foot rope of the actual net behind it; and the float line extends forward above it. This is so that the net can envelop fish before they really know what is happening to them. Hopefully the first they realize is that the net is towering over them and they are being swept back into its interior. The ground rope acts as a tickler, takes most of the bashing, and protects the net.

The head ropes are floated along their length in much the same way as any other fishing net. The ground ropes are slightly different to those on ordinary nets. They are weighted, or often just a length of chain; but since they are moving over the bottom, they must be assisted by bobbins or they will dig in and foul the net. These bobbins are more or less little wheels, and on small nets they are often laminated sections from old car tyres.

Most trawls also have interior cones of netting set back inside them, rather like those on eel fyke nets that we have discussed in an earlier chapter. These act as escape inhibitors and concentrate the catch towards the secured, far rear of the net—the cod end—from which they are removed when the net is taken inboard.

Obviously a net that is dragged along the sea bed is liable to get very worn on its belly. So some sort of protection is needed. In the old days this was often done by lacing on cow hides at crucial spots. Exactly where would depend on how the net flighted. On a small net old rubber car mats or thick plastic sheets would be the sort of thing to use.

As a general rule, trawls are towed with about three times as much warp out as the water is deep; beam trawls on a single rope connected to a bridle; otter trawls on two ropes that are marked so that you can tell that the gear is fishing straight, or as straight as you can get it.

Trawls vary infinitely in design and construction, not only from country to country, but from port to port; and you will hardly ever see two the same. But the above is basically what they are all about. Study the types that are used in your own locality and then make or buy one that you think will suit your purposes most adaptably. In the following chapter I will give a few tips on the construction and rigging of trawls and dredges (which are really mini trawls).

## Working Trawls

The first thing to establish is that you are allowed to trawl in the area you have chosen, so check on that first of all; then find out what sort of nets you are allowed to use. There are often regulations about that as well. If you are thinking of trawling at night—which I would not recommend for a beginner—you will have to show various lights. So familiarize yourself with them.

Having done this basic preliminary work you will then have to make sure that nobody has already set other sorts of gear in the vicinity. If you foul your nets on longlines and fleets of traps, you will not only be liable to make yourself extremely unpopular but also to ruin or lose your gear. Then finally, as if all that wasn't enough, you will have to make sure the ground is clean and suitable for trawling anyway. Without the assistance of a recording echo sounder this will be difficult. But by consulting your chart and towing your rough ground locator around all over the place you should be able to come up with a suitable tow.

Once in position on the grounds, slow down

and steer in the direction that you want to tow in. Make sure that the cod end knot is secure, and that you and your crew are clear, and then start paying the net out. When all the net is in the water, the otter boards or doors can follow it over the side (if you are using them). Hold the net in this position until you are sure that the net is streaming properly and that nothing is upside down. Then gradually increase your speed, paying out the warps (or warp) as you do so. Gently does it is the motto to bear in mind. Don't let the doors hit bottom too enthusiastically or they will bounce and be liable to spin the net. When the net is in position you will be able to tell by the angle and feel of the warps if it is fishing properly. It will soon become obvious if anything is drastically wrong. If the ground you are working over is particularly soft don't pay out quite so much warp, or the ground rope will be more liable to dig in and the net will soon fill up with rubbish.

With a small boat and little power, you will often find that the drag exerted by the trawl will make it difficult to steer the course that you had planned. You will want to go in one direction—the trawl in the other. But once you have got the knack, you should be able to negotiate an acceptable compromise between you. The best towing speed for most trawls is about three and a half knots.

## Obstructions

If the trawl becomes fast on something on the sea bed, you will soon know about it because the boat will stop. You may not realize it immediately, because with the sea moving past you it will be difficult to tell if you are under way or not. A churning propeller will be one warning.

In a calm sea you can just haul back on the warps until you are right above the net. It will then often free itself. If it doesn't, the best thing to do is to pass one warp around the boat and then tow the net off the way that it came on. If it still won't move, probably the best thing that you can do is to lash the two warp ends to a single float and then arrange for some skin divers to try and free it for you later. Never just cut the warps and abandon the net. Someone else might become fast on the same obstruction. And who knows, you may have caught the treasure chest from a Spanish galleon!

If the sea has picked up at all—and why are you out fishing in that sort of weather anyway?—for God's sake don't pull yourself back over the obstruction on the warps. As the sea swells the whole boat will be likely to be pulled underwater if you do. And you will be very soon inspecting at first hand what it is that you have become fast on. Either pull it off in the way that I have just suggested, or buoy it for another day. I would buoy it.

Some writers will advise you to set one buoyed warp adrift and to work back around the obstruction, picking it up again when the trawl comes free. That may be all very well in theory, but in anything other than text book conditions a loose warp is liable to be more of a hazard than a help.

## Hauling

Depending on how big the grounds are, of course, it will be best to make tows of about half an hour in a small boat. But if the boat slows down drastically before then—hopefully indicating a net full of fish, and not debris—you will naturally haul before then.

The first thing to do is to speed up for a few minutes so that fish who are hovering in the net entrance are forced back into the net. Then the engine can be put in neutral and the warps hauled until the doors or bridle come aboard. Then, with all haste, the ground rope should be pulled in. Once this is aboard, the catch have little chance of escape. Now it is all a matter of pulling and heaving until the entire net has been taken in. If the catch is not very big, and you want to carry on fishing, the cod end knot can be undone and the catch emptied into a box or pound for sorting. But if you have got enough for your needs or have caught anything large and unmanageable it will be best to head for home or a suitable beach to sort everything out.

With a larger net or a much larger haul it would be better practice bringing the foot and head ropes in as before, haul in the cod end; then with the main part of the net still in the water, gradually haul in the net bite by bite to empty it. But however you do it, work quickly, because as soon as the fish die they will stop floating and sink, which will make it virtually impossible to get the net aboard. Any undersize fish should of course be instantly returned to the water, which I admit is easier said than done.

## Dredges

As I said earlier on, dredges are rather like miniature trawls in some ways. They are used to catch certain kinds of bivalve shellfish, but you might be lucky and get the odd flat fish and even a few prawns perhaps.

This is a very specialist form of fishing and the exact design will vary for the particular sort of shellfish that you are after. Heavy dredges with spiked leading jaws will be needed to scoop down into the seabed for creatures buried below the surface (like cockles). But lighter affairs with high headlines should be used for bivalves that are likely to hop up off the sea bed as the dredge approaches them (like queen scallops). All dredges are framed to hold them open and are worked in much the same way as a beam trawl.

## Tangle or Ray Nets

These are large mesh nets that are designed to entangle ray type fish as well as shellfish. A typical net would be 100 yds long, set in by half, to 50 yds. It would stand some eight or nine meshes tall to about 6 feet. Although they can be much lower if you are just after shellfish.

The head and foot ropes are normally rigged straight into the meshes. The nets are anchored, marked, floated and weighted like any other ground set net, except that the ground rope should be extra heavily weighted and the anchors more than usually secure to deal with the large fish that you may be after.

When crawfish, lobsters and crabs are around, tangle nets are often baited some way off the ground so that creatures climbing them to feed become caught up in them.

Tangle nets are set on all types of likely grounds, but I would tend to work near rock formations on clear ground if that was at all possible. I know that some fishermen work them purposely over really foul ground. But from experience I would avoid this. A net full of rays is trouble enough without the problem of rough ground.

If you are fishing in an area where lobsters, crawfish, crabs or rays are caught, I would advise you to try a baited tangle net. But keep very quiet about it. I do.

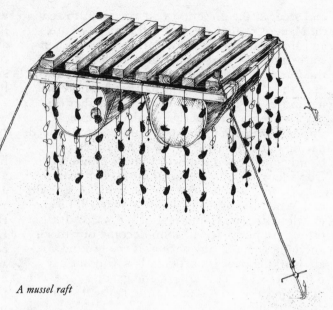

*A mussel raft*

## A Mussel Raft

In their natural environment bivalve shellfish can fall prey not only to natural predators but to pollution as well. If you have access to a suitably secluded and sheltered area of 'clean' sea, it may pay you to start your own little shellfish farm.

Some bivalves can simply be relaid individually in calm shallow water. Then in protected peace and quiet they can happily grow on to maturity. But mussel, in particular, lend themselves to more contrived techniques. Since they naturally attach themselves in clusters they can be artificially grouped in a similar way.

Construct a raft of a size that will match the supply of mussels available, and trail ropes from the sides. Tie the mussels on with wool, and by the time this has disintegrated the mussels will have naturally attached themselves.

Site the raft so that it will not be a small boat hazard, and where someone can keep an eye on your food supply in your absence.

*Ground set tangle or ray net—one no more than a foot or so high will take lobsters and crabs very effectively if it is baited*

# 13. Nets, Knots and Odds and Ends

This chapter is a bit of a miscellany. Tying up (literally in some cases) a few loose ends. Much of the information covers the sort of constructional know how that any practical fisherman needs. I give most of the remainder in the hope of saving you a little money.

### Net Making or Braiding

Braiding is the professional term for constructing nets, and for this you will need a netting needle. Plastic ones can be bought from almost any chandler, but they are easy enough to make from a thin piece of close grained wood. They vary in size according to the meshes they are designed to braid. Very small ones for shrimp netting; but giants over a foot long have been used for various other sorts of nets. I ought to explain that I live in an area where net making has been an important local industry for hundreds of years. Jumbo sized needles like the one I refer to were used to make heavy duty nets for the capture of large African game and suchlike. But to achieve a similar strength, modern synthetic cordage needs to be only a fraction of the thickness of old fashioned twine. So nowadays much smaller needles can be used. One around seven inches long will be suitable for most general work.

You will also need, initially anyway, a smooth, slightly oval-sectioned, piece of wood to act as a gauge to form the netting around. Some people call these 'a mesh', and others call them 'a bar', but mesh is the term that I use. Anyway, mesh or bar, you will probably have to make one of the width that you want, because I don't think that you can buy them. Most fishermen don't use them because they rarely make nets from scratch nowadays. The only time that they normally do any braiding is when they are repairing nets that have an established mesh size that is easy enough to follow.

Two kinds of knots are used to form the meshes, an ordinary sheet bend, and a double sheet bend. For natural fibres, a basic sheet bend knot will be sufficient. But if you are using synthetic twines, an ordinary sheet bend will 'glide'; so you will have to use the doubled version which will lock the knot in position. However, with very small nets this will not matter very much; and if you are making the netting as a covering for crab and lobster traps, it may even be an advantage, because you will be able to adjust the net more easily over the framework.

The netting is formed by tying a loop of the

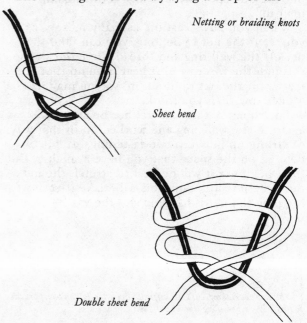

*Netting or braiding knots*

*Sheet bend*

*Double sheet bend*

required mesh size and attaching it to something
that you can work the net up from. Depending
on where you will be working, this can be a nail
in the wall, or a piece of rope attached to the
back of a chair.

If you are making a net of any size, you will
probably be doing it out in the open or in
something like a garage; and if that's the case, a
very good thing to have is a net maker's wall ring.
This is just a metal ring about three inches in
diameter fixed to the wall at chest height with a
spike or staple. In fact if it can be arranged, it's
helpful to have two rings fixed opposite each
other; then you can string up nets between them
to work on them. Fixing one up may seem a lot
of trouble to go to just for making a few nets.
But it is the best tool for the job, and you will be
able to use it to sort out long lines or string fish
up while you skin them. If you can't find
anything more suitable, old metal handles from a
discarded piece of furniture might be one
solution.

You will probably be all fingers and thumbs at
first, but just copy the way that I show in the
drawings, turning the work over as required,
creating meshes that can naturally be added to.
After about half an hour, you will be surprised at
the speed you have achieved.

Initially it will be important to keep checking
the mesh size with the gauge, otherwise you will
end up with small meshes and big meshes. It will
all come with practice, and in no time at all you
will be able to discard the wooden mesh for all
but the odd spot check, using your fingers,
instead, as a gauge.

When you have 'cast on' as many meshes as
you want the net to be long, you can take the
net off the wall ring and thread a length of rope
through the top row. But bear in mind that you
may want the net to be set in, so you may need a
longer row than you think.

The roped net can now either be attached
again to the wall ring and worked on in that way,
or strung up between two fastenings. It will all
depend on the space that you have available. But
for a beginner it will be best to stretch the net
out if he possibly can. This will make it easier to
see how the net is hanging and the work shaping
up.

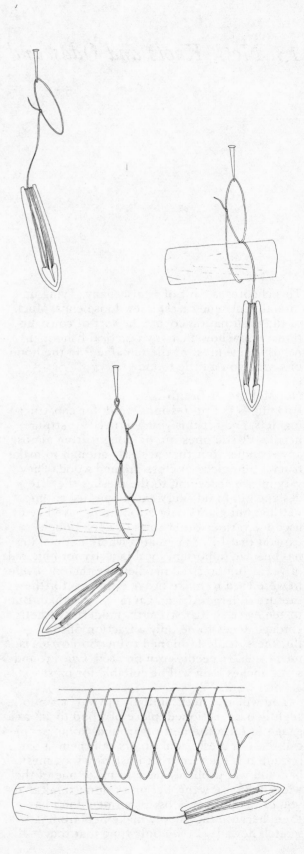

*Step by step net making—it looks difficult, but after half an hours practice
you will be racing along like an old hand*

*Knot for increasing the size of a net*

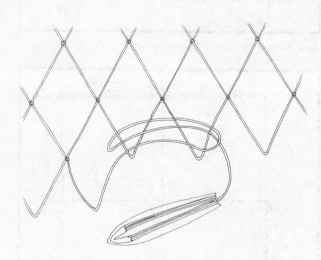

*Decreasing or tapering knot*

## Increasing and Decreasing

If you want to shape your net to make it bulge (for something like a beach seine net) or taper (for something like a trawl), you will have to use increasing and decreasing knots. As the drawings show, the principal is very simple. You merely have to provide less or more meshes to work on for the next row. Remember that, because that's all there is to it.

Hoop nets can be made in one piece this way. Tying a suitable row of meshes around the hoop will give you a continuous row to work on. Then when you reach the required depth, you just keep on decreasing until the net meets in the middle. You can also make hoop nets from the bottom upwards. Starting with just a few meshes looped together around a ring of twine, increasing outwards to the required circumference, then working round in the conventional way until you have enough depth of net.

## Mending Nets

Whether you make your netting or buy it, you will at some time have damage to attend to. So you will have to master this aspect of braiding at least.

If the damage is severe it may be the best course to cut the net right in half, trim the edges, and then just lace it together as you would with a straight forward join. Or you might knot in a new panel of netting if that suits your purposes better. But those sort of solutions will not work with all nets, so you will have to learn how to 'darn' them.

The first thing to do is to trim the damaged area back to the whole unharmed meshes. Then starting from the top, attach the twine and start forming meshes from left to right. At some stage you will doubtless come to a bar of mesh that will be in your way. In other words, if you were to continue with the natural progression of the repair you would end up with double strands. When this happens, all you do is cut out the bar that is already there, and then tie in your new one. This allows you to make your repair with one continuous length of twine, which is obviously better than having to stop and restart all the time.

When you get to the end of your repair row, take the twine down a bar, and then work back across from right to left on the meshes that you have just filled in. Put into words it all sounds impossibly confusing. But study the drawings and then just have a stab at it. All will then become crystal clear.

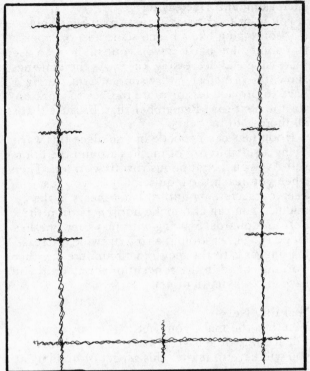

*Trim the damage back to whole meshes*

*Start filling in from the top—cutting out any bars in your way*

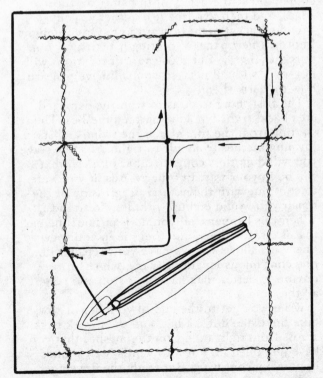

*Take the twine down a bar at the end of the repair row—then work back in the opposite direction*

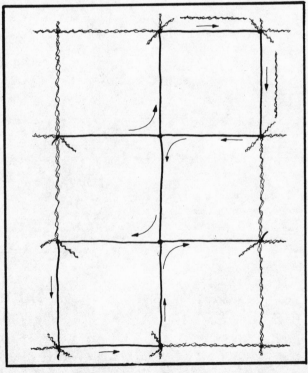

*Go down another bar and work backwards and forwards across the hole until the repair is completed*

## Constructing and Rigging Nets

Apart from traps (and that includes fyke nets and the like), nets for catching fish are of two main types: walls of netting or trawls. The exact way in which they are constructed is very much a matter of local practice and tradition. These sort of techniques have not just developed by chance. They are the distillation of generation after generation's subtle adjustment and improvement. So unless you come from a family of fishermen or are fortunate enough to have experienced, on the spot advice to fall back on, you will not have this endemic expertise to guide you. But without a net in the water you are certainly not going to catch any fish. So the most important thing will be to make up a net of some sort and just start fishing with it. You may be lucky and get adequate catches from the word go. On the other hand you may have to virtually rebuild the net before you get it right for the particular grounds that you have chosen.

### 'Wall' Nets

These include trammel nets, gill nets, and ray nets etc. — those nets that hang more or less vertically in the water. All have a float line and all have a weight line.

The float line is most economically just threaded through the top row of meshes and bound onto it at convenient intervals. But to fish a net low in the water or to cut down on netting, lines can be let down from it to suspend a net well below the float line. But you would still need a headline of some sort. So it would hardly be much of an economy.

Another way of attaching the float line to the net is by means of an additional rope bound onto the float line at intervals, zigzagging down through the meshes, then up to the line again and so on. This method was used more often in the days before synthetic materials. The two ropes would be laid together with opposing twists, cancelling out the tendency for the net to roll up around the head rope.

### Floats

In the old days, the headline would be floated with cylindrical slabs of cork threaded on, or with heavy glass balls secured in bags of netting. Nowadays the standard procedure is to use specially manufactured plastic floats. But if you want to economise you can use plastic containers or even bottles of some convenient size. Plastic balls held in netting also make good floats and markers, and can be bought for a fraction of the price of manufactured ones.

### Ground Ropes

These can be secured to the net in exactly the same way as the floatline. You can either weight the line in some way, or use specially manufactured line that has an integral core of lead. As I said in an earlier chapter, these leaded lines do avoid the tendency of the net to roll up on itself. So you may feel that the additional expense is justified. The alternatives are to make or buy lead weights to thread onto the ground rope, or to attach anything heavy (rocks, chain etc) along its length.

Some nets, even the modern synthetic ones, are weighted additionally by rolling up a yard or two of cotton netting and attaching this above the ground rope. Unlike the synthetic stuff, untreated cotton netting will absorb water, and used in this way, will help to keep the net vertical in the water.

### End Ropes

At the ends of upright nets of any depth it will be advisable to join the foot and head lines with ropes worked in and out of the meshes. On particularly long nets it will also be wise to do the same at odd intervals along the net, as they will help to take some of the strain. These ropes will also be of use at the ends of nets to attach a similar net to increase the overall length.

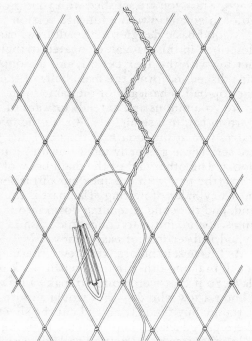

*Joining the head and foot ropes with twine worked down and around the meshes helps to take the strain off the actual netting. Nets can be joined in a similar way. The line should be knotted onto the net at regular intervals*

## Other Rigging

Attaching the anchors and marker buoy lines is all just a matter of commonsense. I know people that attach anchor warps one third of the way up the rope that joins the head line to the foot line. They say that it helps the net to fish better, but I have never found it that much of an advantage. If you study the various illustrations of set nets throughout this book you will be able to pick on a particular method that suits the sort of fishing that you want to do. I tell you what knots to use under the appropriate heading.

## Constructing Trawls

Building trawls is a skillful art. Ideally the main body of the net should stream out so that the meshes travel edge on to the direction that the trawl is travelling in. In this way they offer the least resistance.

Designing large commercial fishing trawls is a complicated and expensive business. In many cases scale models are made first of all, and these are then tested in flume tanks of moving water. The would-be home trawl maker can save himself a lot of wasted effort by doing more or less the same thing.

If you get hold of some fine mesh curtain material, this can be cut and sewn into a miniature trawl that can be tested in the bath. Then, when you are satisfied with your prototype, you can go ahead with a full size version.

A good basic design for a small trawl can be described in this way: an elongated triangle of netting with the apex cut off, and the opposite side dished in, forms the main belly of the trawl, the top half is basically of the same form, but is more voluminous and extends forward of the bottom half in a semicircle. Where the two halves join at the mouth of the trawl, the wings are set. These gradually taper down to join the doors. The other end of the main body of the trawl (the part with the apex cut off) is set down into a cylinder of netting. This part is the cod end, and the cone extending down into it forms an escape inhibitor to concentrate fish in the cylindrical section for easy removal.

As I have said before, very few fishermen do much braiding other than in repair work nowadays. So if they were going to make a trawl—and I know a few who do—they would almost certainly buy the netting and cut the sheets to the repaired shapes before lacing it all together.

In most trawls the netting will decrease in mesh size the nearer you get to the cod end opening. So in a sectionalized trawl, panels of a smaller mesh size would just be introduced.

If you were going to make one from scratch in one piece, you would be tapering it all along the latter half of its length with decreasing meshes, working from about the middle with smaller and smaller gauge bars the nearer you got to the cod end.

## Trawl Doors

These can be bought new or acquired second-hand. They cost quite a lot new, but used ones can come very cheaply, depending on their condition. But if you feel inclined to make your own, it is not very difficult, especially the old fashioned sort that I describe for use with a small trawl.

## Making Otter Boards or Trawl Doors

Deciding on the size and weight of otter boards for use with a particular trawl is a tricky business. They are usually matched to the length of the headline, but since this is a variable factor in relation to the size and design of the trawl, the only precise solution must come through trial and error.

This is all rather unsatisfactory, because to make a pair of boards and the trawl to go with them is no mean undertaking. And if after all that effort the darn thing won't work it will be very discouraging.

Commercial concerns manufacture fairly general purpose otter trawls and experience and experiment will have decided the most suitable doors to go with them. So if you want to make your own trawl and boards, you will have to either copy a standard type, or seek the opinion of local experts as to whether your design is going to be suitable.

But as some sort of guide, I will assume that you have decided to make a small otter trawl with a total headline length from otter board to otter board of around 14 feet. I will also assume that it will have the same general form and proportion of the one that I show on page 105.

For a trawl of this description you will need otter boards that are 18 inches long, 11 inches high, and ¾ of an inch thick.

Many commercially manufactured boards are made from larch, because this stands up to the ravages of salt water particularly well; but oak, wych elm or pine will do nearly as well.

The boards have iron shoes on the bottom and leading edges. These serve three purposes. They protect the boards, assist them by their weight to stay the right way up, and let you know that

*Home made otter board suitable for a small trawl*

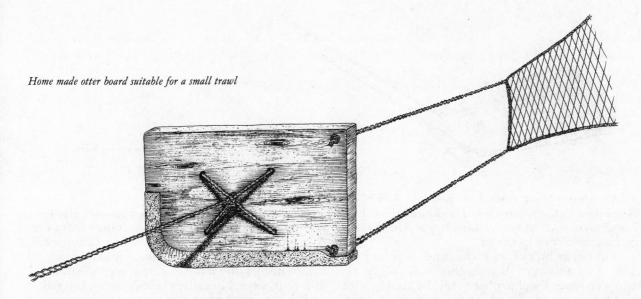

the trawl is fishing properly. That last point needs an explanation. The iron shoes will get rusty in no time at all, and as they travel over the seabed this will be worn off. By examining the wear, you will be able to tell if the boards are working evenly.

Any working farrier or blacksmith will be able to make the shoes, but this may cost you. I have seen trawl boards bound with metal channelling. This could be a cheaper solution. It had been shaped around the curved section by making 'V' cuts on the walls of the channelling.

On a small trawl that was not worked all that often, I think you could manage with a flat strip of metal that just covered the appropriate edges without fitting around it. You would have less weight at the bottom of the board, but that could be overcome by drilling a few holes along the base and filling them with lead.

Commercially manufactured trawl doors have a variety of other metal fittings attached to them — shackles, legs, and all sorts of bolts and brackets. Happily we can do away with all these by just drilling two holes through the board to take the trawl warps and four more to take the cross bridle that the towing warp is attached to. Position the holes for the bridle with a bias towards the bottom of the door. If you get it wrong, just reposition the holes and fill in the duds with plugs or a filler.

## Making Dredges

Dredges that are small enough to be worked by an open boat are easy enough to make at home. They usually take the form of a rectangular cage of iron rod covered in twine or wire netting. The front of the dredge travels on skids of some sort to regulate the depth that a leading rake or tickler chain will dig into the sea bed. It will also be useful if you build in a trap door on the top to assist you in removing the catch.

I have made dredges by welding together steel rods of a type used in making reinforced concrete. But they can just as easily be made if you have no welding equipment by binding the structure with twine or wire. I have on the drawing board a design using some heavy duty plastic tubing that I happen to have acquired. I could write a whole book on materials that you can just happen to acquire. If you have wide open eyes and the cheek to ask (which I have), it is amazing what is going merely for the price of a

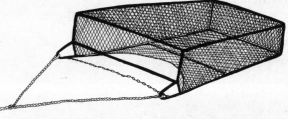

*A light dredge suitable for working from a small boat*

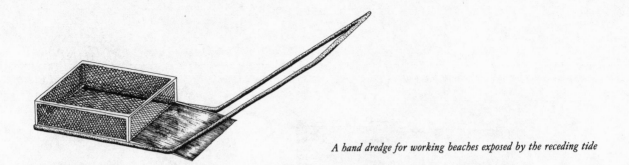

*A hand dredge for working beaches exposed by the receding tide*

polite request. Don't pinch it, just ask; you will often then get far more besides. Remember that. These are words of wisdom from one who has much experience in the art.

I will either bolt or melt the pipes together to form the framework. If it doesn't work out to be heavy enough, I will probably fill the tubing with pebbles or lumps of lead. Then I will bind all the edges with tyre strips. Paying particular attention to the parts that will drag along the seabed. Dredges for working by hand on the sea shore can be made in a very similar way. You merely provide them with a fairly rigid handle.

## A Few Basic Knots

The vast number of knots that are associated with boating are mainly an inheritance from the days of sail. On a fully rigged sailing ship literally miles of rope would be in use, and each one would necessarily have to be secured in subtly different ways. Nowadays things have changed, and the food fisherman will be able to manage very well with a working knowledge of just a few basic knots.

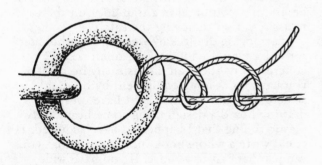

## Two Half Hitches

A good mooring knot. You can make it more secure by passing the rope through the ring twice before completing the knot. If you do that, it will become a Round Turn and Two Half Hitches.

## Fisherman's Bend

A very useful knot. Use it to attach anchors, markers and nets.

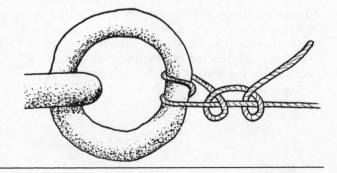

### A Bowline
This is the classic non-slip loop knot. Used on a mooring line it will just slip over a bollard. At the ends of net float and foot lines and on longlines it is an ideal link-up knot. Works well in combination with a Fisherman's Bend.

### Clove Hitch
Very handy for making a line quickly secure to a bollard or post. After the panic is over, you can make it more dependable by adding a half hitch.

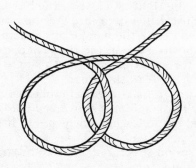

### Double Overhead Loop Knot
A trustworthy and quickly tied line fishing knot. Use it for attaching leaders and weights.

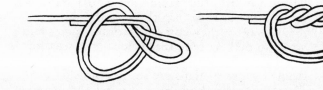

## Preservatives for Natural Fibre

Before the advent of synthetic non-rot materials, natural fibre fishing gear was preserved in a variety of ways. It might be helpful in case of emergency or whatever to have reference to the ways in which it was done.

Cotton twines can be preserved in a variety of ways. They can be tarred if they are to remain fairly rigid in the form of netting on traps, warps, ground ropes etc. If the net or rope needs to remain flexible, it can be treated with an alum solution or a mixture of half raw and half boiled linseed oil. But the most popular way of treating gear that must remain pliable (including cotton and canvas sails) has been with cutch. This is made from the dried bark of various trees by grinding it down and leaving it in water for a few weeks to produce a tannic acid solution in which the lines and nets etc. are soaked. You will need to dilute it before use. It will emerge with the characteristic reddy brown colour. Oak, chestnut and larch bark can be used. As well as acorns and oak galls (growths containing concentrated tannic acid on oak trees—caused by wasp larvae).

Linseed oil is also a very good preservative for wooden boats. You can cut the cost down by diluting it with two parts of paraffin oil.

## Artificial Lures

With a little ingenuity almost all of the artificial lures that are on sale can be made at home. With less ingenuity you can make imitation baits that will work just as well, but which could hardly be offered on a commercial basis. People are not exactly going to be trampled in the rush to buy hooks with pieces of silver paper wrapped around them, so nobody tries to sell them. But the simple fact is that under similar circumstances, homespun versions will work just as well as their mass produced alternatives.

Artificial lures fall intrinsically into various groups: rubber and plastic, spoons, spinners, plugs and flies.

I use the word 'flies' with some reservation. This is normally a term more usually associated with freshwater angling. But I would argue that a feather bound onto the shank of a hook is nothing less than a fly in the general fishing sense, so it will do as well as anything for a group heading.

## Flies

Feathered lures are both trailed behind moving boats and 'jigged' from stationary or drifting boats. Brightly dyed feathers are generally best, and they need to be about one and a half times as long as the hook. The spine is just bound onto the shank of the hook so that the feather trails out over the point. But all sorts of alternatives will work just as well as feathers: thin strips of brightly coloured 'day-glo' plastic, odd strips of worm-like rubber and plastic tubing, even pieces of cloth. Experiment.

## Spoons

If you have ever looked in a fishing tackle dealer's window, you will know what a spoon is. They look very much like the bowl of a spoon with a hook or a number of hooks attached to them. Their main purpose is to wobble through the water creating an attractive movement for predators to become interested in. Some spoons wobble and spin, but the majority just wobble.

Like all fishing gear, spoons are made in various sizes and designs. Make them up as your research tells you is most likely to be locally effective.

## Making Spoons

Take any old spoon—plastic or metal—and cut off the handle right up close to the bowl. For a basic rig, just drill a hole through the bowl close to where you took the handle off, and another on the opposite edge of the rim. Then attach the main line through one hole, and a single or treble hook close to the other.

If you want to make more complicated versions, you can wire on spinners above and below the spoon, and drape feathers or pieces of brightly coloured plastic over the spoon. You can also paint the spoon silver, red, spotted or striped. However you want.

Some spoons are made in a slightly different way. A bar of wire extends through both holes, allowing the bowl to wobble and spin at the same time.

As with most artificial lures, you can bait the hooks with fish flesh or worms, etc., but this is not essential.

## Spinners

These are lures that are designed to attract fish by rotating as they pass through the water.

Once again they come in various shapes and sizes, so make a type that is locally successful.

All spinners have one thing in common. Angled vanes or flaps are set in opposing directions to make them go round and round as they are pulled through the water or held against the tide. Swivels are nearly always set in on the line side of the lure to help keep the movement going.

What the vanes are attached to is very much a matter of personal choice and cunning. You can fashion imitation fish or eels from metal and plastic, perhaps even cast them in resin, but about the simplest way is to make one from a sheet of thin metal. Any old jar or tin lid will do, but the best results will be obtained with something that will flash and shine as it passes through the water. Cut out a triangular shape in which the base is equal to the height. Round off the corners, and punch holes big enough to allow free movement of stiff but thin wire at the apex and at the middle of the base. Bend the top and base edges over slightly so that the wire can go down through both holes. Then bend round the other two corners of the triangle in opposite directions to form the vanes. Form the wire into little rings at both extremities, and fix a swivel to the pointed end to take the line, and a treble hook at the other.

Give the lure a few practice tows in the bath, and when you are satisfied with the way it behaves, make up a selection of sizes for dealing with both large and small fish.

If you run into trouble getting the lure to spin, you can usually sort this out by threading small glass or plastic beads onto the wire to act as spacers and bearings.

Lures like this can be trailed or held against the tide, and depending on the depth that fish are feeding at, you may need to weight the line a few feet above the spinner.

## Plugs
These originated in the United States specifically for catching black bass. But their use has spread all over the world, and now they are used to catch many other kinds of fish as well. They vary in size from around ¾″ up to 5″ or so in length. All are designed to dive and swoop as they are worked through the water.

There are two basic types — those that sink and those that float. But their actions are very similar. Plugs take the general form of imitation fish; but near the head where the swim fins would be, little wings are set at the same pitch on either side. It is this degree of inclination that dictates the action of the lure. At the 'tail' of the plug trail the treble hooks that will actually catch the fish.

Some plugs are jointed in the middle, and some are even made in three parts, the purpose being to compound the action and make it more interesting to predators.

Plugs are used mainly by anglers who work them by continually casting and retrieving them — reeling in quickly to make them dive, slackening off to make them rise. For the hand line fisherman they will only be of much use when trailed behind a boat. But you will have to jig them to make them dive, and get the speed of your boat just right.

## Rubber and Plastic Lures
These can be replicas of the small marine creatures that fish naturally feed on, or illusion lures that will fool fish long enough for them to get hooked.

Rubber tubing can be bound or impaled on the hook, or even threaded over it, leaving just the point and the barb uncovered. Rubber bands can also be used. I have had great success with bunches of them bound onto the shank of the hook — streaming out over the point, partly obscuring it.

Replicas of small fish and eels etc. can be whittled out of solid lumps of pliable rubber or plastic. But an easier way is to cast them in the sort of moulding rubber that all hobby shops sell.

Using either the actual creature or a plasticine master, make up a mould in much the same way that I describe for casting lead weights in plaster moulds. Then just heat up the rubber and pour it in. Most moulding rubber seems to be red, but you can overpaint it in life colours with any waterproof paint. But don't give it too thick a coating or the lure will become stiff and unconvincing.

The hook can be embedded during casting, but it is probably easier to insert it afterwards. To do this, stick a thin piece of wire in the 'mouth' of the lure and thread it through so that it breaks surface where you want the point and barb to be sticking out. Loop the end of the wire tightly round, and attach the leader with the hook on to it. Then just pull on the other end of the wire and draw the leader and the hook through into position.

## Preserved Bait
Especially in the winter months, fresh bait for lining and potting can be hard to come by; so it will be helpful if you have an alternative up your sleeve. Like frozen or preserved food, it won't be as good as the 'real' thing, but it will obviously be better than nothing.

Bait for sea fishing is preserved in two main ways — by freezing and by salting. True, anglers go to infinite lengths to store marine worms in artificial seawater tanks, but that need not concern us, because the cost of doing so is likely to be greater than the value of the fish that they are liable to catch.

### Freezing Bait

Many fish become soft and mushy after home freezing and will not then stay on hooks very well. But they can be used with reasonable effect in traps if contained in bait bags of fine netting or nylon mesh. For use on hooks it will be best to freeze fish that initially have a dense or even tough flesh — squid, cuttlefish, whelk etc. The inadequacies of the home freezer will make them softer, but not so soft that they will just disintegrate in the water.

### Salting Bait

Oily fish always salt down better than white fish, so choose species like herring and mackerel.

Cut off nice firm strips of flesh and lay them skin side up on a bed of salt. The salt will draw off oil and moisture and become rather messy. So keep on renewing it until it remains nice and white.

Now the strips can be removed from the bed and stored between really generous layers of salt in an earthenware or glass crock. If you then fit an air tight lid they will remain in good condition for a very long time in a cool store. Common sense will tell you to keep on inspecting them.

Marine worms can be preserved in the same way.

### Making Lead Weights

Lead weights are often lost when fishing, and although individually they are not all that expensive to buy, over the year replacing them can add up to quite a substantial outgoing. There is little that you can do about the losses — that is all a matter of luck — but you can cut the costs down to a minimum by making your own.

Lead can be bought reasonably cheaply from scrap metal dealers, but if you get into the habit of saving odd bits that you come across in the form of the guts of car batteries and old plumbing etc., the weights will cost you nothing but your time.

Lead melts at a relatively low temperature, so it can be prepared for casting on an ordinary kitchen stove. But saucepanfuls of scalding liquid metal around the house are not likely to make you very popular with your co-inhabitants, or with your insurance company. So you will be advised to practice this particular little craft in as remote a corner of the garden as you can find.

### Equipment

You will need an old saucepan (preferably one with a long, well insulated handle and a pouring lip); a large (again long handled) spoon for taking the scum off the liquid lead; a heat source; some bricks or stones to contain the fire and to rest the grid on; wire to imbed in the weights to form attachments; a mould of some sort, and of course some lead. If you want to be ultra safe you can do the casting over a tray of dry sand. Don't use wet sand or you will have flying globules of hot metal to contend with.

You will need to melt slightly more lead than you think, because when it liquifies, impurities will be burnt off or form as a scum (called dross) on the surface. You should reckon on losing about 10% of the initial weight during each casting.

### Moulds

You can buy moulds for casting lead fishing weights from fishing tackle dealers, but this is rather an unnecessary extravagance, because they can easily be made at home from materials readily to hand in practically any situation.

Weights are relatively simple shapes, so they can be made with basic two part moulds—which can be wood, plaster of paris, or chalk stone (if you live in an area where it is available). Chalk moulds are about the easiest to make, so I will deal with them first.

### Chalk Moulds

In suitable areas, most farmers have a chalk pit somewhere on their land from which they quarry (or rather used to quarry—nowadays more often than not they just buy it in) the soft stone for track making and filling in muddy gate entrances. A sackful of raw material will be yours merely for the asking.

As I say, chalk stone is soft and can be worked without specialist tools. So when you get the rough lumps home, borrow your neighbour's saw (or use your own second best one) and trim the stones into straight sided blocks.

Mark in the centre of one side, and with an ordinary masonary drill bore in from this spot to a depth of about two inches. This will be the pour hole for the mould. The waste lead will be easier to detach, and the mould easier to fill, if the hole tapers conically to the casting. So widen out the hole from the top with a knife or a circular rasp. The mould is now almost ready to be cut in half, but before you do that, saw grooves all around the sides to locate the cords that will hold the mould together during casting. Now cut the mould almost in half, neatly bisecting the pour hole straight down the middle. When you get nearly through the mould, level up the cut and then gently turn the mould over. Now cut into the mould at an angle of 45° until this bottom cut meets up with the downward one, separating the mould into two halves. The point of doing this is to provide some sort of key to locate the two halves. You don't have to do it this way. You can just cut the mould straight in half and plaster in dowels or metal rods on one face, and drill holes to take them on the other, or drill all the way through one side into the opposing face, push the rod through into position, and plaster it in from behind. But the angled cut method works quite well and is probably the easiest way of doing the job.

All that remains to do now is to hollow out the actual shape of the weight. Half on each face of the mould. It helps if you use a template of some sort, this makes it easier to line the two indentations up exactly. But don't worry too much, because adjustments can be made by additional carving if the castings are not absolutely perfect first time around.

## Wooden Moulds

These can be made in exactly the same way as chalk moulds. But use well seasoned wood, or the two halves may warp and the mould will be useless.

## Plaster Moulds

Moulds made from plaster of paris have the advantage that exact copies can be made from existing leads, giving you a much more professional finish and an end product whose weight can be predicted in advance.

## Making Plaster Moulds

For this you will need a flat board to work on, some plasticene or clay to form the mould, some short lengths of dowelling, a bucket to mix the plaster of paris in, and a weight to copy. If you don't have a weight already, just make a model one of the required shape in plasticene or clay.

Roll out a flat sheet of the modelling material on the work surface, and then build up a little wall all around the edges to contain the plaster. Imbed the weight half into the plasticene and do the same with the short lengths of doweling— these will eventually locate the two halves in the correct position. Model one half of the pour hole and lay this firmly into position, hard up against the weight and the retaining wall. The plaster will not adhere to the plasticene because of its oily texture, but to stop it getting a grip on the weight, give it a light coating of vaseline or washing up liquid. Don't coat the dowels, because you want them to become attached to this half of the mould.

Now you can mix up the plaster. Place cold water in the bucket, and get someone to trickle the plaster slowly into it while you gently mix it with your hands. Don't rush it or the plaster will not disolve properly. Eventually you will end up with a mixture that will have the consistency of something like clotted cream. Always add the plaster to the water; never do it the other way round or you will get a mix that is full of lumps.

For uncomplicated shapes, like most weights, the plaster can be just poured into the mould with the aid of a jug or cup. But if you are attempting more intricate shapes it is best to throw it hard onto the pattern, a handful at a time. By applying it under pressure in this way you ensure that you pick up all the detail of the object you are making a mould from. With these more difficult shapes it will also be advisable to mould in air vents apart from the main pour hole, then you will not get air pockets and imperfect castings. Common sense will tell you where these air pockets are liable to occur and where the vents should be sited.

After pouring, wash yourself and the mixing equipment off in cold water. Then wait about an hour for the plaster to harden off.

When you are certain that it has set, carefully remove the plasticene or clay from around the mould, then turn it over and lay it on the board. Now construct another retaining wall so that the other half of the mould can be cast. Don't forget to place the pour hole blank in position. This time it will be the complete shape of the hole and not just half of it. Now coat the whole of the surface with the vaseline or whatever you are using for mould oil — weight, dowels, the complete mould face. You are about to place wet plaster on top of dry, and they will stick together if you don't prevent them.

Mix up the plaster as before and pour it in, forming the other half of the mould. When it is thoroughly dry, strip the mould down and repair

*Making a plaster mould for home made lead weights*

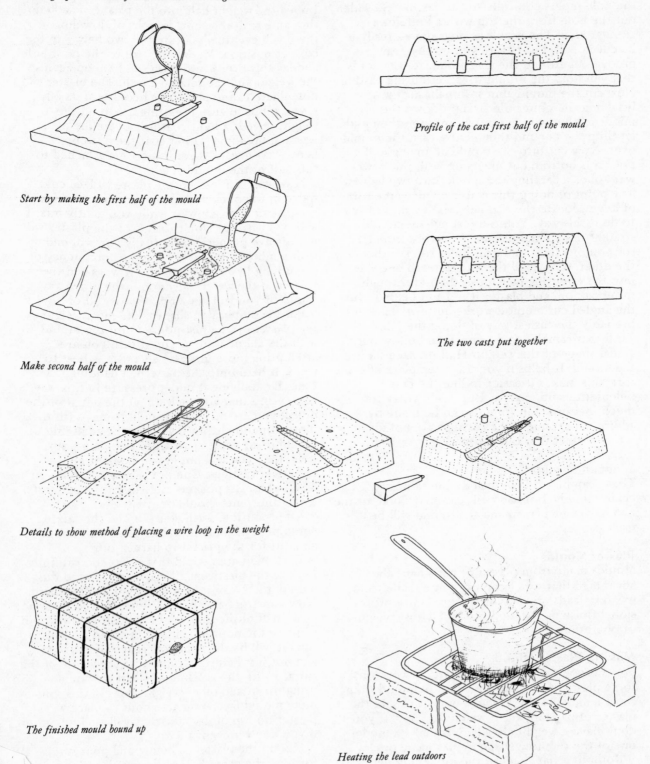

*Start by making the first half of the mould*

*Profile of the cast first half of the mould*

*Make second half of the mould*

*The two casts put together*

*Details to show method of placing a wire loop in the weight*

*The finished mould bound up*

*Heating the lead outdoors*

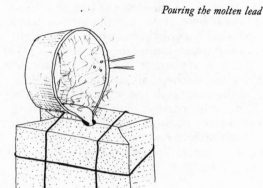

*Pouring the molten lead*

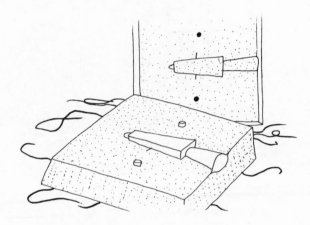

*Breaking the mould*

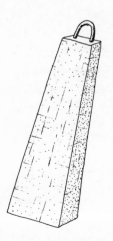

*The finished weight*

any imperfections with a small fresh mixing of plaster.

Although reasonably hard, the mould will take some time to become really bone dry. So store it away in a warmish spot for a week or more before attempting to do any casting with it.

The mould I have described is a fairly straight-forward one. But if you want, you can make one that will allow you to cast a number of weights all at the same time in the same mould. It will be more trouble to make, but it will probably save time and effort in the long run.

## Casting

Whatever type of mould you use, the procedure is very much the same. Unless you have made the mould exceptionally thinly, liquid lead being of a relatively low temperature (as liquid metals go) will not crack or damage it very much. But it will be a wise precaution to make sure the mould is not stone cold. So warm it on or near a heat source before you start. The mould can also be potentially damaged when the final casting is removed; so coat the parts of the mould where lead will run with soot, by smoking them over a lighted candle. This will allow you to free the casting without difficulty.

After sooting, place the attachment wire in position—twist it for a better grip as I show in the drawing—and then carefully tie the two halves of the mould together. You can use clamps instead if you have any big enough.

All that remains to do now is to heat the lead to melting point, and skim off any dross that forms on the surface. Then the lead can be slowly poured into the mould. Keep well clear during this stage of the proceedings, and wear protective gauntlets and glasses.

After the lead has solidified—which will be in no time—and cooled—which will take a bit longer—strip down the mould and winkle out the weight, saw or snap off the waste, and clean up any rough edges with a file.

Weights with a hole through the middle can be made by introducing a tapering wooden core into the casting process, knocking it free when the lead has set.

## Less Complicated Moulds

If you find all this too much trouble to go to, weights can also be made by 'open' casting them in hollows scooped out of wood and stone blocks. You will not be able to get such intricate shapes, but you can always work on them afterwards with a file.

Weights for threading on line can be made with a hole through the middle in much the same way that I have just described. Set the tapering core down into the hollow—recessing it at each end—and then punch it out with a hammer when the lead has set.

## A Tyre Cutter

Inch wide strips of rubber cut from worn tyres are often used by fishermen to bind the edges of traps. They cushion them from buffeting, and protect the netting that covers them.

You can cut the strips with just a short bladed handyman's knife, but if you regularly need any quantity it will save time and effort if you equip yourself with a proper tyre cutter.

If money is no object, just get your nearest practical engineering company to make one up for you from the drawing. If you are less fortunate, reclaim the necessary components to shape and cut to size at home, then get anyone who has any welding equipment to put it all together for you.

The cutter that I show works like this. Start the strips off by cutting into the tyre by hand. Make parallel cuts of the required width right down to the tough inner fabric of the tyre, then place the tyre in position over the curved plate. Slot the knife in the channel, and lock bolt it home in the cut. Grab the walls of the tyre with both hands and rotate it over the plate, dragging the tyre surface through the blade. After a bit of hard work you will end up with a series of parallel cuts across the tyre that will allow you to peel off the binding strips.

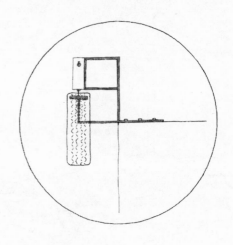

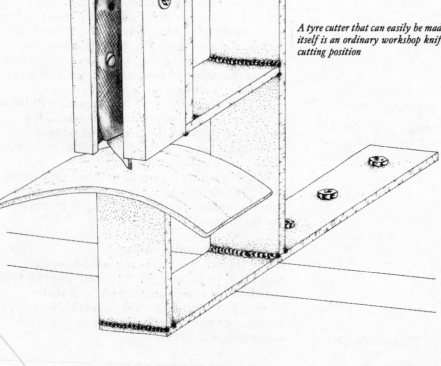

*A tyre cutter that can easily be made at home from scrap metal. The cutter itself is an ordinary workshop knife. The circled inset shows a tyre in the cutting position*

## Protective Clothing

There is a good deal of cheap, waterproof clothing on the market that is all very well for casual day to day wear, and for posturing at the wheel of your yacht, but absolutely no good at all for doing any work in. To stand up to the rigours of the fisherman's life, clothing has got to be tough and not easily torn. So if you are going to buy, *make sure that you get a tried and trusted workmanlike brand.* Then you will not come back split, tattered, and miserable after your first trip to sea.

The best general arrangement is a smock that comes down below your waist with trousers that reach up high on your chest. The gap between the two garmets will then be well overlapped and not let the water in.

Spray and rain are also liable to go down your neck. So unless you want to carry a supply of dry hand towels to plug the gap with, your top garment should have an integral hood. Preferably the kind with a drawstring that will tighten in closely around the face. But remember to tuck in any toggles or ends that may catch in lines or nets and throttle you.

Selecting exactly the right sort of footwear is tricky. In practice you will have to end up with a compromise between comfort, safety, and dryness. Thigh-length fishermen's boots will certainly keep you dry and may well ideally suit your self-image of a seafaring man. But they are cumbersome and awkward to work in, and difficult to kick off if you fall into the water. Ordinary training shoes are non-slip and comfortable, but most will not keep you very dry. You can see that you will be forced into wearing something like a light weight gum boot. But avoid those that have a draw string around the top, because once again they will be difficult to get out of in a hurry.

## Making Your Own Waterproofs

With the minimum of expertise you can make your own lightweight waterproof clothing from proofed synthetic fabric. The average person needs about 8 or 9 yards, but the exact amount will depend on your size and the width of the material. So get some practical advice on how much to buy from anyone who does any home dressmaking.

To avoid the cost of zips and the trouble of sewing on buttons and having to make buttonholes, the garment is secured by drawstrings, elastic, and self-fastening strips or tabs (Velcro is one brand name that I know of). All seams should be reinforced and waterproofed by smearing them with a suitable proprietary fabric adhesive.

Instead of bothering to make a pattern, use a pair of your pyjamas as a basis for your design. Mark out with a special fabric pen (tailor's chalk will rub off) leaving a 1½ inch margin for the seams. Cut out generously; you can always trim overcut seams.

The shoulder straps are elasticated at the back, as are the trouser bottoms—for a snug grip. You don't have to arrange a drawstring around the waist, but it will make you feel less voluminous if you fit one under a 1½ inch band. Velcro pads fasten the shoulder straps on the front as well as the tunic pockets.

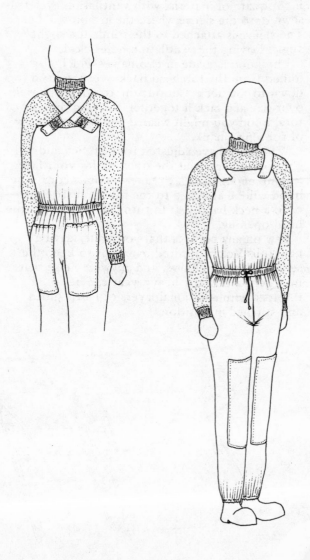

The top is slightly more difficult to make. Fold a length of fabric in half longways, and make a hole large enough to get your head through. Then get someone to pin the sides together giving you a loose and comfortable fit. Remember you may be wearing a heavy sweater underneath. Now extend the neck opening down onto the chest. Turn the edges over and seam them. Insert eyelets for the drawstring, and back the opening with a square of material seamed at the top.

The sleeves are just rectangles of fabric one and a half feet wide, and five inches longer than you think they ought to be. This will allow for turning them in under to form the elasticated storm cuffs.

To allow ample movement of the arms, a five inch square of material with ventilation eyelets is sewn onto the sleeve where the armpit will be. The sleeve is attached to the trunk at a slight angle, leaving the ventilation holes clear.

The hood is made in two halves which are joined from the forehead back over the head down to the neck. Cut out the rough shape well over-size and tack it together, forming the sort of total hood you might wear if you were thinking of robbing a bank.

When you have adjusted it to fit nice and comfortably, cut out the opening for your face leaving enough seam to take the draw cord. The hood will be attached to the tunic, so stitch it onto a neck band that in turn can be sewn to the head opening.

Sew on any pockets that you want, leaving generous Velcro secured overflaps to keep the sea out. Knees, elbows, and anywhere else that may get particularly heavy wear can be reinforced with additional layers of fabric glued and stitched in position.

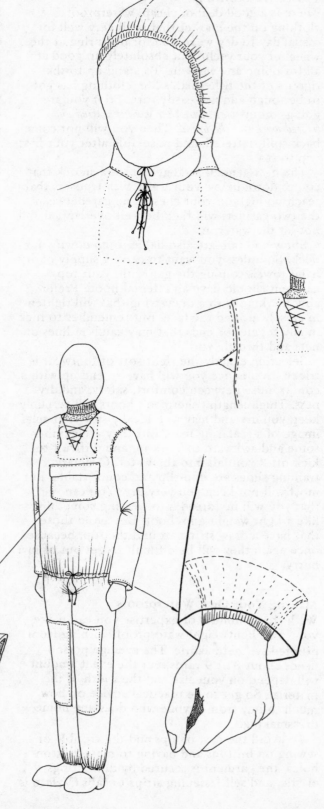

### Glasses

For those who have to wear glasses at sea there
are several problems. The most obvious one is
that spray and salt will get onto the lenses and
fog them up. Unfortunately, as far as I know,
there is little that you can do about this except
to keep a clean dry cloth in one of your pockets
and just keep wiping them. But the main hazard
is losing them overboard. You can get patent
devices that clip on over the earpieces and secure
around the back of your head, but a cheaper
solution is to drill tiny holes at the ends of each
arm and hook on a band of elastic. Not very
elegant, but it could save you a small fortune.

### Watch Your Ribs

A strange heading, I admit, but please do take it
seriously. Broken ribs are a common ailment
with fishermen. They often 'pop' them on the
gunwales of their boats. If you lean over the side
with your ribs against a hard surface to work
gear you will be risking a painful few weeks—or
worse, as I know to my own cost too well. So
watch it.

### Off Sales

I ought to mention to those of you interested in
a source of income that there is a ready market
for much of the gear that I have described
throughout this book. If you have the energy
and enterprise you can cash in on this in a
variety of ways. Obviously you can manufacture
gear for other fishermen. But possibly a more
profitable market looms with tourists and sou-
venir hunters. How about miniature fishing gear?
Crab trap paperweights are one idea that immediately springs to mind. Produce a quality
product that you can be proud of, and you will
not go far wrong in the long run.

# STAGE 3

## The Harvest
## What to do with
## what you catch

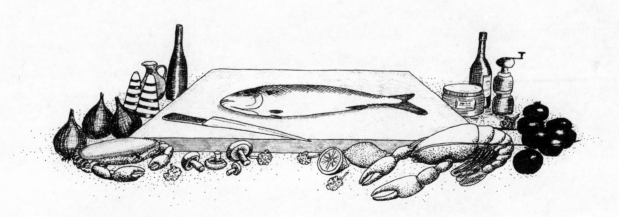

# 14. Processing and Preserving

*They say fish should swim thrice ....
first it should swim in the sea
(do you mind me?), then it should
swim in butter, and at last, sirrah,
it should swim in good claret.*

*Swift*

In this Chapter I don't intend to give you very much information on actually cooking fish. There are numerous specialist fish cookery books that do that far better than I could ever do. But the writers of such books naturally assume that you will have acquired your raw materials from normal retail sources, and so they tend to give very little information on preparing fish from scratch. In this chapter I will try and fill in those gaps, and give you such other information that will allow you to take up the role of middle man and process fish into the forms that you have only previously bought them in. I will also give you some ideas on preservation — putting food by for the days when the fish won't bite or the weather is too wild to work in.

## Cleaning, Boning and Filleting Fish

Most people seem to think that there is something terribly complicated about this. The reason, I guess, is that if they have ever watched anyone doing it, then that person was probably an expert of some sort; and experts do tend to do things rather quickly. But like so many things, if you could only watch a slow motion replay, it would instantly dawn on you that in reality there was really very little to it at all. All you need is a bit of know how, and even less practice.

Apart from a fish of some sort, you will need three things: a decent sized board to work on, a nice sharp knife—one with a fairly thin blade that's not too bendy, and a supply of fresh clean running water.

Exactly how you prepare fish will depend on what the recipe demands, so I will outline all the various alternatives.

## Cleaning

This is the polite parlour way of saying that you whip the guts out. But before you actually do that it's best to cut off the fins and anything else that's sticking out, so that they don't get in the way or tear your hands to pieces. The next thing to do is to remove the scales. Scrape them against their lie with the blunt edge of your knife. Don't do it too vigorously or they will fly everywhere. But since that's probably just what they will do, rinse yourself and the fish off quickly under the tap. Now the gory bit. You can take the innards out either through a slit in the belly or through the gills. I prefer to do it through the belly, because you can see what you are doing better and be certain that you have got them all out, leaving the empty cavity spotless. If there are any bloodstains left, they can be removed by rubbing them with a little salt.

You can throw away the guts, unless you have something else in mind for them. But hang on to the livers and any roe. They can either be eaten by themselves or used in soups, sauces and stock.

## Boning Round Fish

First of all cut the head off, and if you haven't done so already, slit open the belly and remove the innards. Take this cut as far as you can down to the tail, then open out the fish and press all the way down along the length of the backbone. Now turn the fish over and pull all the bones away from the flesh. Most of them will be sticking out and will come away with the backbone, but you may have to dig around for the odd one or two. Put all the bones and skin aside for stock and sauce.

*Above: Preparing a round fish. Skinning and alternative methods of gutting, either through the belly or through the gills.*

*Below and opposite: cleaning and boning a round fish.*

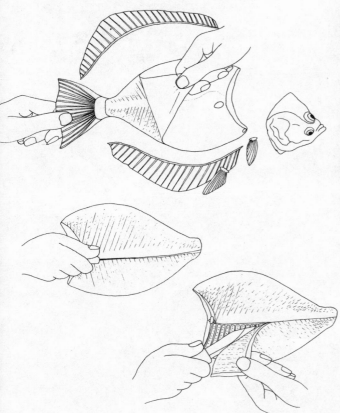

## Skinning and Boning Flat Fish

Skinning this sort of fish is very easy; you simply cut through it just above the tail and peel it off one side at a time. Boning the fish into four fillets is just as straightforward, but needs to be done with some care, or they won't all come away in one piece. Cut all along the central bone on both sides, then with the aid of your knife, work from the head towards the side of the fish all the way down to the tail. Do this carefully to both halves on each side of the fish and you should end up with four nice fillets. You don't have to do all this for many kinds of flat fish, because as often as not they are better cooked on the bone. But if you do, remember once again to retain the bones and skin; they can form the basis of some of the finest fish dishes.

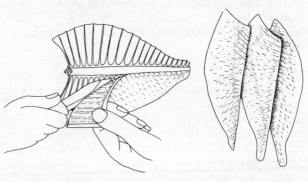

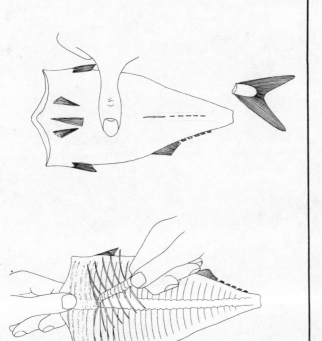

## Preparing Eels

Eels should be alive when you start to prepare them for the table; so you will have to kill or stun them first. If your aim is good, and you can get someone to hold the eel down for you, they can be stunned by whacking them across the back of the neck with a heavy blunt instrument. Another way is to put them in a deep container and give them a really good sprinkling of salt. This method has the advantage of removing any slime, but they do take a couple of hours to die. I find the better way is to kill them by piercing through the spinal column at the back of the neck with a stout skewer.

When the eel is dead or stunned it needs to be skinned. So string him up on your net-making wall ring with a slip knot around his neck. Now

take a very sharp knife and cut through the skin
all around the body just below the rope. Sprinkle
the cut with a generous amount of salt so that it
absorbs any blood that would taint the flesh.
Now take a pair of pliers or pincers, get a grip
on the skin, and start pulling it downwards
towards the tail. It's tricky at first, but once you
get going you can bring your other hand into
use, gripping the skin with a cloth if you find
that helpful. Eventually the skin will peel off in
one piece. Now the eel can be taken down and
chopped into sections as you require. If you want
to gut the eels in the ordinary way, slit open the
belly 25 mm or so beyond the vent so that you
can get at the kidney to remove it. Skins are
normally left on for smoking, in which case you
will have to carefully scrape all the slime off
them. If you have trouble handling them while
doing this, dip them, or your hands in salt and
you will be able to get a much better grip. The
head has no culinary use, so it can be thrown
away.

As with many creatures, after fish have been
killed and even cut into sections, there will often
be some sort of movement and twitching. This
can be rather disturbing initially. But once you
have accepted the fact that this is what naturally
happens and the fish really is dead, there is no
need to worry too much about it. If you are not
a vegetarian, then you (or someone else) must kill
creatures in order that you can eat. Take pride in
the fact that you have done your best to ensure
that there has been the minimum of suffering,
and that the necessary dispatches have at least
been done with some thought and concern.

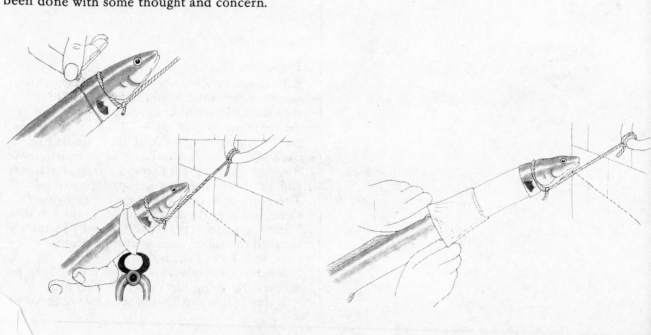

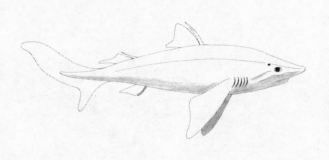

## Skinning Dogfish and Tope etc

Some small members of the shark family make excellent eating, but their skins are rough and tough; so in the first stages of preparation it's best to wear gloves, or handle them with a cloth to avoid getting torn to pieces.

Cut off all the fins, but leave the tail on. Then gut the belly cavity and rinse it out. Cut through the skin around the tail, and then make long cuts from this one all along the backbone and up the underside to the head. Tie the head to the wall ring with a slip knot (or put a large hook through its jaw), and with the aid of a cloth or pincers (the skin is like sandpaper remember), pull off the two halves of skin.

The flesh is then either cut across the body into steaks, or 'split' lengthways into fillets of sorts.

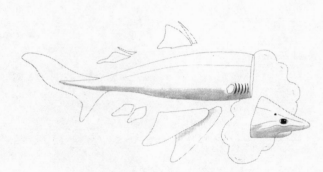

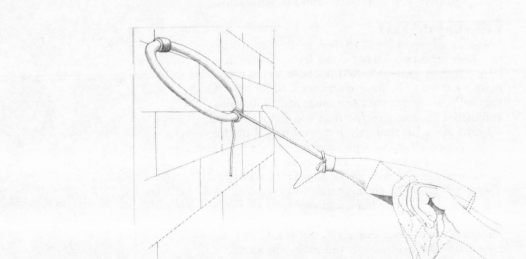

## Preparing Lobsters and Crabs

These are boiled before the meat is extracted. Disregard any recipes that tell you to do otherwise. Traditionally, success lay in having the water salty enough (½ lb of salt to 4 pints of water) and, if you use sea water, which some people swear is the only medium to cook them in, even that needs doctoring to make it salty enough. However, modern medical advice would certainly not recommend using this amount of salt in cooking. You must decide.

All shellfish should be alive immediately prior to cooking, and crabs and lobsters are certainly no exceptions. For humanitarian reasons, some people suggest that such creatures should be killed before the boiling commences — crabs by stabbing a skewer deeply between their eyes, and lobsters by cutting through the spinal column. But I think that although this may seem to us to be a quick and fairly humane death, it is not as painless as allowing them to pass gently into oblivion as the water temperature rises. They say that the least distressing way for a warm blooded creature like a human being to die is to lie down exhausted in the snow, and drift quietly into a deeper and deeper sleep. Conversely, for cold blooded creatures like crabs and lobsters, I feel the most satisfactory way for them to expire is to gradually become dopier and dopier as the water gets hotter and hotter.

## Boiling

Lobsters and crabs are boiled in exactly the same way. Place them in the pan and secure the lid. Bring the water to the boil and then simmer for 15 minutes for the first pound, and then 10 minutes each for every additional pound above that. Remove from the water and allow to cool.

## Extracting the Meat

Lobsters are the easiest to deal with. Just split the body into two halves along its length with a large kitchen knife. Crack the claws so that people can remove their own meat, which is not very difficult, or extract the meat in the kitchen and utilize it in any recipe that you have in mind.

Crabs are a bit more time consuming, but the whole process can be organized into quite a pleasant family activity. And after they have learnt what to do, its a very productive way of keeping even quite young children occupied.

Lay the crab on its back and twist off all the legs and claws. Prise up the flap on the underbelly, get your fingers under it and pull it away from the body. Now the inner skeletal section can be pulled out. This is a curious

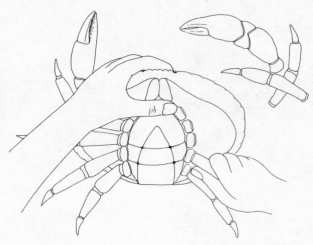

*Preparing a crab*

*Break the legs off*

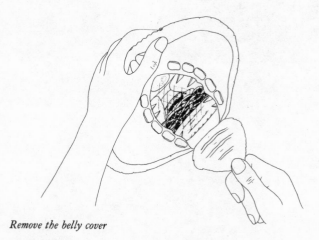

*Remove the belly cover*

*Extract the gut*

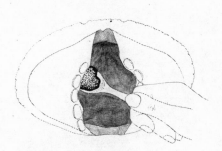

*Remove the brown paste-like meat*

*Snap off the mouth*

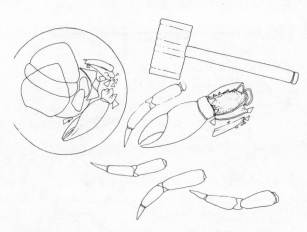

*Break open the claws to get at the meat*

structure of thin bone, meat and gills. Throw the greeny-grey 'dead men's fingers' away; scrape off the brown paste-like meat and put it to one side. Likewise pick out any white meat that will be hiding in the crevices, and snap off the mouth part up near the eyes.

The main body shell contains quite a lot of brown meat, so scrape this out with a spoon and put it separately from the white meat. Crack the claws and legs with whatever you can lay your hands on and pick out all the meat you can find.

There is really very little to it at all; it just takes a bit of time.

For special occasions, you can use the main body shell to serve the crab up in. Break the underpart of the shell back to the natural line out near the edge of the shell, and then scrub it out under the tap. The shell will look more attractive on the table if you paint it with a thin coat of cooking oil.

## Shrimps and Prawns

These should be alive when you start to cook them, and they need to be boiled in the same sort of salted water as lobsters and crabs. They can be cooked in a covered pan for about ten minutes without water. But most people prefer them boiled.

Small European shrimps and prawns will usually be cooked by the time the water comes to the boil, but the larger prawns and American varieties will need up to seven minutes further boiling. Just keep an eye on them, and if necessary, have a few trial runs with just a few before risking the entire batch.

## Shelling Shrimps and Prawns

Take the head in one hand and the tail in the other and straighten it. Now concertina the head and tail towards each other and the shell will come off in one piece. Twist the head off from the body flesh.

## Potted Shrimps

'Melt 3 or 4 oz. of butter in a saucepan, and into it cast a pint of picked shrimps, a blade of mace powdered, cayenne and, if liked, some grated nutmeg. Heat them up slowly, but do not let them boil. Pour them into little pots, and when they are cold, cover with melted butter. One experiment will tell you just how much pepper and spice to use.'

(*Pottery* by A. Potter, Wine and Food Society, 1946)

The melted butter referred to in the recipe is clarified butter. This is made quite easily by melting some butter slowly in a saucepan and removing the scum that forms on the surface. Sediment will form on the bottom of the pan, and the butter should be carefully poured off from this into a clean dry jar.

### Shrimp Waste
The heads and shells of shrimps are rich in protein and are often manufactured into meal for animal feed. I have never tried doing it, but I would imagine it would be just a matter of carefully drying the waste in a low oven until the moisture had all but been removed.

On the continent of Europe small whole shrimp are used for poultry and farmed trout feeding. They are cooked in the normal way for 4 minutes and then kiln dried for 8 hours or so.

### Salting Fish
This is a very good way of storing fish like mackerel and herring. Gut the fish and scrape the scale off with the back of your knife. You can cut the heads off too, if you haven't got a very large storage crock; but they are better left on as they contain quite a lot of oil, and this helps the flavour along. Now rinse the fish clean, and remove any stubborn blood spots with dry salt.

They are now ready to go into the barrel or earthenware crock. Put a good layer of salt on the bottom of the container, and then start packing the fish in one by one. Making sure that each one gets a really generous individual coating of salt.

Fish stored in this way will keep for a considerable time, but when you want to eat them they will need to be soaked in fresh water to get the salt out of them. How long you will have to soak them will depend on how long they have been in the salt. If only for a few weeks, then overnight will do. If for months, then a twenty-four hour treatment will be needed. You won't need to cook them, but they can be heated if you like. And they will need skinning and boning.

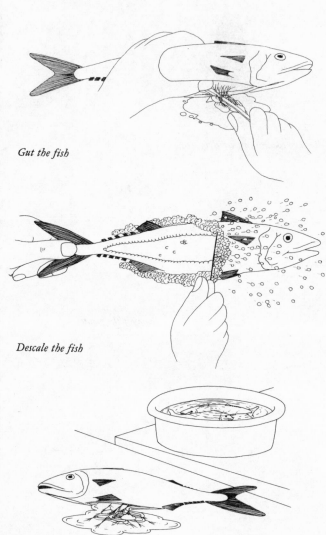

*Preparing a fish for salting*

*Gut the fish*

*Descale the fish*

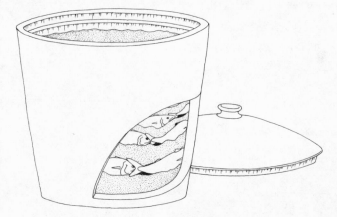

*Wash the fish thoroughly and store it in a crock with salt*

*Making rollmops*

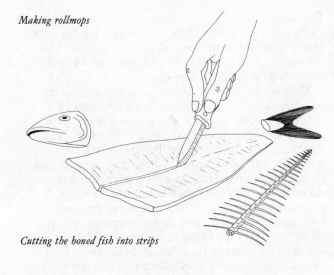

*Cutting the boned fish into strips*

*Roll the flesh up, stick it through with a cocktail stick and store it in vinegar*

## Rollmops

Fish that have been salted in this way can also be made into rollmops. These are an attractive delicacy and are handy for parties or for when you just want to indulge yourself.

Take fish that have only been in the salt for a week or two and soak them overnight in fresh water. Extend the belly cut right down to the tail and then press out the bones as I have already explained in boning fish, Lay the fish out, skin side down, and sprinkle strips of sliced onion all over it. Roll the whole lot up like a carpet, and secure it by sticking something like a wooden cocktail stick through it. Take a suitable jar and pack as many of them as you can in. Then cover them with vinegar and add some peppercorns or whatever pickling spices you care for. Some thin slices of cucumber and the odd gherkin or two will add a finishing touch. Screw the top on the jar, and leave it for ten days before eating. They will keep for a month or more.

## Dried Fish

Oily fish will not dry very well, but round white fish like cod can be treated quite successfully in long spells of warm weather.

The fish need to be gutted and split, and stacked—not more than ten high—between layers of salt so that the brine formed will drain away. So you will have to use something like a large roasting pan with a hole punched in the bottom of it for the purpose. Naturally this will have to drain it into something like a bucket. You will have to contrive a set up that suits your particular circumstances best. You will also need to give some thought to where you will best be able to do all this, because although small fish will have to remain stacked for only a few days, larger fish will need two weeks or so. It helps to speed things up if you weight the pile; this will help to force the juices out.

When the flow of brine seems to have stopped, hang the fish like washing, undercover, in an airy shed or outbuilding. At night bring them indoors and rehang them in the morning after the dew has cleared.

Once they are as hard as leather they can be stored in airtight containers for a considerable time, but before cooking they will need to be soaked in fresh water or milk for at least thirty-six hours.

## Bottled or Canned Fish

In a long and arduous search—and I really do mean that—the following gem is the best way that I have ever discovered of preserving fish without the benefit of cold storage. And by cold storage I don't mean the sort of freezing that you can do at home. I am talking about sophisticated commercial freezing techniques, and the way in which the results can be stored long term in a proper cold store.

If you attend to the instructions carefully, the final results will be equally as good, if not better, than any commercial product. The most important thing though is that fish preserved in this way will keep perfectly well for up to two years—at a pinch, even longer. At an even greater pinch, perhaps even longer than that.

Unfortunately you will need a pressure cooker. So if you don't already own one, you will have to beg or borrow one. Some people manage to do this sort of thing in an ordinary oven, but particularly in the case of fish, I don't think that this is to be recommended. However, I would welcome to be corrected on that point.

Gut the fish, and remove the heads, fins, tails and scales. Leave the skin on, and cut the fish into convenient lengths of something like three inches or so. Pack these sections gently but tightly into half pint glass jars. Keep the pieces vertical and don't force them in too much or they will tend to break up during processing or storage.

When the jar is as full as you can make it, add a ½ teaspoon of salt, a similar amount of vinegar (it doesn't matter what type — brown or white), then pour in one tablespoon of pure olive oil. I know that olive oil isn't exactly cheap, but you must use it, and absolutely no other sort of oil will do instead.

Screw the tops loosely on the jars so that the pressure can escape from them during cooking and place them on the rack inside the cooker. Cover the rack with water. Set the regulator at ten pounds, and when this is reached, cook for one and a half hours. Then turn off and allow the pressure to fall. Tighten the tops hard down, and label and date the jars.

If you use pint jars, just double the quantities and increase the cooking time to three hours.

You can use any sort of fish that you happen to have acquired, but the best results will be obtained with oily fish like mackerel and herring.

After storage the fish will not require any further cooking, and the bones will be soft and more or less edible like those in tinned sardines and pilchards.

## Freezing

I am not a great fan of the domestic freezer. In fact I would define them as electrical machines for extracting the flavour and goodness from food. Self deficiency devices.

This is most certainly the case with fish, and however carefully it's done, home frozen fish invariably ends up with the same sort of taste and food value as any other junk food. Frozen fish cannot possibly taste like fresh fish because it is not fresh fish, and nothing that anyone can do can alter that fact. At home with the sort of domestic equipment that is on sale, you are clutching at straws. True, if you can freeze your own fish within an hour or so of having caught them you may well end up with something that will keep for many months, but the taste won't be a patch on fresh fish. With the benefit of commercial equipment and storage it is possible to produce a safe and stable product that will probably taste more like the real thing. But such products that are on sale have serious drawbacks. They contain additives that may well be harmful to you, and they will certainly have lost a serious proportion of their nutritional value. Very important to me though is that they still don't taste like fish ought to taste. Now that might not be vitally important if the 'new' product was pleasant to eat. But in most cases you might just as well be chewing on a piece of old fishing line for all the gastronomic enjoyment there is to be had from it.

Storage methods like salting, drying, bottling, and to a short term extent, smoking, may seem rather antiquated. But at least the fish still manages to retain some sort of taste. Oh yes, it's a different taste, and it may take a bit of getting used to. But happily there is a flavour there to be commented on—whether you happen to like it or not, which is more than can be said for the bland offerings of the big white box.

But even if I was a devotee, there would be little point in my describing fundamental freezing techniques that are covered in much detail in volumes of specialist freezer books. So if home-freeze fish you must consult one of these.

However, having said all that, there are one or two further points it might be helpful to make on the subject.

As far as fish are concerned, the main trouble with home freezers is that they are unable to reduce the temperature of fish quickly enough, and having failed to do that, they are then unable to store them at a low enough temperature.

Let me expand on that for you. Commercially,

fish are frozen in two basic ways: by the use of an air blast freezer or a plate freezer. With an air blast freezer a stream of cold air is blown over the fish. The plate freezer removes heat by direct contact, sandwiching fish between hollow metal plates through which a liquid refrigerant is passed.

Blast freezers are probably the more versatile of the two, because they can freeze all sorts of irregularly shaped products. Plate freezers are used mainly to freeze whole fish into blocks aboard ship at sea.

Fish are made up largely of water. In some cases it can be as much as 80 per cent of their whole. When the fish is frozen, this water is turned into ice. At 32°F ice crystals start to form throughout the fish muscle. The ultimate size of these crystals is directly relative to the speed at which the temperature is falling. With correctly operating commercial apparatus these crystals will be small, and when fish are thawed after storage, their texture will not have been disrupted and they will be much more like fresh fish.

If the temperature drop is a slow one, as it most certainly would be with a domestic freezer, the ice crystals that form will be large. These sort of crystals rupture the texture of the fish internally, producing fish that will be watery and pulpy when thawed.

Freezing fish with domestic equipment will also mean that the salts and self-digesting enzymes that are present in all fish are concentrated in solution within the body cells. You have in fact created an environment that is ideally suited for them to do their dirty work in. Their main aim in life being, in this case, to spoil fish.

So this very rapid removal of heat is a vital point, and it cannot be done with an ordinary domestic freezer.

To freeze fish satisfactorily its temperature must be reduced from a chilled state (that is well iced at around 32°F) to 23°F in less than two hours. The heat loss must then rapidly continue until it is at least minus 10°F — ideally minus 20°F. Then it is ready for storage.

How do you store it though? Not in a home freezer. In order to keep deterioration to a minimum, fish needs to be kept below minus 20°F, and domestic freezer's don't operate below minus 18°F. Those few degrees are vital.

In very simple terms, that is why I am not very keen on home freezing of fish. The equipment available is just not man enough for the job.

I have promised myself that one day—when I get time—I will collect up a few cast off refrigerators and freezers and have a try at making my own mini blast freezer and cold store. Those who are experts in such things assure me that it can be done. I will do one day—when I get time.

## Smoked Fish

Most fish can easily be smoked at home, providing you with an attractive alternative taste, and at today's prices, a little bit of luxury.

There are two basic methods of smoking: hot smoking and cold smoking. Both produce fish that have the traditional nutty brown colour, but hot smoked products are cooked and ready to be eaten, either straight away or within a few days. Cold smoking is more of a cure, imparting colour, flavour and a certain amount of preservation. You put the fish through a sort of drying, flavouring process, which will allow you to keep them in a cool place for a month or so before final cooking. Both processes are similar, but there are certain subtle differences.

## Making the Smoke

Only hardwood should be used for smoking fish—or anything for that matter. You must never use evergreen or coniferous types. These contain too much resin and will produce a bitterly acrid smoke that will make the fish taste of creosote. Oak is the most popular, but you can experiment with others, or try using a blend — you might come up with a pleasant original flavour all of your own. Juniper wood is a good addition if you can get hold of any.

Seasoned wood is best, and you will need kindling sized chips to get the fire going and wood dust to douse down the flames and provide you with smoke.

## Equipment

Small scale smoking has traditionally been done in a wooden barrel, but these are few and far between nowadays, so you will probably have to improvise with something else. You can use an old oil drum if you can get hold of one, but you may have to burn off any residue left caked inside and then scrape it spotlessly clean, which may not be very easy to do. Old single door refrigerators, with the interior fittings removed, offer alternative possibilities, while discarded wooden cupboards or closets provide yet others. Personally I favour the latter, if only because they are usually nice and clean.

Smoke chambers can be contrived from a whole host of discarded items, even large cardboard boxes. With large boxes you can have hot smoke near the heat source and cold smoke some distance from it.

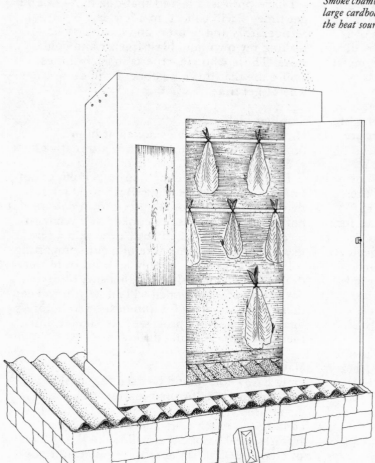

As you will see from the drawings, the fire pile needs to be contained in some way so that draught can be regulated for a nice steady rise of smoke. You don't need anything elaborate, just a metal lid or door of some sort.

The barrel cold smoker needs a cover which can be supported on pieces of wood laid across the top, and a cloth undercover to contain the smoke during the later stages of smoking. A big sheet of triple-folded cheesecloth would be ideal.

With the closet hot smoker you needn't go to all the trouble of cementing the bricks together. In fact it's probably better if you don't, because the gaps left between them will give you a better up draught. The smoke will also need to be diffused, so punch about a dozen inch-diameter holes all over the corrugated iron sheet that rests on the kiln walls under the bottomless cupboard.

Personally my main interest is in hot smoking, but if you regularly wanted to both hot and cold smoke fish it would be very easy to contrive a set up with one smoke chamber that could be supplied with hot smoke from directly beneath it or with cold smoke from a more distant source.

In the old fashioned commercial kilns the fish would be hung up inside on various types of wooden rods (called banjoes, speats and tenters); in the latest mechanical factory kilns if they hang them up at all they use stainless steel rods. I don't suppose it matters all that much what you use; most people will tell you to use metal rods or old wire coathangers. But from a hygiene point of view I favour wooden dowels that can be scrubbed really clean after each treatment. Fish are either tied to these with string or hung with wooden skewers through them in some other way.

Ideally you would equip your smoke chamber with a temperature gauge of some sort, because with cold smoking you won't want to go much

*For cold smoking a separate smoke source and smoking chamber may be a convenient solution*

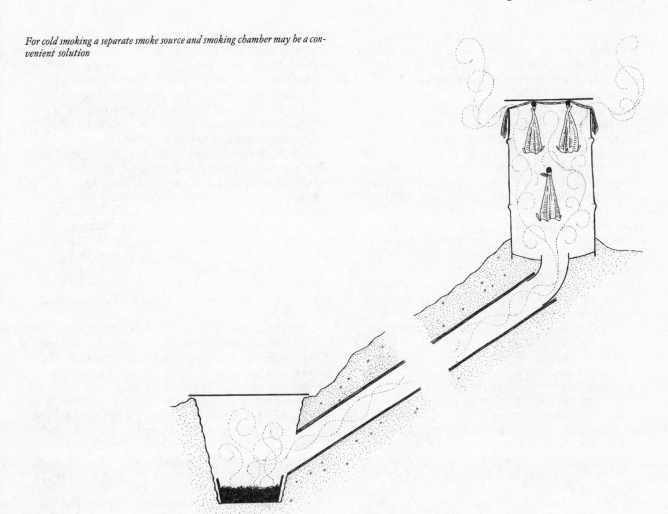

above 70°F, while for hot smoking you may need temperatures up near the 180°F mark. But all this temperature controlling can be very confusing, and I would advise you to do what I do. Rely on your eye and instincts. The very best chefs don't stand around with a thermometer in one hand and a stop watch in the other. They just know by experience how things are doing. So I would say just have a go. No text book in the world can tell you how to emulate the delicacies of the famous Scottish and Nova Scotian smokers; so don't try. Whatever comes out of your smoker will be your own product and nobody else's. You may not get it right the first time around, but it will more than likely taste very nice just the same, and you can learn by your mistakes. There is no great mystery about smoking; it's no more difficult than any other sort of food preparation. All you need is a bit of practice, and you will soon be able to

produce the sort of smoked fish that suits your particular palate.

### Preparing the Fish

Gut the fish and split them wide open, then wash them meticulously, removing any bloodstains with dry salt. With big fish, squeeze out as much blood as you can and then rinse the fish off. The scales of white fish are best removed, but don't bother with other types.

Some people bone, or partly bone the fish, but I don't think we need concern ourselves with all that. Really big fish can be filleted, of course, and you will probably get a better brine and smoke penetration if you treat them in that way.

### Brining

This is the important bit. Some cures involve the application of dry salt, but this is a specialist traditional technique that is mainly used in the preparation of smoked salmon. But salmon is also dealt with by straightforward brining; so I think it will be best if we keep it simple and deal only with that aspect as it standardizes the procedure for all fish.

The purpose of brining is to remove water from the fish, making the flesh firmer, to give it a slightly salty flavour, and to give the finished smoke fish an attractive gloss. The presence of salt in the fish will also to some extent act as a preservative, but that is not a primary function.

Whether whole and split or filleted, all that needs to be done is to immerse the fish in a 70 to 80 per cent brine solution. Commercial smokers measure this salinity with a—guess what?—brineometer. But you can make up a suitable solution with 3 standard cups of pickling salt to every gallon of water. If you are going to be treating any number of fish, the salinity will gradually be diluted as water is extracted from the fish. But don't be tempted to top up the solution by just adding more salt. You will get much better results if you mix up a brand new brew. Then you can be sure that you have got the salinity right, which is important.

The time which the fish stay in the brine solution will depend upon their size. Small fish may need only a few minutes, whereas a ten-pound side of salmon may need 5 or 6 hours. It will depend mainly on the oil content. As a general rule, size for size, white fish will need less brining than oily fish. There are really no hard and fast rules, so you will have to experiment until you find a routine that works to your satisfaction. With really big fish it helps to make some shallow cuts in the thickest parts of the flesh to allow a good penetration of the brine.

As soon as you take the fish out of the brine hang them up in a cool spot. This is very important, so don't delay. After a few hours the gloss will set and they will be ready for smoking.

## Smoking
The motto of the successful smoker must be 'gently does it'. If you try and hurry the process — 'flying' they call it in the trade — you will end up with fish that are rock hard on the outside and more or less in the condition that they went into the smoker in on the inside.

Fish should lose 12 to 14 per cent of their weight during smoking, and the way to make sure they do this is to start off with a low smoke heat and gradually increase it. This is particularly the case with oily fish, and a quick rise in the smoke temperature right at the end of their smoking time will bring oil to the surface, making them look particularly delicious.

Light the fire, and when its burning well start sprinkling on the sawdust. Don't do it too quickly, or you will just put the fire out. When it's smoking nice and gently you can hang the fish in the chamber heads downwards.

How long you smoke them for will depend on whether you are 'cooking' or 'curing' them. Small fish in a small smoker will have had enough in no time at all. Larger fish in a big smoker may take three or four days. The best advice that I can give is to imagine that you are roasting your first joint of meat. When it looks exactly like the ones mother used to dish up it will hopefully be done. Keep looking, testing and most important of all, trying. You will be the one that will have to eat it; so if it suits you, that's all that really matters.

Sometimes fish will 'sweat' when they appear to be cooked and are removed from the smoker. If this happens, put them back into fairly cool smoke and them give them a quick burst of hot smoke and this will put them to rights.

During brining and smoking the overall weight loss should be ideally around 17% of their gutted and prepared weight. So if you've lost too much during salting, you can allow for this during smoking by giving them less heat.

With cold cure barrel smokers, just put the supported lid on the first day; then when you want the heat and smoke density to rise, add the cheesecloth blanket for the final stages.

After smoking has been completed, hang the fish to dry and set in a cool place for a couple of hours. They can then be individually wrapped in plastic film and stored at around 35°. Hot smoked fish will then keep for two or three days, but correctly processed cold smoked fish will be perfectly all right for two or three months.

No matter what sort of equipment you have, never freeze smoked fish. Apart from losing every single shred of taste, salt will be drawn to the surface, defeating the whole object of the exercise, and making the fish look singularly unappetizing.

Eels and some shellfish can be treated in much the same way as other fish, but the procedures vary slightly, so I had better be more specific.

## Smoked Mussels
Cook and clean the meats, and then brine them for 5 minutes. Make up the brine by adding 1½lbs of salt to each gallon of water. Drain the

meats and then dip them in olive oil. Place them on wire mesh and hot smoke them for about 15 minutes on each side.

They can then be eaten, but if you want to store them, cover them in olive oil in 8oz jars and sterilize them in the pressure cooker at 15lbs for a quarter of an hour.

Whelks and many other bivalves can be treated in the same way. Prepared like this they will keep for many months.

## Smoked Eels

Kill and gut the eels, leaving the heads and skins on. Mix up a fairly heavy brine, using 2lbs of salt to each gallon of water, and put the eels in it for 10 minutes. Some palates require an even saltier brew, but if you put too much in, unpleasant white spots will form on the skin during smoking.

Prop open the belly cavity with little wooden sticks and hang the eels in the coolest part of the hot smoker. After about an hour, move them down to a warmer spot and give them another hour and a half or so. What you are trying to do is gradually increase the temperature so that the fish doesn't dry out too quickly and become tough on the outside.

When they are cooked all the way through, remove them to cool, and then brush them with olive oil. If they are chilled, they will keep for the best part of a week.

# 15. Fish Meal

If you keep pigs or poultry, it will pay you to make your own fish meal. In the face of ever increasing costs, and wider and wider international restrictions on industrial fishing;* it is certain that meal prices will continue to spiral upwards. With your own supply of fish, you will make yourself less dependent on that unhappy situation, and yet another overhead could be drastically reduced.

Making fish meal, even on a commercial level, is in principle a fairly simple process. In most methods, the fish, or filleting offal, is firstly cooked, and the resultant liquids drained off. Further heating and pressing removes more liquid, and the remaining 'press cake' is heated until it becomes a fine dry powder. Centrifuges now go to work on the separated fluids, isolating the oil from the remaining 'stickwater', which in turn is evaporated to render a thick, protein rich syrup — which is usually added back to the meal during the drying stage.

The quality of the end product depends typically on the quality of the raw material and the care with which it is processed. Unfortunately this is not always to the highest standards. Often the raw material has been condemned for human consumption, and fish may be in a rancid condition, which will also mean that they have lost a serious proportion of their protein content before the actual manufacturing process begins.

Because of the unpredictable quality of their raw materials, fish meal manufacturers can do little but guarantee the minimum quality of their finished products, which in turn means that you can never know how good — or how bad — the meal that you are feeding to your livestock will be.

*If a commercial fishery catches entirely for the meal industry, it is known as an industrial fishery. About 40% of the total world catch is used to manufacture fish meal and oil.

I have been forced to come to my own conclusions about the situation. My own chickens, for example, will not look at commercially produced fish meal. They just don't want to know. I admit that perhaps they are just a little spoilt. Or perhaps it would be more accurate to say that they are just well looked after. But whatever the reason, bought fish meal is strictly out as far as they are concerned. Put it down for them, and they will look at it, and scratch about in it, and then walk away from it. It is not of the standard to which they are accustomed, so they reject it.

On the other hand, repeat the experiment with some home made stuff, and after the usual no holds barred free for all, not only will there not be a single grain left, but they will be fussing round me asking (in their own way) for more.

So from all this, I must deduce that in some way, my home made meal is superior. I don't know what a laboratory analysis would reveal, because I have never commissioned one (they are very expensive). And happily, my poultry are unconcerned about crude protein contents and oil and mineral percentages. They do not need someone in a white coat, clutching a folder of facts and figures, to tell them what is good or bad for them to eat. They are perfectly capable of deciding that for themselves. Which is good enough for me.

## Making Fish Meal at Home
Perhaps a better subheading would have been — Making Fish Meal Outside the Home — because it must be done out in the open, as far away from human habitation as possible. This is because of the various (nefarious) odours given off during the process. They can be so foul as to defy description. In the league of evil odours, they are undoubtedly the supreme champions, par excellence. So you have been warned. Wear

a face mask, and if you value the continuing acquaintance of family and friends, warn them to keep clear.

I have already briefly described the way in which fish meal is made commercially, and we will more or less be doing the same thing, only on a much smaller scale.

In the section on smoking fish, I have suggested a set up in which you can utilise the heat from a cold smoking unit to dry out the meal. Since most people would want the smoker to be some distance from the house, this will probably be the best solution for most of you. On the other hand, if you don't intend to do very much smoking, you will have to find another heat source.

As a rough guide, the yield of fish meal from whole raw material is about one fifth by weight. So you will be able to judge how much you need process for your own needs, or to achieve an excess for barter. Many specialist books on poultry and pigs etc give the details of how much any stock you have will need; but around 10% of total diet is not far off the mark.

At it's simplest, a backyard process would go something like this. Take a number of whole fish, and place them in a covered heat proof glass or pottery casserole dish. Cook in a slow oven until the fish is almost on the point of breaking up. Remove from the oven, and pour off the liquid — putting it to one side. Press or squeeze the fish to remove as much liquid as possible, and again put these juices to one side. Mash the fish to a paste, and return to the oven in the covered dish. Every few hours, stir the contents in order to avoid overheating on the outsides, and to make sure that the fish is not being dried out too quickly and burning. This is important, because much of the nutritional value of the finished meal can be lost through lack of care at this stage. You can help things along occasionally, by crumbling the fish in your fingers, or by shoving it through a grinder of some sort. The object of the exercise is to reduce the fish to a fine powder, since in this state, moisture can more easily be removed, and subsequent storage made possible.

## The Separated Liquids
The fluid which is extracted from the fish during the process is best placed in a clear glass jar of some sort, where, after having been left for some time — say overnight — it will separate into various levels of density. On top will be oil, next, the stickwater, and finally at the bottom, a layer of protein, mineral and fibre solids.

The oil can be carefully poured off, and put to one side after being filtered to remove any remaining solids left in it (add these back to the meal).

## Fish Oil
Fish oil has various unrelated uses — some of which I shall deal with later. You can add some of it back to the meal at feeding time; but it must be kept separately until then, or it will spoil the meal. I usually add a little salt to my oil to act as an antioxident.

## Stickwater
The next thing to be dealt with is the stickwater. This should again be siphoned or poured off from the solids that have settled on the bottom of the jar.

It can either be filtered — in which case the water would just be thrown away, and the solids put back into the meal — or, it can gradually be added back to the drying meal over a period of time. I think that the latter is probably the best way, for two reasons. Firstly, at some stage your dehydrating meal will probably become overheated, and the return of the stickwater will help to cool it down. Secondly, in this way, most of the protein and mineral solids still retained in the stickwater will be more certain to find their way back into the meal.

## The Remaining Solids
The gooey mess that has finally settled on the bottom of the jar contains a great deal of nutrition, so this should also be added back to the meal. This must be done slowly and carefully, spreading it around as much as you can, or you will simply end up with one large sticky lump wallowing around in the middle of your nicely drying out meal.

The whole process can take four or five days in a very low oven, but you can speed things up by using more heat, in which case you will have to be prepared to give more careful attention to what is happening in order to avoid overheating and burning. When you are sure that as much moisture as possible has been removed from the meal, allow it to cool, and then arrange storage in various small airtight containers. By splitting up the batch, you will avoid any possible contamination from ruining the whole lot, and be able to use small amounts at one time, without exposing all your supply to moisture in the air every time that you take some out.

### What Kind of Fish?

In the North Western hemisphere, most fish should be suitable for making fish meal with, but if you intend to use some obscure variety, check with your fisheries authority. But whole, white fish is undoubtedly the best for making any kind of fish meal. This is because it has a much lower oil content than other kinds of fish, and this means that it is easier to produce a more stable end product. But then again, in our sort of small scale operation, where we will be able to give each batch far more detailed attention than a factory concern would be able to do, I don't really think that it matters all that much.

Commercial meal normally has an oil content of around 6%, and will contain as much as 10% water. Above these levels the meal will oxidise and spoil. I have absolutely no idea what the oil and moisture content of my home made meal is. All I can say is that I have some that has been carefully stored away for three years now, and it has remained in a perfectly stable condition, being just as sweet smelling (for fish meal) as it was on the day that it was made.

# 16. Seaweed

*When descends on the Atlantic*
*The gigantic*
*Storm-wind of the equinox,*
*Landward in his wrath he scourges*
*The toiling surges,*
*Laden with seaweed from the rocks:*

*Longfellow*

You should always bring as much of this home as you can possibly carry. Eat it, or feed it to your livestock, but whatever you do with it, be absolutely certain to put some on the ground that you will be using to grow your potatoes. It will produce the sweetest that you have ever tasted.

Being so rich in minerals, iodides and alginates, seaweed has a vast number of commercial applications. The contribution that it makes to the pharmaceutical industry, in the form of iodine,* is perhaps the most widely known, but to glance down a list of the other derivative uses is a fascinating eye opener — everything from welding-rod coatings and sherbet, to acoustic tiles and toothpaste. Home made welding-rod coatings is going a bit far, so we will confine ourselves (mainly) to the more homespun possibilities — Fertilizer, Feed and Food.

## Fertilizer
Scientifically, there are four principal groups of seaweed:-
Green Algae, Blue Green Algae, Red Algae, Brown Algae.

Of these, the large brown algae — like wracks and oarweeds — are mainly used as manure. This is because they are usually easier to gather in bulk, but any weed that is locally abundant can be used to good effect.

Surprisingly enough, seaweed still plays an important part in the agricultural economies of many countries. Not just the primitive backward ones, as you might expect, but in sophisticated European and American communities as well. The extent of this use is, however, mainly restricted to coastal areas, because of the difficulties involved in transporting the wet bulk of weed, and in siting suitable processing installations to convert it into an easily handled meal. These geographical problems have undoubtedly inhibited the expansion of the seaweed fertilizer and feed industries, but exist they do, and expand they will, as the fossil fuels become less readily available. Methods of application vary with regard to traditional local practice. In some areas the weed is just scattered on the ground in late summer at rates of 10–15 tons per acre, and the debris is raked off the following spring. More generally, it is ploughed or dug in at two or three times this rate; and apart from being less wasteful, results are infinitely more rewarding. But of course — as many an old Scottish crofter has proved — just scattering it on the ground is far better than not distributing it at all.

Other methods involve sandwiching layers of seaweed with other manure and allowing it all to compost down for use as required.

All seaweeds have a relatively high nitrogen and potash content, and because of this, are particularly effective for root crops and cabbages, especially those that will benefit from a fertilizer that has a high salt content — mangolds for example.

Seaweed is also a particularly good manure for potatoes, but the main snag is that it is deficient in phosphates. Potatoes need these and in this particular case, this will have to be remedied. It's well worth taking the trouble to do it, for controlled experiments have shown that when super phosphates were added to seaweed manured potatoes, the crop was twice as large as when phosphates were added to conventionally manured potatoes.

I suppose today's 'modern' horticulturist would simply buy bags of super phosphate and lash it on as per the instructions. But a much better and cheaper answer would be to use fish waste instead. The main problem is that birds and cats are likely to steal it before it gets to work. The best way would be to dry it and grind it before

*Nowadays, iodine is obtained increasingly from mineral sources on land.

putting it on the ground. So if you had any surplus fish meal, or spoilt meal, it would have no need to go to waste.

On the other hand, fish wastes are a very good compost activator; so if it suited your particular needs, it might be a good idea to employ the method I suggested a few paragraphs ago, and sandwich it with seaweed and other manure.

My favourite genius, Lawrence D Hills, of the Henry Doubleday Research Association, offered me this further possibility for growing potatoes. 'You could try putting fish waste along the bottom of rather deep trenches, with some lime on top, then after a layer of soil — to keep them away from the lime — the seed poatoes.' I did, and the results were excellent.

Root crops will not be the only ones to benefit. In France, seaweed is used to great effect on barley (and artichoke) fields. So excellent is the resultant barley that it collects a premium from brewers anxious to have the best that they can lay their hands on. These same Normandy farmers claim that continuous heavy application of seaweed obviates any necessity for crop rotation. There is no definite scientific evidence to back this up, but from what I've seen of it, the same fields certainly seem to produce one beautiful harvest after another.

Tomatoes are probably the most widely known crop to appreciate seaweed as a fertilizer. The commercially marketed variety is usually sold in liquid form. But if you dig in generous quantities of seaweed where you will be placing the young plants, you will not only get better tomatoes, but a general increase in the fruiting period.

Apart from these direct advantages of using seaweed as a fertilizer, there is a great deal of evidence to suggest that its application may play a part in warding off bovine tuberculosis, foot and mouth disease and contagious abortion in cattle. One illustration of this theory can be seen in the Channel Islands off the south coast of England, where in one particular island, Jersey, seaweed is used extensively as a fertilizer, and the cattle are free from these diseases. Surprisingly, little scientific work has been done to prove or disprove all this, but it may be as good a reason as any to start using seaweed on your land. After all, it costs nothing, and it has a natural advantage over farmyard manure in being free from weed and fungoid contamination.

## Feed
Seaweed has been fed to animals since the earliest times, but as with fertilizer, it's use has mainly been restricted to coastal areas. Still in use all over the world today, it is fed either fresh, after storage, or after processing into a meal of some sort.

One of the most basic examples of its use was to be found in North Ronaldsay in the Orkneys, where local sheep were fed almost exclusively on seaweed. A wall encircled the island which kept the sheep on the beaches, and here they would graze most of the year round. Only going to grass during lambing or before going to market.

Typically of sheep fed on seaweed, not only was the wool of superb quality, but winter wool production showed a marked increase in yield.

This high level usage could not be recommended for animals not used to it, and 10% (by weight) of total diet, more in the form of a vitamin and mineral supplement, would be a sensible guide for the backyarder.* Although having said that, it has been shown that after several generations, a particular flock will find digestability of the weed much easier. So it would be quite feasible to gradually increase the amount fed without any harmful effects.

In other parts of the world, the fresh weed is firstly washed, and then mixed with hay and fed to sheep, cattle and horses; or similarly washed, but then compressed into trenches under boards weighted with stones. In this method it keeps very well, but will need to be broken up before feeding. But personally I think the most practical way of storing it for animal feed is to once again wash it, then air dry it in fine weather, and stack it between layers of hay under cover.

Naturally enough, certain animals have particular preferences for different kinds of weed. Horses are said to prefer *Laminaria saccharina* — sugar wrack, as are pigs — when it is fed with bran. Other weeds that will tempt your porker include *Cophyllum* and *Pelvetia*, the latter being used for fattening — boiled and served up with oatmeal. Pelvetia and oatmeal can also be given to calves. Poultry do not appear to be so discriminating, but possibly this may be because the weed that they eat is normally dried and ground first, and when mixed with other food, may not be so noticeable as to create an opportunity for discernment. Anyway, I have found that most 'running wild' poultry show no apparent preferences.

The name of the game is undoubtedly

*In fact this figure of 10% can be taken as a general guide as far as sheep, cattle, poultry, pigs and horses are concerned. But in the case of chicks, the amount should be somewhat lower — in the region of 7%.

experiment. Find out what you have locally available, and see what your stock prefer.

The main benefits come through the mineral trace elements and iodine content of seaweed, because vitamin and other deficiencies can be counteracted, and higher rates of fertility achieved. Experimental feeding of seaweed to dairy cattle has shown that milk production can be increased in this way. In fact in the U.S. a dairy herd with seaweed in their diet once achieved the world record for milk production.

Other controlled experiments have shown that with poultry, egg yolk colour is enriched, and the incidence of thin shells reduced.

Rectifying these sort of problems may not be entirely relevant for most well kept backyard stock. But if you happen to be working poor, mineral deficient land, you could have a great deal to gain.   Although most backyard stock will thrive when seaweed is included in their diet, it is the ruminants that will benefit most of all, with pigs having the least to gain because of digestability problems.

One final point worth mentioning concerns the incidence of goitre in countries where seaweed is used as fertilizer and animal feed. Iodine is known to ward off this unfortunate affliction; so your increased intake of it through eating the eggs, milk and meat of seaweed fed stock will at least make you less vulnerable.

Incidentally, if you want to save yourself a bit of effort in gathering for animal feed and fertilizer, just wait until there have been some severe storms; then make a timely appearance at one of the smart resort beaches. You will find workmen bulldozing the washed up weed into convenient heaps for disposal. They will be glad to let you take as much as you want. But watch out for any signs of contamination.

## Food

For eating, April, May and June are the best months to gather your harvest. At this time of the year the plants do most of their growing and will be at their most succulent. Pick in as remote a spot as possible, away from obvious sources of pollution, and always wash the weed in fresh water before cooking. If you intend to gather seaweed by cutting it from the rocks that it attaches itself to (the best way to gather foodweed) don't cut too close to the 'root' (holdfast) or the plant will die.

**Carragheen, Carrageen,** *Chondrus crispus*
One of the most widely used seaweeds, this small, almost flat plant, varies in colour from almost purple, through to green, and finally cream when exposed to the sun. The fronds divide repeatedly into characteristic fan shaped 'hands', and you should have little trouble in either finding or identifying it.

Carragheen provides the commercial world with a rich source of vegetable gelatines — alginates — and on a domestic level it can be most usefully employed in a similar way.

Apart from that which is nationally produced, a great deal of the Carragheen sold in health food stores comes from Ireland, where after gathering, it is washed in clean sea water, and then allowed to dry naturally in the open air. This needs to be done with some care, because too much sun will knock all the life out of it. So in order to avoid overheating, they dowse it at the appropriate times with fresh sea water. This also eventually helps to preserve it, since the salt from the sea water is left deposited all over the plant. When you want to use the Carragheen, this can be removed by stirring the plant briskly in hot water for a few moments before proceeding with the recipe.

To simulate the same sort of process at home, all you will need to do is to spread the weed out in a sunny but sheltered spot, and wash it with fresh water from time to time. Eventually it will become bleached, and after the less wholesome parts have been discarded, will be ready for long term airtight storage.

## Carragheen as a Vegetable Gelatine

This is probably the most practical way that Carragheen — or the two other main seaweed gelatine sources — Kelp (*Laminaria digitata*) and *Gigartina stellata* can be used. For that matter, it is also probably the most practical way nowadays of including any kind of seaweed directly in a human diet. To suddenly have placed in front of you a salad — or some such dish obviously incorporating seaweed — can be a little unnerving. But when used as a gelatine, the weed dissolves unnoticed into the more conventional elements of the dish. And unless you had been told, I doubt that it would ever cross your mind that you were eating anything unusual.

## Soups, Stews and Jams

These can easily be thickened with Carragheen. Take a cup full of the clean, dry weed, tie it up in a muslin bag, and suspend it in the cooking pot at the appropriate time.

## Some other Carragheen Recipes

*Carragheen Blancmange*
½ oz Carragheen
1 pint of milk
Sugar to taste
Lemon rind

Boil in milk, to which lemon rind has been added, for about 15 minutes until soft and thick. Strain. Add sugar and colouring. Pour into a wet mould and leave till set.

*Carragheen Chocolate Blancmange*
¼ oz Carragheen
1 pint of milk
Teaspoonful cocoa
Sugar to taste
Vanilla essence

Boil in milk for about 15 minutes until soft and thick. Strain. Pour into wet mould to set.

*Carragheen Jelly*
1 oz Carragheen
1 pint of water
6 oz sugar
1 orange, 2 lemons
Colouring
Whipped cream

Pare off orange and lemon rind thinly and boil with water and carragheen for 15 minutes. Strain

juice of lemons and orange onto the sugar, and strain it into the boiling liquid. Add colour. Pour into mould, and when set decorate with the whipped cream.

*Carragheen Cough Mixture*
¼ oz Carragheen
1 pint of water
Juice and rind of 1 lemon and orange
Sugar to taste

Boil the whole lot for about 20 minutes. Strain. Serve hot or cold.

## Sausage Coverings

I also use Carragheen to make very effective sausage skins. There may be better ways, but this is how I do it. Simmer three cups of water and one cup of weed in a saucepan until the weed magically dissolves. Pick out any odds and ends left floating in the liquid, then strain. Place the formed sausage meat in a dish, and pour a little of the liquid over them. Swill the sausages gently around in it, then pour the surplus back into the saucepan and return it to a now moderate heat source. Repeat the process three or four times until a nice even skin has been built up. Store in a cool place.

Doubtless you could do the same sort of thing with cheese, but I have never tried it.

fresh out of chewing tobacco, you might be able to make do with some *Laurencia pinnatifida* — Pepper dulse. They used to in Iceland, but it is more commonly discovered in it's role as a condiment, as perhaps the name might suggest.

## Laver (*Porphyra umbilicalis*)

This is another commonly occurring weed that will be found attached to rocks at most levels of the shoreline. The thin undulating fronds are a reddish purple in colour, but change through to green or brown when removed from the sea.

In China and Japan they use various species of Laver as a body builder for soups and stews, as an ingredient in pickles and preserves, and as a coating for their rice balls. If you are not an oriental, you may be content to stick with the traditional western delicacies — Laverbread and Laver Mutton Sauce.

### Laverbread

Simmer the washed Laver in a little water until it becomes a thick paste. Select convenient portions and roll them in oatmeal, forming flat hamburger shapes. Fry, and serve with bacon and eggs. The cooked paste can be kept in an airtight container for a few days before the final frying.

### Laver Mutton Sauce

Cook the Laver as before. Take just under a pint of it and mix in about an ounce of butter. Add orange juice to taste and serve with mutton or lamb.

Laver, cooked as we have seen, can be used as a vegetable with most meat dishes, as can Sea Lettuce (*Ulva lactuca*) and the similar *Monostroma grevillei*.

*Laminaria saccharina, Alaria esculenta* and Bladder Wrack (*Fucus vesiculosus*) will also happily mingle with the carrots and potatoes. But if you are

## Dulse (*Rhodymenia palmata*)

If you really want, you can eat this one raw in salads, but it is more usual to cook it first. And it takes some cooking. Even after four or five hours of simmering it still manages to remain tough and salty. In New England, the dried leaves are still used as a relish, and although I have never tried it, I would imagine that this might be a much better method of utilization.

## Other uses for Seaweed

At the beginning of this chapter I mentioned the vast number of derivative uses that seaweed has. But apart from those that we have already looked at, there are few that I know of that are practical on anything but a commercial scale. However, I have come across one or two less sophisticated possibilities, and these may be of interest.

Since this is a book that is concerned principally with sea fishing, it might not be a bad idea to kick off with one use that is at least vaguely relevant.

In Alaska, the Indians used the long stipes of the bull kelp nerocystis. They would wash, dry, and stretch it over a period of time, and then use it as fishing line. Now I'm not suggesting that you do the same, but it might be possible to find a different kind of use for similar kinds of 'stringy' weed that you had available locally. Binding the edges of traps to protect them is one possibility that immediately springs to mind.

Seaweed has also been used for stuffing furniture and cushions; and during my research days, I was fascinated to learn that it was also used to *insulate the walls of Radio City in New York*. I am not exactly sure how this was done, but the weed may have been manufactured into tiles of some sort. If you happen to know something of the process perhaps you would let me know. I have come across reference to a factory that once existed in Ireland that made wall and ceiling boards out of seaweed. The weed was mixed with acid of some sort and turned into a hard horny substance. But exactly how this was done, again I am not sure. I tried mixing some Carragheen with the acid out of an old car battery. Absolutely nothing at all happened. I guess that perhaps the acid was not strong enough. Anyway, it has had a year or so to perform any miracles if it was thinking of performing any, and there it still sits in a jar on the shelf — completely unaffected by the acid — looking like some prime specimen preserved in formalin.

More in the line of crafts, the stipes of *Pelagophycus* are made into curios in southern California, and down in South America, stipes from the giant alga *Lessonia* are used as knife handles. The weed is cut and shaped when it is still soft after being taken from the sea, after which it dries out as hard as bone.

I have also come across reference to bangles being woven or plaited out of various kinds of thin, string-like weed, with the indication that certain therapeutic benefits were to be derived by the wearers. Rather like those copper bracelets that people buy in the hope that they will keep their rheumatism at bay.

# 17. By-products

In addition to food, fertilizer and animal feed, the sea and seashore can provide you with a whole range of other useful materials. As always they are free — yours simply for the taking.

## Oil

All fish contain oil in some sort of quantity, but in general terms the ones with large livers will produce most. In some cases the yield can be quite astonishing. Thirty gallons or so from even a fairly small shark. Much more from his bigger brothers and sisters. Personally I like to keep as far away from sharks as possible—and you will probably be well advised to do the same. But the next time the charter boat anglers land one, wait for the weigh in; and then connive yourself and your bucket and knife agreeably to the scene. Plead poverty or scientific interest or whatever else you think will allow you to have your wicked way, and then slit him up the belly. (The shark, not the angler). Once you've got him open you will have no doubts at all as to which is the liver and how you should go about cutting it out. So just slice it cleanly away from the gall bladder and flop it into the bucket. In cold bood, it all sounds a bit ghoulish, but waste not want not, I say. At least you will be able to console yourself with the fact that your actions have ensured the poor old creature's death was not entirely in vain — which is more than can be said for the anglers, who would probably have just unceremoniously dumped the carcass when their 'fun' was over.

## Liver Boiling

For making top grade cod liver oil, only the livers of cod, haddock and coley are used. Cleanliness and freshness are vital to the process, and if you were to attempt it yourself, you would have to be able to start boiling down the livers within half an hour of having caught the fish. Not very practical for most of us, but the procedure is very much the same as it is for producing oil of lesser quality.

## Rendering Down

On a commercial scale, extracting the oil from fish liver is done aboard ship in steam pressure boilers. Steam is introduced at $25 lb/in^2$ and after five or ten minutes the livers disintegrate as the temperature rises to boiling point. When this stage is reached, the inlet of steam is reduced and the contents of the boilers is gently simmered for about 15 minutes.

After simmering, the steam is shut off, and the oil starts to separate from the waste (called foots). For top quality oil the separation time should be no longer than 20 minutes. Prolonged settling will only result in inferior quality oil.

Even though the commercial process is basically quite simple, considerable care is needed to ensure a good end product. The steaming and simmering must not be violent or prolonged, or the oil yield will be drastically decreased. Similarly, the livers must be boiled just enough to break them down, but not so harshly as to produce fine particles that will not separate out.

You can produce your own oil at home in a similar way. The only equipment needed will be an ordinary kitchen steamer. You won't be able to control the steam pressure, but you will be able to get up steam before you place the liver in the steaming tray and adjust the heat source for the simmering.

When the process is finished, the best way to get the oil out of the saucepan is to siphon it off.

If you try to pour it into a separate container, it will just get mixed up with the foots again.

For large livers, or large numbers of livers, you will need to repeat the process several times. Alternatively you could try and lay your hands on a large commercial size catering steamer, or you could perhaps construct one from an old wash boiler.

To render top quality oil needs practice and care, but it is quite feasible to do so on a small scale. And just how much cod liver oil are you going to need anyway?

## Fish Oil as Fuel

Oil produced in the way that we have seen, and as a by-product from the fish meal factory, can be used as a primitive light source.

All you need is a small jar to hold the oil, a wick of some sort and a slice of bottle cork. You can use any old piece of string for the wick, but you will get better results if you get hold of some of the proper stuff from a hobby shop that sells candle making equipment. Make a hole through the middle of the cork and thread the wick through, so that about half an inch is protruding. Then just float it on top of the oil in the jar. Give the wick time to soak up enough fuel; then just light up.

If the oil is of really rotten quality, it will tend to smoke and smell a bit. You can cover up the smell by putting a few drops of anything that smells nice into the oil. All you can do about the smoke is to make a resolution to take more care the next time that you make any oil.

If you are worried about the fire risk, don't be. If the flame comes into contact with the oil in the container, it will just go out. You can put lighted matches out in this sort of oil.

Doubtless some of you who are more technically minded than I am will be able to construct rather more refined and effective lamps and burners than the primitive one that I have described. If you are able to, let me know all about it, and we will try and include your suggestions in future editions of this book.

It may also interest you to know that some commercial concerns will buy fish oil from you — assuming, of course, that it comes up to their required standards, which need not necessarily be all that high — and they will often provide drums for you to store it in. You might make enquiries about that as a possible source of extra income.

## Oilskins

While we are on the subject of oil, I ought to mention oilskins. Not that they have much to do with the sort of oil that I've just been talking about, but they do have a great deal to do with fishing—or rather they did in the not too distant past.

In the days before PVC and the more modern lightweight-waterproof materials, fishermen protected themselves from the elements with oilskins. This was made by coating cotton cloth with boiled linseed oil, and is quite easy to do at home if you want to or have need to.

All you need is a fairly stiff brush, and if possible, some assistance in stretching the cloth out to allow a good, even penetration. Brush the oil on quite vigorously, and then place the garment over some sort of framework to hold it open as it dries out. An old chair with some lengths of wood lashed to it will serve as well as anything.

You may or may not need to make further applications of oil. It depends on how thickly you have painted it on, and exactly what sort of cloth you have used; but what you are aiming for is a nice, thick, plasticised finish. When the garment dries out, it will turn yellow and take on the appearance of cured animal skin and be waterproof and airtight.

The problem with this sort of clothing is that it does tend to be rather stiff and heavy; and because it's airtight, you can run into ventilation problems. Lighter oilskins used to be made using silk instead of cotton as a base, so you might experiment along those lines if the need should ever arise.

Anyway, whatever their limitations, oilskins will keep you dry. And however you look at it, that must be an awful lot better than getting soaking wet.

## Fish Glue

Old fashioned fish glue was basically an impure gelatine made from boiling down fish waste—fins, heads, skin and bones etc. And you can do the same at home should you ever have need to do so.

If you have already tried making fish meal in the way that I described in Chapter 15, you may have made some fish glue without realizing it. During some stage of that process you may have noticed the odd sticky lump of dark toffee-like material floating around. Well, to all intents and purposes, that was fish glue.

To make a decent amount of glue you will

need quite a mound of fish waste. So you will probably be best off attempting it when you have been processing fish for storage in some quantity.

As with making fish meal, the whole procedure is best performed out in the open, because the smell can be rather unpleasant.

Place the fish waste in a suitable pan, and add as little water as you can get away with. You need just enough to get the whole lot simmering away nicely. If it looks like drying up at some stage, just add a bit more water. It can take quite a long time to reduce the contents of the pan down into a sticky, glutinous mass—all day maybe. But if you keep your eye on it, it will be pretty obvious when it has reached the required stage. While the glue is still hot, spoon it out into paper rings set out on a sheet of glass or something like that that's very smooth. Then when your glue cakes are cold and hard you can just ease them off and store them in their rings.

When you want to glue something, all you do is melt one or more of the cakes in a proper glue pot or a double saucepan of some kind and apply it with a brush.

## Beachcombing

If you have regular access to a beach, it is madness not to make use of the flotsam and jetsam that comes ashore on every tide. Rope, fenders, netting and floats are all liable to appear at some time or other; so collect as many odd bits as possible, and you will be surprised at the gear that you can make up. Pick a quiet spot, and correspond your visits with the ebb tide. Virtually anything you can think of is likely to appear, but your most frequent find, apart from oil waste, will certainly be our dear old friend, Mr. Driftwood. Now I mention him, not for the obvious reasons that he can be burnt or used to make traps, but for what an old man that I know does with him. Mostly he selects pieces that at some time have been machined into regular shapes, and these he carts off home. In his shed he has a bench circular saw, and by running the wood through it, he reduces it to thin strips about an inch wide. These he nails at an angle onto frames, with another row going in the opposite direction on top of them. After a slosh of creosote they can't be told apart from the expensive lattice-work fences that they have on offer in the perfumed gardens of the horticulture centre. He uses the cash they bring to help eke out his pension, but by varying the mesh, they can be put to far better use around the backyard.

A simply made wooden sledge is useful for collecting on a high yielding beach, as is a very large sack or bag that you can stuff oiled up rope or netting into for later treatment with detergents at home.

## Shells

The sea shells that you acquire, either from fishing or from your beachcombing expeditions, can be used domestically or, hopefully, as money earners.

The most obvious use of shells for the self supporter is as a source of calcium for poultry. The best commercial kind is described as oyster shell, but any other type of shell will do equally as well. To prepare them for feeding, all you have to do is crunch them up enough to pass through a quarter-inch garden sieve; but be careful first to discard any that are affected by oil waste or any other sort of pollution.

Shells can be used around the home both decoratively and functionally. Oyster and clam shells will do duty as ash trays, soap dishes, and even on the dining table to hold individual portions of seafood. I have even seen a cruet set made out of four, carefully matched limpet shells. Supported by smaller shells glued to an oyster shell base, one held salt and another served as a container for mustard. The other two had been glued together to form a pepper pot, with a corked hole in the bottom of one, and a series of smaller holes drilled in the top of the other to let the pepper out. Spoons for the mustard and salt had also been fashioned from odd pieces of shell.

If you live in a part of the world where you are likely to come across large and exotic shells, these have more elaborate possibilities around the home as lamps, toothbrush holders and even plant pots. You may even be able to gather shells on a commercial basis for collectors. But if you live in this sort of area, you will be liable to know more about those sort of possibilities than I.

Shells are also often used to make jewellery and novelties, and very nasty most of it is too However, if the idea does appeal to you there is plenty of literature on the subject. Most of it won't tell you how to make anything of any merit, but it will at least teach you the basics of shellcraft. I'm not much into shellcraft myself, but a while back I did do quite well selling a few crab claw pendants. These were made from the discarded pincers of edible crabs. Boiled clean and cut down to size they were glued into commercially manufactured mounts—very cheap if you buy a load of them—and strung on neck chains.

*Crab claw pendant*

## Sandpaper—Leather

The skins of the shark family have since ancient times been used as an abrasive, and you can make use of them at home in just the same way.

Freshly acquired skins should be scraped clean on the inside and then soaked in a heavy brine solution for a week or more. This will help to slow up any bacterial action. For general use, the skin should then be cut into small manageable squares, and when dry will serve very well for woodworking and the like.

If you keep on returning these sections to the brine and then reusing them, they will, in a sense, become tanned. And although not fully treated leather in the conventional sense, they can be used to make small craft items.

Eel skins are particularly worth saving because they remain soft and pliable without any other treatment than an initial wash. In the past, strips of eel skin were often used to joint the top section of flails. Nowadays, rectangular sections can be used as very effective hinges.

## Cuttle Bone

If cuttle fish inhabit your local sea area you are sure at some time to find their bones stranded on the tideline. Being a kind of mollusc, the cuttle fish is closely related to the squid and octopus, but instead of having an exterior shell, its flabby tentacled body is built around a central core of light cellular bone.

As you stroll along the beach, your first indication of the presence of a cuttle bone will be that you will spot something gleaming white amongst the weed and debris that has been washed up by the tide. Your first thought will probably be that it's going to be yet another piece of plastic, but on closer inspection you will discover a curious little light weight slab around five inches long. It will have something of the appearance and texture of expanded polystyrene, and the general shape of a miniature one man hydroplane.

When I was a small boy, we used to gather cuttle bones and sell them to the owners of cage birds. They would wedge them through the bars of their incarcerates cages so that the unfortunate inmates could relieve their boredom by pecking them to pieces; no doubt at the same time sharpening their beaks, and presumably absorbing some beneficial calcium. They are still sold in pet stores for the same reason, so who knows, you may be able to find a market for them.

Cuttle bone has also been used to erase marks

from paper and parchment, and when reduced to a powder, as a dentifrice, and somewhat similarly as a polishing compound for the softer metals like silver. In fact it was also used for forming moulds for small silver castings (it carves very easily), and I have used it for casting lead weights in.

No doubt the theory would not be totally acceptable to the dental profession, but with a mixture of powdered cuttle bone and some seaweed gelatine (and some flavouring if you wanted it), you would have the ingredients of what could at least be an emergency toothpaste.

# INDEX